China Born

———

Henry Noyes

CHINA BORN

Adventures of a Maverick Bookman

CHINA
BOOKS
& Periodicals, Inc.
San Francisco

Cover design by Robbin Henderson
Cover photographs by Gary Bulmer and J.B. Leatherman

Library of Congress Catalog Card Number: 89-60880
ISBN 0-8351-2199-2 (paperback)
ISBN 0-8351-2198-4 (casebound)

Printed in the United States of America by: **CHINA
BOOKS**
& Periodicals, Inc.

Contents

Illustrations

A Note on the Spelling of Chinese Names and Terms

Chinese names and terms have been transliterated with differing systems over the years, and now the modern *pinyin* method has become standard. In the first five chapters the older methods of transliteration are applied, while chapters six through the end of the book use the *pinyin* system.

See the Glossary on p. 219 for some transliteratons of Chinese names and places, and also abbreviations and explanations of terms.

✻ 1 ✻

China Childhood

Morning in Canton at Pui Ying Middle School

The weather is open, sunny, even crisp on most Canton winter days. But the day in January my grandfather died was dark, night glooming into an overcast morning, dampness penetrating to the bone, as if the very earth lamented his passing. Even the usual street cries from the hawkers of beancakes and Chinese doughnuts in the village surrounding our missionary compound were muted. *To-fu* seemed to come from deep underground and *yao-cha-quei*, usually so shrill in Cantonese opera style as to defy the human ear, was drowned out by the swish of rain on the palm trees outside our bedroom window.

'Get dressed, Billy, Henry,' Ah Quei commanded in English, imitating my mother's tone of urgency. She never spoke English to us unless delivering orders from above. As usual I pulled sheet and pillow over my head, but our amah was not in a playful mood. My father then came rushing into the bedroom to take over. He yanked Billy and me out of our bunny pyjama suits. 'Boys, your grandfather wants to see you.'

Before breakfast? I wondered as he insisted we dress up in our Sunday best. My mother handed baby Richard over to Ah Quei and Billy and I were then tugged and pulled by both parents downstairs, across the school campus, and on up three flights of stairs in the old school building to my grandparents' apartment. As we scrambled up to the third floor wondering what all the rush was about, we heard the rising-falling inflections of boys in the Pui Ying Middle School chanting their lessons in Cantonese. I wished I were old enough to do singsong with them.

As we were towed into my grandfather's room, I wondered why he was still in bed. He often came over to our house to play with us on the floor, but I had never seen him in bed before. His white beard bushed over the white sheets. His hands folded across his chest were like a stone buddha's. His eyes stared over our heads, focused on some unseen object.

It was a solemn occasion the meaning of which Billy and I could hardly guess. It was like suddenly being called to the bedroom of God or Santa Claus. And why was my grandmother, who was the cheeriest person I knew, sitting beside my grandfather on the bed with her head bowed and face clasped in her hands so tight that her fingers were bloodless? Her hair was wilder than usual. Tears beaded down her cheeks, though she tried to scrape them away with a futile gesture of the backs of her hands when she saw us. She never said prayers like this, the only time she was ever solemn. It was frightening. She jumped up, seized us by the arms, brought us to the bedside. She placed my grandfather's right hand on Billy's head and his left on mine, then ran out of the room sobbing.

But my grandfather gave us a cheerful, almost hearty smile, his eyes flooding with an inward light. He didn't have to say he loved us; we knew. It was like a transfer of energy that his very powerful spirit was transmitting to inspire us for the rest of our lives. 'God gives and He takes,' he said, almost in a whisper. 'He has given us you two boys because continuing the Noyes family must be important to His scheme of things. He gives life to you and takes earthly life from me.'

My brother and I were blissfully happy to be the centre of attention and of his affection, especially when he added, 'We will be together again in heaven.' But suddenly I felt a heaviness. Why did he have to go? Heaven seemed a terribly long distance away, even farther than the moon or the sun, way out somewhere beyond the farthest stars. Besides, my grandfather was one of my most important defenders in the sibling rivalry between Billy and me. As if in response to my thought, he went on to say, 'Billy, you're the eldest brother. You have the greatest responsibility for the younger ones. God, who sees even the smallest sparrow fall, will keep His loving eyes on you. Be tender and thoughtful to your younger brothers. Might doesn't make right, you know. Will you promise?'

Billy was eager to please our grandfather. 'I promise.'

'They will need your love. So will your parents. You have much energy to burn. Use it wisely. Be a credit....' His voice trailed off in an indistinguishable whisper. Then he seemed to gather strength again and began to comb my hair gently with his fingers. His touch and his smile made me feel there was a sun inside my body. 'You were named after me and your mother's father. That's why we christened you Henry Halsey.' Then he chuckled, 'You were a roly-poly little rebel that day.' He looked over my head to where my mother and father were standing. 'Remember how he cried out in protest when I baptized him? It was as if he was saying that he would have to test out the faith of his fathers first before he would follow in our footsteps.'

My mother laughed in a funny, tense sort of way as she said, 'But Father, you know the water was cold!'

'I am not blaming, but praising the child. He will make a good Protestant.' My grandfather's hands patted our heads, then circled affectionately through our hair as he went on in a sort of benediction to say, 'Our Heavenly Father has given you boys two wonderful parents. They will raise you as good Christians to continue His work here in the mission field. In His own time, my children, we will all be together again – for ever.'

Then my mother took us by the hand to the kitchen. My grandmother was beginning to cheer up. 'I'll look after them, Mary.' She fed us with homemade peanut butter on bread she had baked herself. As usual she kept bustling around the kitchen as if she could never keep her hands and feet still for a moment. 'Now your mother will take you along home, but be sure to say goodbye to your grandfather and give him a big kiss.' A smile came streaming out of her eyes, which were red and tired-looking like my father's. 'He loves you very much.

You may never see him again ...' she lamented with an Irish crooning '... on this earth.'

My brother was two years older and bolder than I was. 'Where will we see Grandpa again?'

'In heaven,' she said with a deep breath, crying and smiling at the same time.

My brother was brash. 'So why do you cry, Grandma? Isn't heaven a nice place to go?'

'Your grandfather will be missed on earth by all of us,' she answered, with a prayerful glance to the ceiling. 'Now, children, have some cookies, and then it will be time to go.'

My grandfather's room was filling with relatives and missionaries resident in the compound. They all seemed to be shadows of their everyday selves, gaunt and lifeless, standing with arms or hands folded and a melancholy darkness in their eyes. My mother's sister Helen had come over from Shamian with her husband, my Uncle Bill. He was a purchasing agent for the Sloane Furniture Company, my Uncle Bill, with glasses and a square face somewhat like my father's. He could afford to buy more toys for my cousin David than my father ever could for us. Why hadn't David come across the river with them? I wondered. Although my mother and Aunt Helen seemed old to me, they were still in their twenties, both beautiful in a plump and freckled sort of way – but dismally sad, with eyes downcast.

As we kissed our grandfather goodbye, my Great-Aunt Harriet and her lifelong companion, Electa Butler, arrived from Truelight Seminary on the Canton side of the Pearl River. With my grandfather's advice and aid, the two women had founded one of the first girls' schools in South China to teach more than sewing and good manners. Their curriculum, adapted from the Christian West, included mathematics, history, some science, and of course Bible study. Miss Butler had a white cloud of hair overhanging a rosy face; in fact, she was the only one I saw who came into that room with any red in her cheeks. Aunt Harriet's face was stark white like my grandfather's, even a little green in the light that filtered through the slats of the bamboo shades. Her hair was pressed tight to her head as if glued down. As usual, she wore a deep-bronze-coloured dress with just a touch of white lace at the neck. And as usual she seemed remote and kindly, like an angel down from heaven. My grandmother barely nodded to her, smiled at Miss Butler in a fleeting way, but gave an effusive hug to my Great-Aunt Martha.

Aunt Martha's bulk was always impressive, even over-whelming. As she came into the sickroom, my father helped support one side of her body and a cane the other. She wore a dark silk dress like Aunt Harriet's, but voluminous as a tent. Years before, at the turn of the century, her husband, Dr Kerr, had left her to administer the institution for the insane and the blind which they had jointly founded. Aunt Martha herself was relatively indestructible and carried on their mission work a quarter of a century after his death – with a great heart open to the whole handicapped world. In spite of the solemn occasion, she gave us a loving smile which made the wrinkles undulate across her face. We were favourites with her, and she with us. She would have hugged us to death if her arms had been free.

My mother began to give us warning glances as she saw us edging behind Jim Henry and Selden Spencer, who had just come up the stairs. My father's chief assistants, they were resident in the compound with their wives and children. They were accompanied by Wong Yuk Shung and Mo Man Ming, both former students whom my grandfather had ordained into the Presbyterian ministry. My brother and I wanted to stay on stage in the exciting, though puzzling, drama, but my mother took us both by the hand and, after a goodbye wave to our grandfather, we started down the steps two at a time. She was crying now and didn't try to hide her grief from us. So we suddenly felt very sober, part of a tragic ritual, as we recrossed the campus, slowing our pace to conform to her grief.

Pui Ying Middle School, founded by my grandfather in 1879, was located in the village of Fati across the river from the main city of Canton. It was segregated from the village by high walls and on one side a canal. The missionary compound was extensive enough within its walls to contain two large school buildings, one a dormitory with classrooms on the ground floor. My grandparents' apartment was on the third floor of this building. The newer Severance Hall was a large four-storey building with an assembly hall and a gymnasium on the ground floor, classrooms on the second, students' and teachers' residence quarters on the two upper floors. The hall was named after the Cleveland millionaire, also a Presbyterian, who had donated funds to my father to build this structure. It still stands today in the heart of Fati, though compound walls and other buildings have long been torn down and restructured elsewhere. Other buildings in those days were a beautiful little gatehouse with an upturned tile roof to recycle evil spirits back into the upper atmosphere and four missionary family residences with spacious arched verandas on two floors, surrounded by bamboo groves.

Our house was a large square building, a mansion in comparison with any of the houses any of us have lived in since. As we reached the entrance, rain was dripping from the pomelo tree overhanging the front door. Its large yellow fruits glistened as if they were having their faces washed. Palm trees stood at the corners of our house, shedding water in driblets from their fan-shaped leaves. I wondered how the bats who housed themselves up there in the inner fibre centres of the palms could keep dry when it rained. We could hear them squeaking like rusty hinges on small gates.

My mother insisted we change our clothes at once and called our amah to supervise. Ah Quei was a motherly peasant woman from an upriver village saved by my parents, as I learned later, from 'a life worse than death' and converted to Christianity. In some ways Billy and I loved her even more than we loved our own mother. When our mother and father were away doing missionary work, she would tell us stories that had demons and dragons in them, bad devils as well as good spirits. We also loved her because she had carried us on her back when we were babies, sung songs to us, and when my mother was not watching filled our mouths with pre-chewed food. We had learned our first words from her and preferred to speak her up-country dialect to our parents' more correct Cantonese.

'Ah Quei,' my mother ordered, 'help the boys put on their everyday clothes again. Then feed them. They haven't had a proper breakfast yet.'

I whined about being cold because I did not want to take

off my new blue coat, worn especially in honour of my grandfather. It was the first article of clothing in my memory that had been bought for me specially. It had arrived just in time for Christmas in a crate from Montgomery Ward all the way from America. All my other clothes were my brother's cast-offs. This beautiful coat was mine only. But Ah Quei had had her orders, and she gave me mine. 'Take it off, like your mother said!'

After breakfast I watched my mother nurse brother Richard. He seemed always to be hungry, screaming like a cat for milk, then grunting like a pig when he was feeding. I felt left out of my mother's affection and went into my room to sulk. Why did my younger brother, my older brother too, get all the attention? In self-defence I had adopted a family of my own whom my father helped name from the victims prepared for the fiery furnace. I called them impressionistically Adrack, Meshak and Tobedwego. I kept them in a toy house with their heads and legs sticking out of windows and doors. They talked to me any time I wanted to put words into their mouths: some Chinese, some gobbledegook that only the four of us could understand.

'If you go to heaven, Adrack, and you see my grandfather. . . .' But I stopped. My grandfather wasn't there yet. So I changed heaven to America, which was as much Shangri-la to me, both far away and unreachable. I put the question straight to Meshak and Tobedwego: 'Which would you really like to do, go to America or to heaven?' They were easily prompted to say America. Then I responded, with parental sternness, 'Take it from me, you are just going to stay right here in Fati and help me feed our chickens.' All three, chastened, travelled under my arm downstairs and out by the back steps to the patio on one side of which were the five servants' quarters, on the other side the henhouse.

One of the hens was cackling, another reaching her appointed time to lay. She was my favourite bantam hen, a deep-brown-coloured little bird with glistening feathers of gold and purple at her neck, and bright yellow feet. 'You see, children,' I confided, 'Yellowfeet is going to lay an egg. Let's help her.' In a moment she stood up without needing our help and, with visible contraction and expansion of her sphincter muscle, plopped a steaming brown egg into the nest. With great excitement I tucked my three children under my arm and raced upstairs to deliver the egg into my mother's lap. Baby brother was still clutching at her breast, but his eyes were squinting shut. 'Can I have a drink, too?' I asked. After all, though one of my mother's breasts was in service, the other seemed most enticing.

She smiled away my request. 'You're a big boy now, not a baby. Ah Quei, bring Henry a glass of milk.'

Before I had time to feel rejected, there was a sound of rushing heavy feet up the stairs. My father appeared at the door, grey in the face, looking more unhappy than I had ever seen him. 'It's all over.' He sat down on the bed near my mother and began to cry, just like I did when my big brother hit me, with great heaving sighs.

'He's had a very long and useful life,' my mother said as she buttoned her blouse and put Richard back into his crib. Then she put her arm round my father's head and drew him to her breast, as if he were a baby again. 'Your father was a great man, Will. Everybody's going to miss him.'

Billy came running into the room, then slowed to tiptoe when he saw our father crying. 'Has Grandpa gone to heaven?' he asked excitedly. 'That's where I want to go.'

My father paid no attention to my brother, only to his own grief. 'Fifty years in the mission field. So wise, so tolerant, how can we equal him? He gave his life . . . ' was all he could say for the moment. Then, turning to Billy and me, he said, as if he was angry with us, 'Your grandfather won't be with us any more – on this earth.'

That night my father put us to bed, praying for a long time on his knees. 'Will I go to heaven?' I asked him after the 'Amen'.

'One day,' my father answered in his preaching voice, 'if you are good and if God wills.' He left it up to predestination, not giving me a direct answer.

My father shut out the light in our bedroom as he closed the door. It was suddenly very dark, the time when I was afraid snakes, particularly cobras, would come slithering up the stairs, make holes in our mosquito nets and get into bed with us. Also tigers. But darkness that night brought a new fear. Maybe I wouldn't be good all my life. Maybe I would never see my grandfather again. But out of the dark his face appeared to reassure me. I could feel his hand on my head and almost hear him say, 'Be not afraid.'

My grandfather would reappear in my dreams and waking reflections for years after his death, even down to the present. He was a model of wisdom and kindness for me to imitate, a father figure even more important than my father himself. It was easier to idealize the dead, since my living father kept disciplining us from day to day, but death had removed my grandfather from criticism and reproach for ever.

My Grandfather's Funeral

In a land where some of the most impressive obsequies in the world had been solemnized for five thousand years, especially for emperors and dukes, my grandfather's funeral by comparison was a modest affair in the tradition of early Christian burial. For me, however, it was the most impressive ritual I had ever taken part in. The service was held in the auditorium of Severance Hall, where a closed casket of polished ebony was placed in front of the pulpit. It rested on a long refectory table covered with a white sheet. White calla lilies in two large vases in Ming blue and white were placed at head and foot, and flowers of many colours were banked below.

'Is he really in that?' I pointed and whispered to my mother. But she didn't hear me, she was so far away in her own thoughts.

Assembled students and teaching staff of Pui Ying, all dressed in funeral white, were deathly silent as the hall filled with visitors from all over the Canton area who came to pay their respects to the memory of one of the early missionaries to China. The American consul general and vice-consul were assigned to the front row by the student usher. They were accompanied by my father's friend, Captain Jim O'Neill of the US gunboat *Spitfire*, anchored off Shamian, and by six of his sailors who had played tennis on our court in happier days. The sailors winked at Billy and me as if the world had not come to an end yet and they would be back one of these days to play tennis and trot us around on their shoulders. The British and French vice-consuls and accompanying personnel were ushered to the second row of seats; then American businessmen and their wives from Shamian, my Aunt Helen, Uncle Bill and his partner among them.

I could recognize many of the teachers and preachers who came from the Canton missions, teachers and students from Aunt Harriet's Truelight Seminary and from Canton Christian College. But there were dozens of people I had never seen before and when I asked my mother who some of them were, she whispered, 'From the Baptist mission, the Methodist mission, the Missionary Conference and the Presbyterian Hospital. Now don't ask any more questions.' She was tense and seemed ready to burst into tears at any moment, but I felt elated that so many people would come to honour my grandfather.

The service was opened with a prayer and the first tribute was delivered by Wong Yuk Shung, an honours graduate of Pui Ying, who spoke in Cantonese with a wonderful tone flow up and down the scale. 'Our departed brother has been with us here in the mission field for forty-eight years of service. He travelled over the dangerous ocean for one hundred and nine days and nights bringing the light of Christianity to dispel our darkness. He was stoned and persecuted by the sinners he came across the ocean to save. Like Stephen, who was stoned before him for propagating the true faith, he persisted in his divine mission. Like Daniel he braved the lions of heathenism and idolatry in their dens.

'When he arrived in Canton in 1866, there were scarcely twenty Christians to carry the cross of Jesus. Now we are many thousands, a great and swelling army to raise high the gospel light kindled by the Reverend Henry Varnum Noyes to enlighten ignorant souls in every corner of our land. He has taught us to arm ourselves not with guns or explosives but with the words of the New Testament, which he has helped to translate into the vernacular for the benefit of those of us who are not scholars. And therefore we remember our deceased brother as a great teacher. We have met at his feet and learned many important lessons. And we followers of Dr Sun Yat-sen are glad indeed that our beloved Henry Varnum Noyes brought us books and the Bible, not guns and opium. So God rest his soul in eternal peace!'

When Wong Yuk Shung mentioned opium and guns, there was a nervous shifting of heads and bodies in the front two rows of consular personnel and a swaying back and forth in the assembly like a ricefield in a breeze. And before he left the pulpit, Jim Henry was already taking his place as if to correct a false note in the harmony of the service. 'Yes, Henry Varnum was a great teacher,' he boomed as he seized the pulpit with a firm hand to steady it and himself. 'Not only Pui Ying Middle School is his work, but the little mission schools of the Canton area and, of course, upriver. As an Ohio farm boy he had learned what it was to plough a straight furrow, and to reap and toil in the Lord's vineyard. As a teacher coming from a country village – Seville, Ohio – he understood the need of ordinary people for education. As a chaplain in the Union Army during our American Civil War, he wrote to his father back in Seville: "I have seen soldiers perish – almost like animals without seeking the grace of God – by the hundred. War attaches a dreadful penalty to victory. But through His grace, I was able to bring to conversion hundreds of wounded and mutilated soldiers at the point of death. Think what it is, Father, their souls are saved. I was with them at the end. And when I think of other peoples of the world who die without hope of life eternal, I hear His voice speaking to my Christian conscience: Do you want an easy life for yourself, or are you willing to accept God's challenge? In China there are 300 million souls who will go down to eternal darkness. I feel called upon to bring the light of salvation into their lives." And so our brother Henry Varnum came to China, not to lead an easy life or to profit himself ...' – Jim Henry focused stern eyes on my Uncle Bill and his business partner – '... no, he came with higher principles. He introduced the best of Western education to South China, one of the early pioneer missionaries. Certainly the studies of history, geography, mathematics, science are all vitally important in the development of the new Republic of China, but above all he was a believer in Bible study as the foundation of education. He was also an advocate of all-round development, as we know from our programme here in Pui Ying. The Chinese feudal style of education he called a failure. Let me again quote his words: "The poor

Chinese boy is doomed to long years of drudgery in stuffing his mind with Chinese characters and memorizing the explanation. The Chinese need a complete revolution in their way of studying. They need to be taught to think for themselves." Henry Varnum believed that a healthy mind and soul can only function at their best in a healthy body.'

Jim Henry paused to sweep the teachers and students of Pui Ying with an encouraging glance and give his words a chance to sink in. 'He placed as much emphasis, therefore, on sports and gymnastics as did the Ohio colleges of Wooster and Oberlin which he and his worthy son and successor, William Dean Noyes, attended in their student days. "Nourishment without exercise", he said, "gives us a body fat, lazy and useless, and even worse, the literary stoop." The old ideal of the frail student wearing glasses and scorning any kind of physical work or exercise as unscholarly was anathema to the founder of our school. He was responsible for a whole new concept of education which will be of tremendous importance to the new China. He is of the same school of liberal thought as Dr Sun Yat-sen in promoting modern education.

'And so are all of us he leaves behind in the mission field to continue the great work he initiated. His son survives to carry on as principal of Pui Ying. Also, his wife and companion, our dear sister Arabella. She has served the women and girls in this area as an evangelist and organizer of women's Bible-study classes and has assisted Harriet Noyes and Martha Kerr in this great work. Our beloved sisters, Harriet and Martha, perpetuate his work in institutions of supreme importance to the Chinese people. His daughter-in-law, our sister Mary, and eventually his grandchildren, I am sure, will continue his work in the mission field. Our brother we bury today was more saint than man. We can be sure that he will be at the gate of heaven to receive us all when our time comes, God so willing!'

At the end of the service, I was astonished to see my grandmother throw her arms around Aunt Harriet. I had never seen them embrace before, or my grandmother show her the slightest sign of affection. As she returned my grandmother's embrace, Aunt Harriet actually had tears on her face. She was usually so self-possessed, like a stern angel, that I couldn't believe she knew how to cry. She and my grandmother were ushered into the first rickshaw together as the funeral procession assembled.

'The procession was such as had never been seen before,' Aunt Harriet wrote that evening to her four sisters back home in Seville. 'People wondered who it could be who was being laid away with such honours. The students of Fati walked, some before the casket carrying six white banners like scrolls which were inscribed with the main facts of our dear brother's life, and the others followed. It was a lovely quiet afternoon. The sun shone through the trees and all nature was at peace as we left the grave of our loved one covered with flowers.'

The sun was out full in the afternoon sky as the casket was lowered into the earth. But cheerful as the day was, everybody seemed very sad, with heads bowed and eyes not meeting, except furtively. My Aunt Martha was weeping great glistening tears, moistening handkerchief after handkerchief. Years later I was surprised to come across her letter to her sisters in which she had written almost blithely the evening after the funeral: 'God has given us such a brother to give back to him, a shock of corn fully ripe.' Her letter was fresh with reminiscences of the farm life that brothers and sisters had shared in the early days with my great-grandparents, Varnum and Lois, and of the rustling of unfolding leaves in Ohio cornfields. And there was regret, too, that her favourite brother would not rest in the shade of the elm trees, back home in the Seville cemetery.

My father was sunk into his own reflections at the supper table after the funeral. Finally he blurted out, 'Wong should have had more sense than to talk about opium and gunboats. I know the way my father felt. He didn't approve of violence and he would never carry a gun, even though his life was often threatened. But Wong took advantage in front of the consular people. What are they going to think of Pui Ying? That we are anti-British? Anti-American?'

It was not tactful for my mother to say, but she did, reflecting back some of my father's anger, 'But, Will, if the Chinese feel that way . . .?'

'They have no right to,' my father cut her off. 'Those days are finished!'

A long pause followed. Finally my mother broke silence. 'The *Spitfire* is still anchored off Shamian.'

My father and mother both seemed miserable to be involved in an argument on such a day in front of us, but these arguments were to increase over the years and involve us more and more in choosing sides.

Tactfully my mother finally changed the subject. 'It was wonderful, Will, to see your mother give Aunt Harriet a hug, after being so jealous all these years. It took your father's death. I am sure he would have been happy at their reconciliation.'

'I'm sure he would. Too bad it didn't take place sooner. My mother has that stubborn Irish streak in her. Even my father couldn't help her overcome her jealousy, though he was a great force for bringing people together and helping them solve their problems.' There was quiet at the table until my father finally said, 'We can only walk in his shadow.'

In the years that followed, it was difficult for my father to be more than Henry Varnum's shadow. He was less of a visionary, less of a pioneer; also, less of a saint. He could not always count on his temper, especially when mother or wife offered him advice, and then he had periods of penitence for his explosive anger. My grandfather had been naturally serene; whatever the calamities of this world, there was always the light of the next shining in his eyes. My father was more enmeshed in the affairs of this world, living on into a century and a country that demanded more tact and less heroism from foreign missionaries.

My mother was more in tune with new developments than my father. Behind an expression that combined sweetness with a suggestion of martyrdom she had a way of making her opinions prevail, even though my father disagreed. There were many whispered arguments Billy and I were not expected to hear, and one in particular that broke out into the open over the growing demands of Chinese nationalists. Teachers like Wong Yuk Shung, whom my grandfather had taught and ordained, began to speak out with the new republican spirit, even to go so far as to indicate preference

for a Chinese principal for Pui Ying. This my father simply
could not understand, he who felt more Chinese than
American, had spent nine-tenths of his life in China and with
the help of a dictionary could identify twenty-five thousand
Chinese characters. But my mother tended to agree with the
new trend, at the same time beginning to question the
absolutism of Presbyterian dogmas. In a land where native
religions had a similarity in ethical principles with Christianity, she found it difficult to view Buddhism and Taoism as
heathen. There were 'heathen' moral tenets with which
Christians could unite: brotherhood and sisterhood, respect
for parents, love of children, and so on. My father, however,
believed, as his father had before him, that 'Taoism blinds
with superstition. Confucianism has no light to throw on a
future life, and no motives sufficient to enforce even the
morality which it teaches. Buddhism is destructive, crushing
out all the sensibilities of the human heart and finding refuge
from misery in losing consciousness of either pleasure or
pain. Tried by the Chinese for eighteen hundred years, it has
never lifted a shadow from the darkness that still rests thick
on those ancestral tombs where more than a hundred
generations sleep.'

Buddhism still seemed the greatest challenge to Christian
conversion for my father as he continued to walk in the
shadow of Henry Varnum's dogmas until the summer of
1916. His two-week visit to the Buddhist monastery at Feiloi
undermined his rigid antagonism to 'heathen idolatry'. This
visit was an experiment in inter-faith and inter-culture
between West and East promoted by my mother and her best
friend at Pui Ying, Julia Spencer, Selden Spencer's wife.

The trip upriver from Canton on a small paddlewheel
steamer was a great adventure for Billy and me. On deck all
sorts of bales and boxes were being shipped upstream; also
pigs strapped on their backs with feet kicking up through
rattan containers, their squeals as piercing as the whistle of the
little steamer. Through flat paddy fields we finally reached
mountain gorge country, transferred to a smaller boat, and
were towed upstream by a team of coolies. The monastery
was built on a sandspit projecting downriver like a large index
finger. Mountains towered above at neck-breaking angles as I

tried to look up to their tops.

The visitors' wing at the monastery had a beautiful view down canyon, blue and so deep that the sun appeared for only three or four hours around midday. The towpath was just under the windows of the guest house. Day and night we could hear the groans and work chants of coolies pulling junks up current. Their faces almost touched the ground as their bodies strained and twisted forward under the ropes. I wondered why they didn't put more coolies on the tow so they wouldn't have to groan so much and could walk upright. I felt bent and hurting in empathy just to watch them. But at night with the lanterns the tow crew seemed like spirits from another world engaged in some kind of strange ritual.

One very hot afternoon, with the cicadas shrilling, my brother and I had scrambled halfway up the mountain on the flagstone path and were returning sweaty and dirty. A refreshing pool appeared at a bend under trees. Fulfilling a natural body urge, we stripped and plunged in. It was a delight. We splashed and bubbled water and felt that life had never been closer to the heart's desire – or cooler. The white faces of two monks appeared at the bend in the path, and as abruptly disappeared. The pool seemed all at once dark and haunted. We scrambled into our clothes and ran down to the security of the guest house.

My father was soon summoned to a conference with the head monk, who politely invited him to pull up stakes and take himself and his family back to Canton on the next boat. 'Your children have profaned our sacred pool. I must ask you to leave.'

In answer, my father launched into an humanist interpretation of our profane act. 'My children are not of an age yet to understand profanity. They are innocent of evil intent. I will explain to them that they must not again bathe in the sacred pool.'

'How old are your children?' asked the head monk.

'Eight and six,' my father replied. 'We would feel it a great honour to be permitted to stay.'

The head monk took only a moment to consider, then accepted my father's explanation with a generous smile. 'What you have said is true. Children of that age are innocent of intent to profane. You may stay.'

Talk at the supper table that night revolved around my
father's account of our bathing in the sacred pool and the
reasonableness of the head monk. 'I wonder', said Julia, who
was an opponent of any kind of dogmatism, 'what would
have happened in the reverse situation. Would Christians
have been so tolerant?'

'If you're talking about the Catholic monasteries, who
knows?' said her husband, with a disapproving glance. 'But
I'm sure Protestants can be equally tolerant.'

'The monks seem to be very understanding,' my mother
reflected.

'Yes,' said my father emphatically, 'if only they would
accept Jesus and not worship idols.'

'Perhaps they think our rituals are heathen,' my mother
persisted. I remember the silence at table, then Julia laughing
hilariously and saying, 'Mary, you've hit the nail squarely on
the head!'

My father closed off further discussion in his that-will-be-it
tone of voice. 'That is not the issue.' His face was red, but he
suppressed his anger. And Selden Spencer looked at his wife
as if there were things he would say in private to her later.

Julia, however, was incorrigible. 'Our beliefs must seem
very strange to them. Buddha is so calm and Jesus so tortured.
Maybe they think by having us here that they will convert us
to Buddhism.' She said this so lightly that the adults round
the table had to smile. And Billy and I, glad that tension was
reduced, laughed out loud, though we didn't know exactly
why. We no longer had to feel like culprit sinners.

When the monastery gongs summoned the monks to
vespers, we stole up to the great temple to watch the
yellow-robed brothers gather for prayer. The Buddhas in
benevolent repose with their backs against the walls were
larger than life, beautiful in blue and gold, creating an air of
calm in an atmosphere flowing with sweet incense. Were
these *idols*? How could they be evil, when they were so
beautiful in their attitudes of contemplation, so peaceful with
their multiple golden arms interlocked across multiple folds
of their golden bellies? Why didn't I have more than one set
of arms? I was thinking what I could do with them, when the
big gong stopped beating and the monks began to chant in
unison. I felt there was a force lifting me up to the blue and

gold vault of the temple. I wished I knew the words of the chant, but some of them were so simple and distinct that I could quietly join in.

The world seemed at peace, until I saw my mother and father with the Spencers appear at the visitors' end of the lofty hall. Punishment loomed for being out of bounds, so we scattered back to visitors' quarters like a pair of temple mice.

The next day at tiffin my father said, as if he regretted his sharpness the evening before to Julia and my mother, 'Their services are impressive. They seem devout and very sincere. And they don't live by oppressing the peasants. The members of this order grow their own food. They are not parasites, like the contemplative orders.' My father came from the kind of Ohio farm stock that believed, 'He who doesn't work, neither should he eat', anticipating the more recent slogan of the Chinese revolutionaries. At the same time he was all too conscious of making concessions that would have been heresy to his father. Times were changing, and beliefs with them. Still, in all conscience, my father had to make a stand on the ancestral rock of faith and add, with eyes focused on mountains high above our heads, 'I only wish they believed in our one God.'

Last Days in China

Our summers were usually spent on Cheung Chau, an island fifteen miles south of Hong Kong in the South China Sea. When June came, with its floods and subtropical heat and dampness, we would take a riverboat eighty miles downstream to Hong Kong through the lush green ricefields of the Pearl River delta.

On the way we watched peasants ploughing the underwater fields behind slow-footed water buffaloes. Along the tributary creeks, peasants rotated the treadmills that raised the level of water in the rice paddies, like their ancestors for forty generations. I don't remember seeing a pump the whole trip.

My father would explain that the system was feudal. There were water towers which the landlords could use as observation posts to oversee the labour of their peasants. In the walled compounds, full granaries insured against hard times of drought and famine for the landlord and his family. Landlords would double the price of rice. Then the peasants had to borrow money from the landlords just to go on living, and they had to pay back double what they borrowed. It was a hard life and my father said he pitied them plodding after water buffaloes, knee-deep in muddy water; turning the treadmill for endless hours generation after generation; pasturing the stock year after year, century after century; dying poorer than their fathers before them. Christianity offered a much more hopeful way of life, he said. Also Western-style farming, where farmers owned land and tools. 'More and more Chinese will learn how we do things in the West and in the long run will put an end to the feudal system.' I did not understand too well what my father was saying, but I was always happy when he took time to explain things to me and was impressed by all the things he knew and I did not. One day I would be a teacher like him. However, one of his explanations puzzled me. When we saw a dead baby girl floating on the river, a bloated little corpse, I asked him what had happened. He only shook his head: 'Too many mouths to feed.' How could that be? We always had food on the table.

That night our boat anchored outside Hong Kong Harbour. Because of World War I regulations, we would have to dock in daylight the next morning. Great jets of light circled clouds above the harbour and Victoria Peak. My father said these were to detect possible German enemy agents in boats, submarines or Zeppelins should they try to attack the British crown colony. I knew the United States and Germany were at war because my father had tried to enlist as a chaplain in the US army – he hated the Kaiser worse than the devil – but the consular office in Canton rejected him because he had flat feet. If the harbour was likely to be invaded, how safe were we just outside? I wondered. But as I watched the cones of circular light, I was more concerned about the dead baby girl whom I had seen with my own eyes than with German submarines. Why didn't her mother and father feed her so she wouldn't have to die? And why didn't they bury her in a grave, the way my grandfather was buried?

In Hong Kong there was one particular person I always wanted to see before we boarded the little steamer for Cheung Chau. She was a girl four or five years older than I, both of whose arms had been bitten off by a tiger. Yet there she would sit patiently on the Bund, drawing a needle through embroidery by using her mouth and two arm stumps. I marvelled at her skill. What would I have done without hands? I could not even sew with hands.

I wondered if the tiger which had bitten off her arms was the one I saw in summer 1917 on Victoria Peak. We stayed there for a month in the mansion of a rich English Presbyterian while he was home on leave. The white, spacious building stood high on Victoria Peak overlooking the crowded harbour 1,800 feet below. Every evening after supper I used to venture down a trail which wound through trees to a deep pool. I could hear the sambur deer barking like dogs and occasionally see their bodies disappear between the trees. I was watching one of them drink at the pool below when there was a warning bark, more like a shriek, and the deer leapt away out of sight. Out of the gloom a beautiful striped animal appeared at the poolside and began to lap up water like a giant cat. I turned and raced up the hill. 'I saw a tiger', my voice and eyes blazed at my mother, 'down by the pool.' My father, big brother and I, at a safer distance, ran down the trail. When they saw the pool, but no tiger, my father laughed. 'You always had a good imagination.' The tiger had drunk his or her fill by that time and must have disappeared as abruptly as the deer into the woods. My father and brother had proved to their satisfaction that I was a liar. It hurt. I was never able to overcome the credibility gap, but I can still summon that tiger in memory and watch it emerge from the dark trees and slurp up water from the highest pool on Victoria Peak. Years later, when I read Blake's poem, I knew my tiger was like his:

> Tiger! Tiger! burning bright
> In the forests of the night,
> What immortal hand or eye
> Could frame thy fearful symmetry?

The only one who believed my story was the armless girl on the Bund. With tears in her eyes, she said that it must have been the same one. *She* believed me.

Cheung Chau was a dumbbell-shaped island with a beach like a handle connecting the two ends: one tree covered and not populated; the other partially built over with a fishing harbour and village and, beyond on the headlands, summer homes of foreign missionaries. My father had levelled off the top of a hill on a promontory out of reach of storm waves and in place of the hilltop had built a stone cottage, presumably protected from the full force of typhoons. This was our summer home, with a sweeping view over miles of ocean, limited only by clouds and blue islands.

When we arrived at the village dock, the little steamer puffed and panted, making a great display of churned water and tangled seaweed. Upside-down sea turtles, flippers waving wildly but not designed to help them roll over, were already assembled at dockside for the return trip and the soup kitchens of Hong Kong. Crates and baskets of dried fish were stacked on the wharf waiting to be loaded, and there were live fish in oblong vats. Slopes around the village were white with drying fish that stank in the tropical sun. Acres of nets smelling of fish and salt water were spread out to dry. Children, mostly naked in the village streets, watched us wide-eyed but would not return our greetings. In our sun helmets and khaki shirts and shorts we must have seemed like creatures from another solar system.

At the turn of the village street I would try to talk to the parrot, which had green and gold feathers and a head that glittered with all colours. But she was shy with strangers and issued a stream of curses in Chinese at us only when we were halfway up the hill. She was said to be one hundred years old, older than any person alive in the village. I believed it – she had such an old crackly voice, sounding much older than my grandmother.

I shall never forget the summer mornings when my father took us down to the beach to watch the fishermen draw in their nets in a great U shape, first in boats, then springing out into shallow water and with rhythmic grunts hauling a ton or two of flopping fish and eels, sea urchins and starfish up on the beach. The early sun turned beads of water and sweat on their half-naked bodies into jewels of light as they pushed wheelbarrows loaded with their catch up the hill to the village. They left the most brilliant tropical fish, sea urchins and starfish on dry land to flop and gasp and die. As Billy and I put some of these inedibles back into the ocean, I wished I knew a language fish would understand to warn them not to come back into that bay if they wanted to go on living.

I remember the shark fins that came triangularly knifing into the bay towards the beach where we swam on hot afternoons and the shouts and whistle blasts that went up from our shark-fearing missionary parents; the poisonous snakes glistening an evil green as they looped down from bamboos that shaded our barefoot path to the beach; and the sea turtles which came wallowing through the waves like self-propelled rafts to flipper themselves awkwardly up the beach in the cove below our cottage to lay eggs in the sand. On the trail down to the cove was a natural cave with skull and crossbones we had chalked at its entrance after reading *Treasure Island*. One day we found a massive python coiled in possession of our pirate hide-out. Its eyes suggested that we should find another cave or be squeezed, and the very next morning, right inside the brick bathtub in our cottage, I discovered a cobra with hood up, poised for the kill. So life was a path to tread with caution, especially barefoot – to advance when possible, and to retreat when necessary.

I still remember the way the moon, eye-dazzling, paved its phosphorescent freeway across the ocean from Lamb Island to Cheung Chau. On summer nights, with warm arms around me, my mother would sing, 'Baby's boat's a silver moon'. At times like that I thought she was the most beautiful person in the world, and the most loving. I felt no constraint then and was happy and free to sail off to sleep on the words of her song. It was in those Cheung Chau summer nights and days that I felt life was at its full, as if my father, mother, brothers and I were a family of birds in one nest.

Nor could I ever forget the ocean and skies in their stormy moods when life on earth, including my own, seemed threatened by forces far above and beyond human control. I can see again the thrash of palm trees below our cottage in the cove and the splash of waves a hundred feet in the air above the rocky promontory during typhoon assault; also the unlucky missionaries, whose temporary mat-shed summer houses, less typhoon-resistant than our stone cottage, were first flattened then blown to smithereens by hundred-mile-an-hour winds, who came crawling uphill on their bellies with fierce ramrods of rain beating on them.

Abruptly our life in China came to an end. My mother's health broke down. Passage was booked on the *Ecuador* for 1 January 1919. My father was to remain behind for six months 'to wind up his affairs'. What that meant I had no clear idea, but it sounded like something my father would do.

It was not until the last day of 1918, when we were leaving Canton, that my mother told me Ah Quei was not coming with us. The thought in addition that I would not see my father for six months gave me a feeling of desperation. 'Who wants to go to America?' I complained. 'I want to stay with Ah Quei and my father.' But by the religion of my forefathers and the decisions of my parents I was predestined to embark on the *Ecuador* early on the morning of 1 January and, after waving farewell to my father, growing smaller by the minute, to be transported out of the port of Hong Kong into the South China Sea as land dimmed out under a driving rain cloud.

I would not see that coast again for the next fifty-six years.

2

Seville Family Noyes

The House on the Hill

The first stage of our trip from Toronto to Seville was by train, the second by lake steamer from Buffalo to Cleveland. We boarded the *Erie Queen* at a time when day and night were contesting the sky after a rather dismal sunset. For once the whole family was travelling together, all six of us. I had not been on a ship since the *Ecuador* landed my mother and us four boys in San Francisco Harbor back in January 1919. We were happy to have our father with us this time, and excited to be travelling by water again.

We were excited also because it was the Fourth of July and firecrackers were flashing and popping along the waterfront. Confetti sparks fountained out and flecked our faces with weird colours. Foam from the propeller churned a silver river out into the dark waters of Lake Erie. It became a night of magic and adventure.

For once, I had my father all to myself. My mother had taken my younger brothers to the cabin to bunk them down for the night and go to bed herself, early as usual since her health was not good. My brother Bill was somewhere up in the bow trying to impress two girls. My father and I leaned over the stern rail together like habitual fellow-travellers. We watched the fireworks burn out over Buffalo and the moon and stars once more establish their hegemony over sky and water.

My great-grandfather, Varnum Noyes, preparing his sermon for Sunday service at the First Presbyterian Church of Seville, Ohio, which he founded.

Henry at the age of five in front of the family summer home on Cheung Chow

My father, the Reverend William Dean Noyes

My mother, Mary Stevenson Noyes

My maternal grandmother in a sedan-chair on a visit to China in 1914. This mode of transport is now banned in the People's Republic.
Below left: Our house at flood time. My father is feeding a marooned goat on the veranda. *Below right*: Billy and Henry in the garden of their house on the Pui Ying School campus

'It was like Chinese New Years in Canton,' my father reflected. He had my hand firmly in his grip, as if afraid I might fall overboard. 'Do you remember that far back?'

'That's easy,' I answered. 'I remember the strings of firecrackers in Fati. They were popping and smoking so we could hardly breathe. And the cash in the red paper us kids used to get for New Years.' The mention of money made the smart aleck in me add, 'Hey, Dad, how about a penny for my thoughts? It should cost you more than a penny, though, because I've got lots of them. Millions!'

My father checked his change. He had two Canadian pennies. 'You won't be able to spend them till we get back to Toronto,' he cautioned. 'So what are two of your thoughts?'

'I'm thinking about a long time ago. You were holding me by the hand, like now.'

'When was that?'

'I suppose in Canton. The first thing I can remember. It must have been at the railway station. There was a very bright light....' I hardly knew how to describe the power of that light, since it involved a feeling for my father which I did not know how to put into words. It was as if a star had exploded and obliterated everything else, including the real stars above. My eyes were on fire and my body seemed to shrink down to insignificance. There was no shield to ward off the light, or defence against terror. Then I felt a hand securing mine. It was my father's hand, powerful and warm. Like an evil dragon the locomotive roared past, showering us with cinders. But I was no longer afraid. The blinding light had passed, and the lesser light of coach windows went flashing by. The stars began to glimmer again above my head in a wondrous universe without terror as though I was absorbed in and absorbing all things on earth and in the heavens – by a father's love which had no limits. But how could I put such intense feelings into words? 'It was a train engine,' was all I could say. 'I thought it would run over us. But you took my hand. Then I knew everything would be all right.'

My father seemed very pleased to be part of my earliest memory and laughed as he said, 'So here's one penny. What next?'

'I'm thinking about how we came back from China on the

Ecuador. We got into a typhoon. The big waves broke the transoms up top. We had to take off our shoes and go wading to the dining room. Then the dishes started crashing to the floor. Mother stayed in her bunk almost every day till we got to San Francisco. She was really sick the whole way over.' My eleven-year vocabulary wasn't up to describing the incredible delight of seeing land again and cruising through the Golden Gate, or the excitement of nosing into harbour just ahead of the *Empress of Asia*. What a beautiful sight! The crack ship of the Orient Line was steaming behind us into port in the sun of that early January morning – and our little *Ecuador* homing in a ship's length ahead! 'Bill and I changed all the diapers for brother Geoff. We never knew babies were so dirty.'

'You forget, you were a baby once yourself,' my father sermonized.

'I disremember,' I laughed, and went full speed ahead with my story: 'There was a sailor who played bear on us. He growled in the deckhouse where they kept the shuffleboard. And the albatrosses and gulls kept flying after us without ever taking a rest. When we got to San Francisco, buildings kept bending back and forth. I couldn't steady them.'

My father had left China six months after we did and joined us in Auburn, New York, in the summer of 1919. He had a beard at that time as bushy as my grandfather's, but black and prickly to the kiss. My mother said, 'Will, you look just like a Bolshevik!' That was the first time I had ever heard the word Bolshevik, and it didn't sound like a compliment the way my mother said it. Then she added, 'Shave it off, for my sake!' He would do anything in reason for my mother, like shaving off his beard, but he was faced with a very difficult decision when he learned from the doctor that her illness was tubercular. 'It would be suicide for her to go back into the Canton climate. She needs rest and quiet.' So my mother spent the next two years in bed, or near it. Since her father had died of tuberculosis in 1906, the killer disease had clouded her life as well as ours. In all conscience, my father had a most difficult decision to make. His career was China-orientated from earliest childhood. Except for several years in the United States studying to prepare himself for the ministry at Wooster

College and then Auburn Theological Seminary, he had spent his whole life in China. He was happy to follow in his father's footsteps – more of a plodder and less of an initiator, but like Henry Varnum a staunch Presbyterian. He was also head of the Synod in Canton, succeeding my grandfather, and a consultant to a whole mission of Presbyterians who turned to him for solutions to every conceivable problem in the mission field. Now that the problem was his, who could advise him whether to put the Canton mission first and return to China, or his wife and family and stay in the United States? My father would have been happy to hear Henry Varnum say, 'Son, whom God has joined, let there be no separation.' But hearing no voice, he resorted to prayer.

His answer came shortly, as he believed, from the intercession of the divine will at the moment when family funds had reached zero: an offer came to him from the Home Mission Board of the Presbyterian Church of Canada. The appointment gave him charge of home mission work among Asians, with Overseas Chinese as a main concentration. It involved frequent travel across Canada from Halifax to Nanaimo and an occasional trip to Newfoundland. He officiated at baptisms, marriages, and burials of his far-flung oriental parishioners. He also visited them at their places of work in laundries and restaurants. He could interpret for them in court on charges of gambling or opium-smoking.

Their life was hard. They sent most of their wages back home to support wives and children barred from joining them in Canada by the Oriental Exclusion Acts, modelled on those of the United States. If Chinese smoked opium occasionally or played mahjong for pennies, it was because they were not permitted to have a normal family life. Although my father never approved of these practices, he did not consider them heinous enough sins to justify incarceration, particularly as families back in China would also be penalized by lack of financial support and would probably starve to death. Finally, my father reasoned, as I had often heard him say at the dinner table, that if non-Orientals in the United States and Canada drank and smoked over bridge and pool tables, often for fabulous stakes, why should Orientals be singled out for discriminatory punishment? Many a time I went with him to court and learned at first hand what it meant to defend oppressed people – especially those who did not know the English language too well and whose parentage was not Anglo-Saxon or early American, like our own family.

My father was less of a theologian than a social worker. It was characteristic of his mission that he would be called upon to solve interracial problems, and he would always respond without thought of self. When a telegram came in from Nova Scotia, one evening when we were at supper table, with the message: 'Authorities have imprisoned leper Chinese origin in boxcar without food, drink, toilet arrangements. Come', my father was furious. He slapped his napkin down on the table without finishing his supper. My mother helped him pack and off he rushed to catch the night express for Halifax. Our family life was constantly interrupted by such emergencies, in addition to his scheduled cross-country trips. Any normal family life was therefore impossible. My mother by default, in spite of poor health, became head of the family and more and more asserted her decision-making power. She managed our slim budget and helped us four boys to solve our many problems of adjustment from China, to the United States, to Canada. Not least of these was the name-calling we were subjected to. In Canton we had been called *fan quei chi*, foreign devil children; in Auburn *Chinks*; and in Toronto, with less stigma attached, *Yanks*. With all the strains and stresses of adjustment, we were always happy when the whole family could do something together. The trip to Seville was one of those rare occasions.

When my father put me to bed that Fourth of July night, my two younger brothers were already contentedly sleeping in the bunk they shared, Dick's feet in Geoff's face, and vice versa. But I could not give in to sleep, elated as I was from the talk with my father and the beauty of fireworks blazoning the night sky and the moon silver-plating a pathway over deep waters. The very next day I would see for the very first time the family home in Seville which I had heard about all my young life, and actually meet my fabulous great-aunts who had all been born before the American Civil War. With such excitements ahead, I could sleep only in short spells with one dream succeeding another in frightening disorder.

In Cleveland the next morning, our whole family of six boarded the electric interurban that jolted us forty miles south across the Mongahela Valley to Seville through clouds of smoke and steam from steel mills. Flames from open-hearth furnaces were as eye-blinding as the sun. My father seemed happy but nervous as he briefed us on his student days and vacations spent with his aunts in 'the house on the hill'. He pulled out a packet of photographs and, passing them round, shouted descriptions over the roar of the rocking train. 'That's the old farmhouse on the hill. When my grandparents came out from Massachusetts, they lived in a log cabin back in the 1830s. But when my grandma's father came out to Ohio to visit and found his daughter living in such primitive quarters, he took my grandfather in tow to the nearest sawmill. They bought enough lumber to put together a New England-style farmhouse – with their own hands, of course. That's the part they built together, at the right of the photo. Then later my grandfather added this wing to accommodate a family of eleven. At the back of the kitchen he added pantries and toolrooms, and on the second floor six more bedrooms. So it's quite a place.' My father pointed to an upstairs window. 'That was my room when I spent vacations here in my Wooster days.'

My Great-Aunt Mary, the smallest and youngest aunt, met us at the station with a great demonstration of affection, giving my mother a specially warm hug. 'Myohmy, it's wonderful, Mary, to see you looking so full of health after all your trouble. And these are the boys? Splendid. Will, you can be proud of them!' Village friends of my father had come to welcome us. He was 'Willie' to them, a Christian hero who had won many battles against heathenism for the good Lord in faraway China. For all of us, it was an adventure into the past. As in the photograph, the family farmhouse occupied the crest of a hill. My three senior great-aunts, also just like their photographs, greeted us from the front porch with wildly waving handkerchiefs. The floodgates of love and reminiscences were opened wide. My four great-aunts had taught school all their lives before retiring and, having no children of their own, overwhelmed us with long-stored-up affection. We were Will's and Mary's boys, the four young hopefuls of the Seville branch of the Noyes family, sole descendants of the six daughters and three sons of Varnum and Lois Noyes, who had come out to Ohio from New England to cultivate and populate the wilderness.

After all the hugs and kisses, Bill and Dick and I scattered to explore the farm. The barn was falling apart, the henhouse was occupied by spiders and transient flies, and the great strawstack in the barnyard was grey with the wear and tear of many winters. We found domesticated strawberries growing wild in what had once been a garden. We filled our mouths and pockets and went racing back to the creek to splash naked and then to build a dam to deepen a swimming hole. We finished the afternoon making the horses across the road from the farmhouse stampede to the far end of the field. As midgets it gave us a great sense of power to provoke fear in mighty stallions, but for our bravado in chasing them we almost got hooked on the horns of an angry cow. Ingloriously, we flattened on our bellies and crawled under barbed wire to escape with our lives.

Supper was preceded by an extended blessing by my father before we were permitted to take up fork or knife, but Aunt Sarah's cooking was a reward for patience, especially her chicken and dumplings. She was a woman to keep her thoughts to herself, unlike my other aunts, who overflowed with enthusiastic talk and advice around the dining table. Aunt Sarah tolerated children in an abstract way, but showed none of the loving tenderness of her three sisters. She cooked while Aunt Mary served. When she finally sat down at table, she would stare out of the window at the road to the village with a sort of unfocused regret that the world had long passed her by. When Mr Lincoln was mentioned, however, her face glimmered with a little warmth and she would tell stories about the Civil War and family history one after another in a faraway stream of consciousness which rarely trickled down to the twentieth century.

After supper there was serious talk in the front room, where the adults sat in rocking chairs aged in oak from the days of my great-grandfather Varnum. I felt embedded in the family atmosphere in that room where my great-grandmother had spun, woven and dyed the blue and white sofa covers and cushions and crocheted the antimacassars. The room was overfurnished in Victorian style with teakwood cabinets, their glass-curved fronts reflecting grotesquely the flames of kerosene lamps. The adjoining music room was an informal museum with treasured cloisonné vases, silk embroidered garments formerly worn by mandarins and their ladies, silk and ivory fans and golden back-scratchers – a sort of Marco Polo collection sent from China by my grandfather and my great-aunts, Harriet and Martha, who were still in China and a cause of anxiety to the senior Noyeses.

'I am very happy to hear that nothing happened to them during the troubles in Canton,' my mother was saying. 'Since the Versailles Treaty, the Chinese have been very upset with the treatment meted out to them. I can hardly blame them.' She was so engrossed in the discussion that she had completely forgotten Billy's and my bedtime.

'Why do you say that, Mary?' asked Aunt Emily, with a kindly smile. 'I've often wondered myself why President Wilson could agree to turning over the German concessions in China to Japan. Hattie and Mattie were most unhappy about the Treaty.'

'It was outrageous,' said my father, his face colouring with anger. 'After all, the Chinese labour battalions served bravely in France and the Middle East. China made her contribution to winning the war. Even before I left China in 1919, things were boiling over. Anti-Japanese riots were breaking out in Peiping on 4 May, and troops crushed the demonstrations. We can be proud of the girls in the American Board Mission School who marched in the streets to the President's house and demanded the release of the students who had been jailed for making speeches. But these new riots in Canton are of a different order.'

'Will, can you really call them riots?' my mother asked. There was a strong appeal in her voice, also a challenge.

My father's face reddened. 'It was a terrible tragedy when the seventy-three Chinese were killed in Canton this year. It set our whole mission work back. But can we expect residents of Shamian to allow a mob to destroy them?'

'If the Allied Powers ...' my mother began. But my father had heard her arguments before and assumed the right of final authority in the Noyes home, like a patriarch of the old order.

'We know, Mary,' he interrupted, 'that Dr Sun Yat-sen was reorganizing the whole country along the line of the Three Principles, but this mob was just turning the clock back. I'm sure their actions didn't have his sanction. He's a Christian . . .'

'I think the Chinese people shouldn't be treated like children any more,' my mother persisted. 'How can they accept US leadership in the mission field if we have no respect for China as a nation?'

My father was too irritated to trust himself to reply. There was a tense silence between my parents, who still leaned towards each other as if in confrontation. For myself, I felt painfully tense, hoping the difference between them would soon be resolved. Even if I didn't know what it was all about at the time, I believed my mother was 100 per cent right when I listened to her and I was equally certain my father was also 100 per cent right, whatever differences he might have expressed. Aunt Sarah relieved the situation by asking, 'Will, what exactly are the Three Principles?'

My father seemed happy to explain, in his scholarly way, 'Nationalism, democracy, the people's livelihood.' He enlarged on these while my mother sat with eyes lowered. She had heard his definitions many times before and was reserving judgement on other matters under suspended discussion.

On Our Knees

After breakfast the next morning, my father read from the Bible. My aunts were so happy with his reading that they urged him to read another chapter, and yet another. They seemed especially happy when praying was about to begin and the younger ones of us knelt down, put our elbows on chair cushions, and were supposed to close our eyes. My aunts were blissfully content to close their own eyes and gently rock to the rising and falling intonations of my father's praying voice. With an audience part willing and part captive, he lengthened out his prayer to half an hour that morning, blessing our ancestors as far back as the Norman Conquest,

when they had first settled in England. He blessed particularly our two young ancestors who had taken ship with the
Huguenots back in 1634 and sailed to Medford Harbor, in
the new colony to be called Massachusetts. Nor did he forget
my pioneering great-grandparents, who had founded the
Ohio branch of the Noyes family in the 1830s. He urged God
to spare the lives of Aunt Harriet and Aunt Martha in this
perilous moment of human history and to bring them back to
the family home safe in His appointed time. He prayed for
the good health of my mother and our four aunts and
everybody else in the room, winding up with the hope that
his four children would follow in the footsteps of their
predecessor Presbyterians.

There were times, like that morning, when Bill and I
became supersaturated with prayers and tributes to ancestors
and church services. In a carefully planned plot, we decided to
make ourselves scarce at church time on Sunday morning. We
didn't let Dick and Geoff in on the subversive plan, afraid
they would divulge all to our mother. We spent a good part of
the week, while my father was away looking up college
friends and professors at Wooster, burrowing a tunnel in the
old strawstack. The only one who caught us in the act was
Aunt Mary, and somewhat hesitantly she allowed herself to
be sworn to secrecy.

Sunday morning after prayers, Bill and I made ourselves
scarce in the strawstack, patching up our cave entrance from
inside as well as we could. In half an hour we heard the dinner
bell ring, which on a Sunday morning meant 'get ready for
church'. We breathed with caution. Finally Aunt Mary's
voice came shrilly through the straw: 'Boys, I feel so badly.
But we shouldn't do this. Your father's such a good man and
he's asking everybody where you are. And I won't, I can't, I
really can't lie to him. Please come along now. I won't tell
him where you've been. I promised you I wouldn't.' But the
straw in our hair told the story when we followed her back
into the house.

When my father conducted a service, he always told a story
for children before he gave his formal sermon. That Sunday
he told a story about two boys hiding in a haystack. The
moral of the story was that nobody could hide from God,

whose eyes could see through anything, barn doors or haystacks. My father carefully avoided looking in our direction. Bill and I smiled at each other, and at Aunt Mary. She gave an amused little laugh, but sobered again at once when Aunt Emily frowned at all three of us in mild reproof. Her eyebrows said, as plainly as words, 'There's a time and place for mirth, but not in the church our father built and gave to the community.' A bronze plaque at the church door gave tribute to Varnum Noyes for his generosity. It also commemorated him as the first Presbyterian pastor to set up pulpit in Seville in the early 1830s. The sanctuary was therefore too hallowed ground in family tradition for casual jokes and smiles – especially during Sunday morning service.

I will say for my father, although his prayers were long, his sermons were short. He preached that day on Ruth amid the alien corn. It was an easy transition to praising Aunts Harriet and Martha for continuing their mission amid the alien corn in a country rocked by civil disturbances. Women in the congregation began to dab tears with their tiny lace handkerchiefs at my father's eloquence and the thought that two courageous sisters in religion, whom they knew personally and loved, were continuing to propagate the faith in a hostile wilderness. Then my father appealed to the men in the congregation who had helped to support Pui Ying Middle School financially: he talked about the mission of his grandfather, who came west from Massachusetts to convert the heathens on the American frontier, and of his father, who crossed the seven seas (three of them at least *en route* from New York to Hong Kong via the Cape of Good Hope) to convert oriental heathens. He ended with a diatribe against the Treaty of Versailles as a barrier to spreading the true faith in China. It was forbidden to clap in church, of course, but I noticed after service that most of the parishioners put an extra bill or coin in the collection box on the way out.

I was proud to be the son of the preacher, and glad after all that Aunt Mary had rousted us out of the strawstack. I was also proud to be the next generation in a long line of pioneers and felt like a young saint on the mission road, especially during the hallelujahs of the last hymn. My Aunt Clara, who was the organist, managed to put tremendous soul into her playing, gentle as she was at other times. She had a soft nature, a beautiful face, scarcely wrinkled, and a voice that sang rather than spoke. Her eyes were as bright as bluebirds flashing in the sun. Of all my great-aunts I felt most romantic about her, dreaming that she was a young princess, not related to me at all, and that I was the young prince from the next-door castle. I was blissfully happy when she invited me into the music room that afternoon. As she rehearsed hymns on the foot-pedalled organ for the evening service, I pretended to leaf through the hymn book, but my mind was away romancing. When she finally moved over to the piano in a sort of Blue Danube glide, surprisingly graceful at seventy-five, and her fingers began to dance through a Chopin waltz and then to breeze through the Moonlight Sonata, she became in my fantasy the very archetype of romantic beauty. Her fingers, flying like a hummingbird's wings, were so much more flexible than Aunt Sarah's or Aunt Emily's. Their fingers were knotted up with arthritis and moved clumsily in pain. Sometimes Aunt Clara played wistfully slow at the thought of my grandfather lying buried in a far country. 'For my brother Henry you were named after,' she whispered, smiling and crying at the same time. 'He was the only member of our whole family not to be buried in the Seville cemetery.'

I felt oppressed by her tears and the memory of my grandfather's funeral. 'Why did he have to go to China?' I asked, with the feeling that predestination might have treated him unkindly.

'He was called to save souls,' she answered simply. 'And he chose China, rather than Africa or India, because he was greatly impressed by the Taiping when he was a divinity student at Hudson.'

'Who were the Taiping?'

'An early Christian sect in China, farmers mainly, who wanted to set up a heavenly kingdom on earth. Your grandfather thought of joining them in his student days, as I remember. Instead, the Lord called him to serve as chaplain in our own Civil War. It was fortunate for him that he didn't go out to China at the time, because the Taiping Rebellion was crushed in 1864 and twenty million died in the most destructive war in human history. Although they overran four-fifths of the Chinese Empire in their heyday, your grandfather thought it was a great mistake on their part to rely on swords and guns, instead of conversion. He knew that the best weapons for Christian soldiers were the Bible and the Ten Commandments. When the Taiping dream of creating a heavenly kingdom on earth became a dreadful nightmare and they themselves turned on each other and brothers killed brothers, as in our Civil War, your grandfather felt the divine challenge to carry true Christianity to the misguided millions of China. So, as you know, he gave up all thought of self and an easier life at home for his perilous mission in a foreign land.

'Now, Henry, I must finish my rehearsal for evening service.' Abruptly she went back to the foot-pedalled organ. With the urgency of duty on a Sunday, her voice crisped and her back stiffened. My archetype of grace and beauty transformed herself into the official choirmistress of the First Presbyterian Church of Seville.

Ancestors from Noah to Noyes

Early the next morning the sky was dark, with thunderclouds threatening a dreary day in the house on the hill. During prayers the rain pelted the windows, and through half-shut eyes I could see the drooping heads of cows and horses, their hides plastered down by the rain, sheltering under the elm trees across the turnpike. At the final 'Amen', I had an inspiration to brighten my day. I asked my Aunt Clara if she had any of my grandfather's old letters. It would be fun to read what he had to say about Canton. Maybe, even, he had written about Billy and me to his sisters back home. What fun to find out what he thought about us!

'There's a trunk full of old letters and diaries in the attic. I'm afraid the spiders and termites have made nests of them all. Will,' she said, turning to my father, 'maybe you'd like to show Henry what's left up there – in your old room. We were talking about the Taiping yesterday. I remember my brother Henry wrote a report for the Mission Society when he was attending seminary at Hudson back in the 1850s. He kept most of those reports, I'm sure you remember, in that leather-bound journal of his. Maybe it's still up there.'

My father took me upstairs to the attic room he had occupied in his college days. The old brass-bound trunk, which had travelled back and forth to China half a dozen times with my grandfather and grandmother, was green with mildew and blanketed with dust and cobwebs in disrepair. As my father prised open the lid, a flutter of winged termites blinded us for a moment. Among the bundles of letters, my father extracted a faded crimson volume with golden title and subtitle: *Noyes Genealogy, Vol. II, Descendants of Rev. James Noyes.* 'Go to, son. You'll find the whole family history – our branch of it at least – in this book published by a Colonel Noyes in 1904. From Noah to the twentieth century. Sorry, I can't stay and excavate the archives with you. Your mother and I have to go to Wooster for an alumni luncheon in our honour.'

I was glad to be left alone to travel back along the highways and byways of family history. Some of the diaries and letters were so tunnelled by Canton white ants and Seville termites that I had to use more imagination than eyesight. But the *Noyes Genealogy*, with its coat of arms engraved in gold on the cover, had survived in faded mint condition. A dove with an olive branch in beak was poised for flight above a gold shield surrounded by golden vine tendrils. The dove was preparing to take off after forty days and nights, I guessed, to check water levels for Noah and family. I did not stop to think that, according to the Bible 'begats', everybody alive was descended from the Noahs and that we were not an exceptional family, even though our name was similar. Colonel Noyes, however, made a point of bringing our Norman ancestors into the direct line of descent. It was exciting for me at age eleven to voyage with Guillaume Noiès – our name was interpreted by the Colonel at this stage in family history to mean walnut, possibly hard head – across the English Channel in 1066 in the van of William the Conqueror's army-navy. In return for helping to defeat Angles and Saxons in their own country, Guillaume was rewarded with a county-size estate near Norwich and serf labour enough to cultivate it for himself and his heirs for several centuries.

Family good fortune must have sagged sometime in the six centuries following the Norman Conquest and twenty undocumented generations – undocumented, at least, in our direct line – for our last English ancestor, also a William, owned little enough property as a parish preacher, and even that was forcibly confiscated by King Charles I. William had refused to use the prayer book of the Church of England in his Sunday services. In his sermons he had also identified the golden calf as a symbol of corruption in His Majesty's court and was therefore denounced by Bishop Laud's FBI as a roundhead and a subversive. Sons James and Nicolas, as might be expected, had negative feelings about the divine right of kings and, after setting sail from the Port of London in the good barque *Mary and John*, landed safely on the shores of New England in 1634.

From that time on, for the next eight generations, our ancestors were preachers and teachers in the New World. I had counted how many of them had served in the American Revolutionary War – eighty-two anti-redcoats altogether – and had already reached the count of 205 ancestors, including my Great-Uncle Frank, who had served in the American Civil War on the side of Mr Lincoln, when my brother Bill shouldered his way through the cobwebs into the attic room and grabbed the *Genealogy* out of my hands. 'Bully!' I shouted at him, but I was getting tired of counting Civil War ancestors and began to plough through a bundle of old letters. 'Hey, Bill!' I shouted again, this time with excitement. 'Here's a letter from our great-grandfather in 1831 inviting our great-grandmother to come out to Seville and marry him. How about that?'

Bill had finished ruffling through the *Genealogy* and was reading from the 1865 diary of Aunt Clara, who turned fifteen that year. 'Listen to this, boy,' he gloated, as if he'd found gold. 'This is important history. April 10th. Aunt Clara writes: "The news came in the paper that General Lee and his army had surrendered and so our little town's cannon is going off." That was the end of the Civil War. And then on April 15th she writes: "President Lincoln is dead. He was at the theatre last night and was shot by an assassin. Who ever expected to hear such news?" That's history! How do you like that?'

In the meantime, I had located our grandfather's journal with a hundred and fifty pages in his handwriting, old-style like an engraving. 'Hey Bill, here's his article on the Taiping Aunt Clara told me about yesterday. Do you know who they were?'

'So what?' Bill ignored me and continued to leaf through the 1865 diary. 'Listen to all the sobs when our grandpa left the house on the hill to go to China. Aunt Clara wrote on January 20th – that was in 1866 – that "The whole family has probably spent our last day together on earth, but may we all spend a blessed eternity in Heaven." Just like our grandfather,' Bill interpolated, 'the day he died. Remember what he said? Here's some real sob stuff: "Farewell meeting in the evening. Father made some touching remarks, and Henry also. He closed with the verse of the hymn, *Yes, my native !and, I love thee.* We all wept most of the evening to think that the parting is so near, near, just tomorrow, and we shall bid them a long farewell." ' Bill smiled at me, as if reading from Aunt Clara's diary was great fun.

I thought it must have been a very sad occasion, not one to smile about, so I changed the subject: 'I'll bet you don't know why Grandpa went to China in the first place?'

'So, smarty-pants, I give. Tell me all about it. To save souls, I bet.'

'Sure. But also our Aunt Clara told me it was a lot more than that. He wrote this article here on the Taiping. They were Christians. Read it. They believed in everybody having the same property, and women were in their armies. They were a bunch of farmers like our folks believing in the Ten Commandments. When they were all wiped out, our grandfather wanted to go and carry on their work. You know, Christianize four hundred million Chinese – or as many as he could.'

By this time, Bill had wrenched the journal out of my hands. 'Here's something more interesting than all that ancient history. What our grandfather thought of drunkards.' I read some startling passages over Bill's shoulder: 'Alcohol is a tyrant more cruel than Nero and harder to escape from than was Pharaoh of Egypt.... In Cromwell's England, drunkards were enframed in whisky barrels and made to walk in the public streets to be ridiculed.... Blood from the head of a man who used whisky has been known to burn....'

Outside, the sun had broken through clouds and was beginning, anaemically, to filter through cobwebs spun across the dormer windows by a band of guerrilla spiders. 'Come on,' Bill ordered as he chucked the family archives back into the trunk and slammed down the lid. 'Let's go out to the old swimming hole,' piously adding, with a wink, 'We've had enough of ancestors and drunks for one day!'

'You can joke about it like a fool if you want,' I protested in a holier-than-thou tone of voice. 'Besides, you got drunk yourself, smarty, at that banquet Dad took us to. Remember, on the houseboat in Fati?'

'You've got a great imagination. So you saw a tiger on the Peak of Hong Kong!'

I wasn't going to be sidetracked into defending my tiger. 'You drank two of those small glasses of rice whisky when our father wasn't looking. Then you started acting like a worse idiot than usual.'

'You're nuts, I never did any such thing.' Then Bill resorted to Chinese slang, as if that proved his point: 'You're just a *kongtaiwah*!' We went on shouting at each other: 'I'm not a big fat liar!' 'You are!' 'I didn't!' 'You did!' all the way back through the woods until we reached our swimming pool.

My Great-Aunt Emily

Our three weeks went by like a flash. Before we knew it we were packing for the return trip to Toronto. The last night in Seville was hot, as Ohio nights can be in June. It was also prayer-meeting night. But I didn't want to go. I wanted to spend my last evening with Aunt Emily on the front porch watching the yellow-hot sky grey out in the west and the stars come out to match the fireflies in the cornfields. Aunt Emily was already seventy-nine. I might never see her again. I had learned to know and love her in three weeks with a devotion second only to my love for my mother and father.

By conventional standards she was as homely a woman as I had ever seen. The wrinkles, the discoloured skin in patches, the snubby nose, and the warts gave her a certain distinction of ugliness. But what a warm spirit burned in her eyes, a glowing brown that radiated good humour through her glasses! All her life she had bolstered the morale of parents, brothers and sisters with utter selflessness and a chuckle that defied discouragement. Her hearty laugh must have carried her through many a downing situation as the first woman to graduate from Wooster College. She had scorned the male superstition that women should stay home; or, if they had to have a career, teach grade school, for which a college degree was not necessary. College was for men. Why would a woman be studying science, mathematics or theology when there was no way she could become a professor or an ordained minister, or have a scientific career? God had settled that question in the Book of Genesis when He made Eve out of Adam's rib. With Victorian fortitude, Emily ignored male platitudes and ably outranked many of the bigots in their own chosen subjects. She had learned from her mother, my Great-Grandmother Lois, that a woman had a right to be a person. She had the inner conviction that life could be happy and that a woman could enjoy it equally with men. God was on her side, she knew, when women won the vote in 1919. 'It was His will,' she said proudly when she mentioned voting for the first time in 1920. When she retired from the teaching profession she became the gravitational centre of the Seville Noyeses around whom her three younger sisters orbited. They looked to her for difficult solutions and judgements. The first week in Seville I was awed by her, the second I admired her, and the third and last I loved her with the passions and insecurities of an eleven-year-old finding a solid foundation for his affections.

'How many did you make it?' she asked. We were counting the freight cars in a long train a quarter of a mile away across the fields.

'One hundred and sixty.'

'I make it one hundred and sixty-one, but it's too late to count again,' she chuckled. 'Now if you listen, child, you can hear the corn grow!'

'I can hear it! But why can't I hear the corn grow in the daytime?'

'You can, but you have to listen carefully. There are so many other noises, but at night, most of the world sleeps.'

'Not the owls,' I reminded her. We could hear them hooting from the maple bush a mile down the road.

'In the daytime,' Aunt Emily went on, bubbling out her words as if they were rising from a deep well of knowledge, 'the sun makes growth even more rapid. It warms the leaves and helps them make chlorophyll. That's the green in the leaves which is like bread and butter for trees and plants. And the sun gives his golden abundance to the corn as it ripens. Each kernel is like a baby sun and when you eat corn it's like eating sunshine.'

'Why are strawberries red then, if the sun makes everything green or yellow?'

Aunt Emily was amused. 'You're going to make a great theologian or hair-splitter. Our strawberry patch has gone back to wilderness now, hasn't it? But our kitchen garden used to be beautiful and tidy. My mother, your great-grandmother, saw to that. She had a green thumb. She planted those strawberries close to seventy-five years ago when she first came out from New England. The farm was like the Garden of Eden in those days. We used to grow or make almost everything we needed: corn, potatoes, carrots, beets, turnips – everything. We used to spin and weave wool from our own sheep into blankets and clothing. We churned our own butter, made cheese, apple cider, even made our own sugar. The men in the family used to spend a week or two in the maple bush down the turnpike . . .'

'Our father took us down there yesterday,' I interrupted. 'We saw where they camped out and an old vat with rusty holes they used to thicken the sap in. Dad said they used to have a cabin and sat round the stove at night smoking pipes and telling stories.'

'Can you believe it?' Aunt Emily was on her own track. 'We didn't even know what a banana was in the days your Great-Aunt Harriet went out to China. She wrote us a letter about how she crossed the Isthmus of Panama on the back of a donkey – of course there was no canal then, or transcontinental railway – and on the way she ate what she described as an overripe apple with a heavy yellow skin which she had to peel off before she could eat the fruit. We didn't know what she was talking about – neither did she!'

Aunt Emily paused to shift time gears. 'Now, of course, life is very different. We can't look after sheep and cows any more. Mary had to give up even raising chickens last year because of her arthritis. Now we have to depend on our teachers' pensions and buy almost everything we need in the village or from Montgomery Ward. That's the trouble with getting old. We become so dependent.' She smiled benevolently at me, as if it would be a long time before I would fully understand what she meant. 'Yes, things are very different in these days, with automobiles speeding down the turnpike at twenty-five miles an hour. Takes my breath away! It's hard to believe we'll have electric lighting in a year or two!'

'My Uncle Roe in Cayuga makes his own electricity,' I volunteered. 'He's got one of those little gasoline generators that goes pup-pup-pup. And he's put a couple of light bulbs in the henhouse with an alarm clock that turns them on at five o'clock in the morning. So the hens lay all winter.'

'Just what I meant,' said Aunt Emily. 'Your mother has told us what a scientific farmer her brother is. Well, that's progress. It seems only yesterday they put in our telephone. Now we could hardly do without it.'

Aunt Emily was at last running out of steam, her face sagging from fatigue. Abruptly changing the subject, she began in a preachy voice to say, 'Now you boys are the only descendants of our whole family, we think you have a wonderful opportunity in your lives to perform a great service. Your two grandfathers were preachers and your grandfather Noyes a missionary into the bargain. Your father has told me that the day your grandfather died, almost his last words were to you and Billy. He hoped you both would go out to China when you are grown and continue the work he started in 1866.'

'I'd like to, but I don't know if I'm good enough.'

'God will help you decide that. He's wiser than you or I.

He will give you the confidence you will need. Now it's time for bed. But first, listen again!'

We both listened a moment to the corn leaves rustling open. 'I can hear them!' I said, with the excitement of a new discovery. Aunt Emily was like Mother Nature herself revealing the secrets of growth, but in her own body she was stiff-jointed and aching as I helped her pull herself upstairs to her room, leaning on me and the banister.

My mother was reading in bed, a history book on China. No wonder she had such a lot of information about Sun Yat-sen and the Versailles Treaty, she was always reading. 'Aunt Emily thinks I can make a missionary,' I blurted out, 'like Grandpa, when I'm grown and go back to China. I'd like that!'

My mother's flicker of interest hardly corresponded to my enthusiasm. 'You will decide later, when the time comes. But now it's time to go to bed. We have a long trip ahead tomorrow.'

As I pulled the sheet up to my chin, I thought: Anyway, my grandfather would have been very happy at what I said, even if my mother wasn't. I could see his white beard and feel his hand stroking my head. His face enlarged and smiled encouragingly as the room widened into an ocean and I was sailing with him on a ship that docked in Hong Kong Harbour. Victoria Peak, rising above us, was replaced almost at once by a two-storey tropical mansion with screened verandas and palms at the corners and a pomelo tree shading the front door of the house I was born in. I woke with the secret assurance that the most important decision in my life had already been made. I would go back to China when I was grown and complete my father's interrupted mission.

But between the dream of an eleven-year-old and its fulfilment, time was to cast a long shadow. It would be fifty-three years before I would return to China, and then with a mission vastly different from my father's.

❋ 3 ❋

Transitions

Student Days in Canada

I came back to Canada on a tremendous high and, for years afterwards, had massive support from aunts and uncles on both my mother's and father's side to go back to China when I grew up and settle the unfinished missionary business of the Noyes family. In my more stagy moments I could see myself cast in the role of Little Shepherd of the Chinese Hills, with Bible in one hand and knotty staff in the other, going out to pastures in rural China to convert half a billion souls to the Christian way, rather than the Taoist or Buddhist way. But adolescence, with all its zigs and zags, put my religious fervour to the test. For a time it was possible to bend my faith between a father's conservative theology and a mother's liberal philosophy. More and more, though, I came to agree with my mother that Buddhism and Taoism were respectable religions and that Christianity should move over and make room, especially after reading the *Tao Te Ching* and certain Buddhist scriptures she borrowed from the library for me.

By the time I graduated from grade school, the double transition from China to the United States to Canada no longer created problems of adjustment. It was an advantage, rather, when I went on to high school, to have been born halfway round the world and to have lived under the Stars and Stripes for two years. Most of my fellow-students had been born and raised within a few blocks of Humberside

Collegiate Institute on Toronto's West Side. They respected and envied me for being a world traveller. And I will say they were tolerant of what they considered certain oddball tendencies, such as the conviction I expressed in oral compositions that I was chosen by the forces of progress to campaign against the Fu Manchu and Yellow Peril stereotypes in and out of class.

I was inspired to speak out by my father's trans-Canada campaign against the Oriental Exclusion Acts, for which he organized a united front of Protestants, Catholics and Jews. I was also impressed with the direct action of Anne Leung, who lived with us for five years like an adopted sister. It was unbelievable to me, knowing Anne and her friend Jean, that Chinese were not permitted to sit downstairs in the cinemas of downtown Toronto, only in the balconies. One afternoon Anne and Jean were accidentally sold main-floor tickets at the Palladium. When the usher refused to seat them, they began to scream. The manager rushed out of an inner office to enforce quiet, but Anne and Jean hollered all the louder. In lower key the manager apologized for the mistake at the ticket counter and tried to woo them back upstairs into the balcony. But Jean and Anne went on shouting, and by this time some of the audience were giving them support: 'Aw, give the girls a break!' A few youngsters cheered and clapped, just to get into the act. Oldsters growled, 'Shut up, you young fools!' The manager scuttled back to his office and immediately the confusion ended. Anne and Jean sat in seats of their choice and the show went on. That was the end of discrimination against Orientals at the Palladium.

Through Anne and my father I was in frequent contact with Overseas Chinese, but rarely with anyone direct from the Republic of China. When I was a sophomore student in Modern Languages at the University of Toronto, however, we had a young visitor from Canton. Chen Yung, a recent graduate of Pui Ying Middle School, was on his way to England to study at the London School of Economics. On a stroll in High Park down to Lake Ontario, Chen told me an amazing story: 'The whole student body of Pui Ying was kidnapped by the communists in 1927 and transported to a camp in the guerrilla areas behind White Cloud Mountain.

We were treated well, fed well, and given orientation classes in Chinese history – the kind of history we never learned at Pui Ying. The communists showed a great fondness for us students and sent us back home after six months to our parents. They said that the youth of China were the hope of the Chinese revolution and that one day the warlords would be overthrown and foreign control replaced by an independent people's government. I hope they were right. My people have suffered for thousands of years under oppressors. It's time to take our destiny into our own hands.'

'Did you tell my father?'

'No, I didn't think he would approve.'

'Just as well,' I agreed, 'I'm sure he wouldn't. But what an exciting story about the old school! I never heard anything good about Chinese communists before.'

'In that case,' Chen went on, 'you've probably not heard about the May 4th Movement?' I shook my head. 'It was a student revolt to begin with against the Versailles Treaty which ceded the German concessions in China to Japan. It led to the forming of the Chinese Communist Party in 1921 and to massive strikes of workers and sailors in Hong Kong and the port cities. Didn't Dr Sun Yat-sen become unpopular in the West when he advocated a radical policy for the Kuomintang? An alliance with the Soviet Union, unity with the Chinese Communist Party, and concern for the welfare of the working masses. Chiang Kai-shek has reversed Dr Sun's famous Three Principles and taken the motherland back to feudalism.'

A few weeks after Chen's visit, the bombardment of Shanghai by the Japanese air force and navy hit the headlines of the Toronto papers and became of immediate concern to the college crowd, especially in the student commons and the coffee shops. At Flo's the serious students of history and political science came into their own. Debates opened up from table to table, corner to corner in her basement café. 'It's just another of those Far Eastern crises,' came from one corner; and from another, 'The Japanese aren't stupid enough to add 600 million starving mouths to feed out of their already skimpy ricebowl,' and from a third, 'Bullshit, it's the beginning of World War II and every able-bodied Canadian male will be in uniform next week!'

At Flo's the debate continued to rage all week. 'It's a dangerous situation,' Stanley Ryerson, an outspoken radical, summed it up. 'It's Japan's turn now for more imperialist adventures to externalize its internal problems in the world-wide depression. 'It's Japan's turn now for more imperialist Powers see war as a solution to their problems as well. The only force to stop a second world war, theoretically, would be the League of Nations representing the will of the world's peoples. But it looks like the so-called Great Powers have turned the League into a debating society.'

'That's the danger!' The voice was familiar. I turned round to identify Norman Endicott, one of my professors in the English Department at University College. He was earnest, as usual; his eyes seemed to shape his words as he leaned forward to add, 'Japan sees China as a raw-material base for Japanese expansion. It's inevitable, with the zaibatsu structure of Japanese society, that they will try to take over and run China with their military machine, the way they have Formosa and Korea. Chiang Kai-shek's not going to stop them.'

'Mao Tse-tung may, though,' said Stanley.

'Who's Mao Tse-tung?' A sceptical voice joined the discussion. 'A magician?'

'You might say so,' Norman answered. 'Don't under-estimate him. My brother Jim, who's a missionary in China – I was born in Chengdu myself – gets occasional information from Chinese friends about the guerrilla areas. The Chinese communists have apparently won over the support of large sections of peasantry. That means trouble up ahead for Chiang and Madame.'

Since my brother Bill and I were both of draft age, a serious debate developed at home around the supper table as well as at Flo's. My father thought that the Canadian and US governments should support China to the limit. Bill and I shared his hatred of Japanese aggression, but we were not so keen to be involved in a war in the Far East.

We were not drafted. The Western Powers had laid the basis for Japanese aggression at Versailles and were not about to support the Chinese Republic until later in the thirties when their own interests were threatened.

In the meantime, although I was worried about the war clouds gathering over Asia and Europe, I was more concerned about my own career. A product culturally of the sceptical twenties with literary gurus T.S. Eliot and Aldous Huxley in the ascendant, I had already shifted focus from training for the ministry to working for a PhD in English, which was a prerequisite for a university career in Canada. My father offered to borrow money from Aunt Emily to see me through two years at the University of London and suggested we spend a week in Seville in the summer of 1936.

It was a nostalgic experience for both of us. The family home was more like a museum than ever, with its Chinese silk fans and embroidered gowns and screens that had been sent over from Canton by my great-aunts, Harriet and Martha. They had returned to Seville to enjoy their retirement for only a short year or two in the 1920s. My aunts Clara, Sarah and Mary had lived on into the 1930s. But all of them had passed and left my Aunt Emily sole survivor of my great-grandparents' family that had once numbered nine children, including my grandfather. With a skin as wrinkled and brown as an autumn ploughed field, Aunt Emily at eighty-nine was a woman of amazing graciousness and humour. Her eyes smiled up with her customary warmth. She was now confined to a wheelchair after breaking both hips and suffering from arthritis in her back. When my father broached the subject of a loan for me to study abroad, she responded at once: 'Certainly, child, I will be happy to lend you the money.' Although I was twenty-six she still called me *child*, the way she had back in 1922 when I was only eleven.

'Are you sure it won't be a hardship for you?' I asked.

'Why, not at all,' she answered. 'We had hoped you would follow in your father's and grandfather's footsteps to continue their mission in China. Still, being a teacher is one of the great callings, and I am sure the Lord wanted me to put aside money for just such a good purpose. I do hope for your sake, though, that war doesn't break out before you finish your studies abroad.' As a retired history teacher, Aunt Emily took keen interest in world events. 'The radio is a blessing, now that I can't read much, but it brings such bad news these days. War is so terrible, and Hitler and Mussolini are such threats to world peace! I do hope that God in His mercy will take the weapons out of their hands. After Ethiopia, now it's Spain, as if they intend to involve us all in a second world war. If they do, I just hope I won't live to see it.'

Her wish was granted. She died at the age of ninety-one while I was still in London, but not before she had heard on her radio that Japan had invaded China, occupied Peiping, Tientsin, and Shanghai, and massacred 300,000 Chinese civilians in the capital city, Nanking; and that Hitler's air force and navy had blitzed two Spanish cities, Guernica and Almeria, totally destroying buildings and people.

London 1936–39

My two years in London doing research at the British Museum were ominous years for world peace. In all conscience, it was impossible for me not to take sides in the Spanish Civil War from the time I arrived in England in autumn 1936 with a Canadian passport stamped 'Not valid for Spain'. Ninety-five per cent of British writers, including H.G. Wells and J.B. Priestley, whom I admired, supported the Spanish Republic in the counter-revolutionary war launched by Franco with the open support of the Axis Powers. As I began to understand the non-intervention policy of the US State Department and the British Foreign Office, my politics moved steadily from centre to left.

A chance meeting at the Unity Theatre – one of those chance meetings that lead to a lifetime relationship – speeded up the process. Gertrude Sirnis had studied law at the London School of Economics and was currently an organizer for the National Association of Women Clerks and Secretaries. Our next rendezvous was at the Albert Hall, where a giant rally was called to protest the policy of non-intervention and to raise money for Spanish refugee children housed with English families. H.G. Wells chaired, and in his introductory remarks gave the historical background of the Spanish Civil War and the failure of the League of Nations to form a united front against the fascist Powers. Later in the programme when Wells introduced Paul Robeson, the audience rose to cheer them both. In his powerful bass voice, unequalled in the twentieth century, Robeson spoke and sang of the courage of the Spanish and Chinese people in their resistance to Hitler, Mussolini, and Hirohito. When he sang *Chi-lai*, the battle hymn of China, the audience joined him, singing and humming the *Internationale*.

The mass rally, the first of its kind I had ever attended, was an overwhelming experience. As we were leaving the hall, Gertrude drew me over to the literature table. 'With your background, here's a book you should read.' She handed me a copy of *Red Star Over China*. 'By one of your American journalists, Edgar Snow. They say it's a red-hot item! Have you heard about it?'

I was ashamed to say no. 'I've always been interested in China,' Gertrude went on, 'ever since cousins of my mother went out there years ago. When I was at LSE, I took an active part in student affairs. I used to give talks at Toynbee Hall denouncing the Japanese occupation of Manchuria. When I'm not so busy with my organizing job, *Red Star* is at the top of my reading list.'

I stayed awake all that night to follow Mao Tse-tung and the Chinese People's Liberation Army across mountains, rivers and treacherous grasslands to set up a new Soviet-style government in the mountains of Shensi in a village called Yenan, where the inhabitants lived in cave-dwellings. Yenan was already headquarters of a revolutionary government that had jurisdiction over a population of 100 million Chinese, mainly peasants.

'You should read Snow's account of the Long March yourself – six thousand miles!' I advised Gertrude at our next rendezvous. 'Mao Tse-tung and Chu Teh have trained in a new-style army that integrates with the peasantry and national minorities. Chiang Kai-shek's armies have a history of robbing, raping and brutalizing the peasant population and conscripting their sons. But the revolutionary armies are volunteers, instructed to take nothing from the peasants without paying, not even a needle or thread; to help with the harvests, respect women and religious customs, and much more. *Red Star* is a terrific book! Snow thinks China will get rid of its oppressors after five thousand years, the old as well as the new, and become a real people's republic.'

'Jolly good, and about time,' Gertrude gloated with me. 'The Chinese have nothing to lose but their chains, and the women their bound feet.'

As springtime had come to London in a burst of unexpected sunshine, Gertrude went on to issue an invitation: 'Maybe you'd lay aside your books for the weekend and we could take off for Southampton to visit my folks. It's primrose time in the New Forest. We'll rally our friends for a picnic.'

On the drive to the south coast we talked about H.G. Wells, Paul Robeson, Edgar Snow – a highly political kind of courtship. I told Gertrude how my grandfather had been inspired by the principles of the Taiping. 'Strange, I feel the same type of compulsion to go back to the China Edgar Snow describes – one day. As he says, the slumbering giant of Asia is waking up. I would like to take part in the awakening. Would you?'

Before saying, 'Maybe some day,' Gertrude gave me a quizzical glance, as if asking what I was proposing. In London I was rarely able to be alone with her, since politics and job were priorities. But that evening, after supper, we found a hillside lane to stroll down hand in hand. The sun had just set over Southampton Harbour and the moon was rounding up above a skyline of rose and rhododendron hedges. 'Maybe we should try Canada first?'

Again Gertrude's answer was, 'Maybe some day.'

Ten months later, after many more rendezvous and political meetings, Gertrude and I were married in London and went to Davos, her birthplace in the high Swiss Alps, for a skiing honeymoon.

In the following year I completed work for the PhD and accepted a teaching position back in Canada in the English Department of the University of Manitoba. On 10 September 1939 we sailed from Southampton, a week after Neville Chamberlain announced that we had fallen on evil times and declared war on the Axis Powers. Gertrude's sad family, shouldering gas masks, gathered at the dockside in the shadows of barrage balloons to wish us a safe voyage as they waved us off into an English Channel infested with Nazi submarines.

It was reassuring to know that the *Aquitania* was carrying a substantial shipment of gold bullion from the Bank of England to purchase tanks and ships in the United States. Besides, there were close to a thousand anxious Americans aboard, including John and Robert Kennedy, whose father was US ambassador to the court of St James. He assured the passengers by telegram that the British navy would guarantee us safe passage, and it did, through the Channel. Four destroyers accompanied us past Land's End. Then the *Aquitania* took off at top speed in a zigzag course, with engines pounding until the old ship threatened to rattle apart. We heard from a deck steward that she had never sailed so far so fast and that it was a miracle she arrived in New York Harbour 'in one piece'.

Before we sailed, Gertrude's grandmother, aged ninety, had given us her blessing, like the good Forsyte she was: 'When you get to the New World, buy yourselves a piece of property, and if the house burns down, you'll still have the land.'

World War II and After

During World War II and the Cold War that followed, we had more important things to do in Canada and the United States than to buy a piece of property. Gertrude and I both came from families highly motivated to pioneer in fields of their faith and choice – mine in the religious field, hers in the political. Her father, Alexander Sirnis, was a Latvian journalist and linguist who, with her English mother, worked on translations of Tolstoy journals with Chertkov in Bournemouth. When he contracted tuberculosis he moved with his wife and two children to Davos to try the high-altitude cure, which Thomas Mann was later to make the theme of his *Magic Mountain*, with Davos as its setting. Shortly after Gertrude was born, in spring 1914, the family moved back to

England at the outbreak of World War I. Her father spent the last two years of his life translating the writings of Lenin and Karl Liebknecht into English, to the end a strong advocate of socialism.

In my own case, the example of my father's lifelong campaign against the Oriental Exclusion Acts provided me with a strong incentive to take part in political and social movements. Social and self-fulfilment were for both of us two sides of the same coin, motive forces for rising to a higher level of consciousness and being. In the process we both had the age-old urge to raise a family, hoping to contribute to the progressive trend in human evolution.

As we look back at the twenty years between 1939 and 1959, we remember the many activities into which we put our energies with the conviction that our years were well spent, and the additional conviction that the experiences gained made it possible for us to meet the greatest challenge in our lives in 1959.

I remember two experiences especially, during this period, that strengthened our conviction, both concerning China: the first while I was head of the Creative Writing Department at the University of Missouri in Columbia; the second when I was an organizer for Henry Wallace's Progressive Party in Chicago. The atmosphere of Columbia, which was ineptly styled the 'Athens of the Middle West' by the local chamber of commerce, was conservative to the core, but the School of Journalism had a liberal orientation and a worldwide reputation. Edgar Snow was still remembered as a distinguished graduate, especially by two radical journalist students from China.

The morning after Kuomintang agents came to our house to ask if the two students were communists, I went to the registrar's office to protest. The assistant registrar, a progressive Southern woman and a good friend, welcomed me: 'You're just the person I wanted to see.' She lowered her voice to add, 'Henry, this must absolutely go no further. The administration has given *carte blanche* to two Kuomintang agents to snoop around campus and investigate the "loyalty" of the two Chinese students registered in journalism.'

'Yes, that's what I wanted to see you about, Jean. The two

agents came out to the house yesterday with a gift of one of those beautiful stone plaques, grey veined with black, which they said was quarried in one of the Yangtze gorges. They knew from some source,' I laughed, 'that I was born in China, so they asked me confidentially if the two students were communists. I told them I was not on the faculty of the School of Journalism and hadn't the slightest idea. As I showed them the door, you should have seen the way they eyed the Yangtze artefact, but there was no tenet in the whole Confucian canon that would have permitted them to take back a gift once given.' We had a good laugh together, then sobered as I put Jean squarely on the spot: 'What are you going to do about it?'

'What can I do?'

'That's for you to decide, but I know for certain that the snoops here and in China won't prevent students here and in China from supporting the revolution.'

It was a relief for Gertrude and me to find a larger arena for progressive activities. The Abraham Lincoln School in Chicago offered us the opportunity when I was appointed extension director in the last year of the war. My new job gave me a chance to review the latest books and reports on China for my current events classes and I was often invited to give talks to larger audiences, even Kiwanis* and Rotary clubs. Our teachers were experts in their fields; they encouraged discussion, glad to teach in an institution that gave them freer rein than the traditional schools and colleges to criticize the established order, to support equal rights and job opportunities for women and ethnic minorities and, in the international sphere, to support the United Nations concept of self-determination for Third World peoples. As the horrors of the concentration camps were exposed in the last year of World War II, special classes were given in the rise of fascism in Europe and Asia and reactionary movements in the United States that had supported or tolerated Mussolini, Hitler and Hirohito. We had special rapport with Jewish groups, many of whose members had lost relatives in the

---

*Kiwanis: an organization founded in 1915 for the promulgation of higher ideals in business, industrial and professional life.

Holocaust. Other ethnic groups were keen to hear about Russian socialism and the Chinese revolution approaching its climactic period – especially the older people. The Board of the School defined our primary aim as 'education for action' and our instruction as 'people's education'.

When the School closed its doors three years after the war, I went in summer 1948 to work as an organizer in Henry Wallace's Progressive Party, which presented an alternative programme to the 'Cold Warriors' of the Democratic and Republican Parties. While still Vice-President in the Roosevelt administration, Wallace had tried in vain to persuade Chiang Kai-shek to unite with Mao Tse-tung and form a new Asian democracy modelled after the United States. The China question remained high on his agenda in his election campaign. As a result a number of Overseas Chinese students joined the Wallace for President Committee at the University of Chicago and one of them, a journalist from Canton, invited me to speak at a forum in the student union.

I was matched against a returned missionary who praised the great achievements of the Republic of China under the Christian leadership of General Chiang and Madame. They had defeated the Japanese with American assistance and would soon rid the country of bandits and communists. When the reverend missionary sat down with the smile of a saint, two students let out a vociferous cheer and clapped loudly, but failed to enthuse more than a faint applause from the rest of the eighty students present. My friend, Kacheng, then introduced me as a person who could be called an Overseas Chinese, since I had been born in Canton. 'Our second speaker', he added, 'is an expert on contemporary Chinese affairs.'

The students looked up hopefully as I began to refute the first speaker's arguments and prove that Chiang was an authoritarian and an enemy of democracy. I traced the progress of the Chinese revolution from the first Chinese soviet in 1931 through the Yenan period down to the current victories of the People's Liberation Armies and the defection *en masse* of the Kuomintang troops. 'It is too late in Chinese history to turn the clock back,' I advised in conclusion. 'If I were one of you I would go home to my motherland and take

Henry on the Great Wall

Henry and his son, Chris, on the steps of the main entrance of the Great Hall of the People

At Nanniwan, near Yanan. *Left to right*: our interpreter, Yang Aiwen, my guide and host, Wang Hongshen, myself, and three cadres directing a cadre reform school, the dormitories of which are in the background.

Left: Fan Jingyi, the director of the Foreign Languages Publication Bureau, welcomes Henry to a reception in the Great Hall.
Below: Peasants working in rice-fields near Guangzhou (*photo Gary Bulmer*).

part in freeing my people from the control of feudal landlords and foreign elements, help build an independent China. I will look forward personally one day to returning to Canton and seeing the Pearl River and my native city liberated from foreign gunboats.'

The majority of the students rose and applauded, and I am sure they were as happy as I was on 1 October 1949, when Chairman Mao Tse-tung announced the founding of the People's Republic of China from the Gate of Heavenly Peace in Peking: 'Our nation will from now on become one of the family of peace- and freedom-loving nations, working bravely and diligently to create its own civilization and happiness and at the same time promote world peace and freedom. Our nation will never again be insulted, for we have stood up!'

A year and a half later I received a letter from Kacheng postmarked Guangzhou (Canton). 'I am now working for Xinhua News Agency,' he wrote. 'Thanks for your encouragement last year. Victory is ours. Forty out of our eighty Chinese Student Club members are now back home busy constructing our New China. Our new constitution guarantees equal rights for women and national minorities and freedom to believe or not to believe in any religion. Come and see the great things we are doing in your birthplace – as soon as you can.'

❋ 4 ❋

China Syndrome

A Challenge

The year 1959 was a turning point in our lives, a year when we were called upon to use all the ingenuity and experience we had accumulated in a lifetime. On 1 October, by coincidence China's National Day, our longtime friend Paul Romaine phoned me to say, 'Henry, I hear you're no longer working at Pettibone Mulliken.'

'That's correct. When I applied there three years ago for a job in the tool-and-die department, I neglected to put down my university education on the application form.'

'They fired you for that?'

'No, not really. The real reason, I was a shop steward, filed and won too many grievances; and also locked horns with the works manager in bargaining sessions. Now I've had to file my own grievance with the Machinists' Union and the Labour Relations Board. But they're slow to act.'

'You think you'll get your job back?'

'Not a prayer. The cards are stacked.'

'Then I have something here that might interest you: a letter from Imported Publications and Products in New York. They supply me, as you know, with books and magazines from the Foreign Languages Press in Peking.'

'What's the deal?' I was excited without yet knowing why.

'If you come down to the shop this afternoon I'll tell you more.'

Paul Romaine ran the only independent bookshop in downtown Chicago. He handled bestsellers and popular fiction to pay the rent, but his chief interest was in progressive publications and his store was known as the best place in town for avant-garde books and magazines. Despite the inquisition of Senator Joseph McCarthy, symptomatic of the deepening freeze of civil liberties in the Cold War period, Paul continued to handle radical writers of the 1930s: John Steinbeck, Agnes Smedley, Jack Conroy, Clifford Odets. As liberal leaders of the New Deal became McCarthy's special targets for political assassination, left-led coalitions and united fronts dwindled. In Chicago the Abraham Lincoln School was defunct. Henry Wallace's Progressive Party shrank to a holding operation of the isolated left before bowing off the stage of US political history like earlier third-party movements. The American Peace Crusade had spent its energies in one giant rally at the Coliseum. The Congress of Industrial Organizations was being shredded from the top down by loyalty oaths and anti-labour legislation passed by an intimidated Congress. Romaine's bookshop was one of the few progressive institutions to survive the 1950s – the New Dark Age, as Paul called it – and he continued to handle *Moscow News, China Reconstructs* and the *Peking Review*; also, to display them in his window on La Salle, the Wall Street of the Middle West. He had such an affable, pipe-smoking disposition that even officers of the law stopped in to browse and ask him questions like: 'What the hell is Marxism–Leninism? And who is this Mao Tse-tung?'

Paul's wife, Marguerite, welcomed me with a cynical smile as she stood with arms akimbo behind the cash register: 'You're a notorious character. Read what the *Chicago Tribune* writes about you, in case you missed it.' The clipping she held out accused me, in usual *Tribune* style, of taking part in a worldwide conspiracy, and asked: 'Why should a professor otherwise want to work in a machine shop?'

'Why indeed?' Marguerite mocked.

'Why not?' I took her up half seriously. 'Gertrude and I decided to work with our hands to round out our characters. The days I could make a living as a freelance writer and organizer of large meetings for progressive causes ended with the New Dark Age. Besides, Chris and Nicky are great kids but they eat like pigs and need new shoes every three months. And seriously, I miss the day-to-day association with fellow-workers who usually say what they mean and mean what they say.'

'Paul's got a proposition for you.' Marguerite nodded up at Paul's office, a mezzanine pigeon loft from which he could keep his eye on customers and also watch the passing crowd of bankers, stockbrokers and lawyers in La Salle Street.

Paul was not a word waster. He motioned me to a seat with a twist of his pipe and handed me a letter. 'From Margaret Cowl. She's a remarkable person. Single-handed she's organized the import of publications from the Latvian and Lithuanian Socialist Republics, the USSR, and also China. She has the right kind of guts. Her father died when she was only fourteen. She went to work in a garment factory, hid in the toilet when the child-labour inspector made his rounds, and for years supported her mother and younger brothers and sisters.'

The letter invited Paul to take over the import of publications from China, since Margaret, at sixty-five, was about to retire and wanted to slim down her imports. 'If you can't do it yourself,' she wrote, 'can you recommend somebody who's qualified?'

Paul came straight to the point. 'You're the only person I know who's qualified, meaning that you are deeply interested in China and have wide contacts in the progressive movement.' He gave me an encouraging smile. 'You've used my China section like a library for years. You're a natural, China born ...'

'But wait,' I objected. 'I don't know a thing about the book business, accounts, marketing ...'

'That's easy. Marguerite and I can teach you the basics. What's it going to be?'

'First, a family conference.'

'You'd be a schlemiel to turn it down.' Paul spoke as if he had already made the most important decision in my life for me, and began to sort out a stack of invoices.

'Does Paul make all your decisions for you, too?' I asked Marguerite on my way out.

'He's right. You'd be a fool to turn it down,' she said, with an urgency in her voice and eyes. 'China's on the map to stay – 800 million strong – in spite of the silence or abuse of the US media. You could do both countries a favour in helping develop two-way understanding.'

A Family Business

Our family conference took place the following evening in the café of the Greyhound bus station. My trip to New York was an occasion of prime importance which required a group send-off. While Chris and Nicky were talking excitedly about taking canoe trips on the Grand Canal and riding camels across the Gobi Desert, Gertrude and I were discussing the pros and cons of transforming ourselves from proletarians to petty-bourgeois entrepreneurs. When my bus was called, Gertrude advised me in parting, 'Investigate it all first before we make up our minds.'

Twenty-four hours later I was sitting across a restaurant table from Margaret Cowl in the great American metropolis. She was a lively person for one soon to retire, with grey hair, glasses, and a youthful and alert manner. 'Paul gave you a most favourable recommendation, which I value, since we are old friends. He wrote that you've been a machinist for ten years and before that the extension director of the Abraham Lincoln School. The Chinese will be specially interested in your experiences as a worker and teacher in people's education.' Margaret was sizing me up with a friendly but critical eye, as if to make sure that I measured up to Paul's recommendation.

'But do you think the Chinese will balk at my missionary background?'

'Why should they? I'll send them a copy of Paul's letter. Your problem would be more with US regulations. Since the US Treasury bans export of capital to the People's Republic of China under the Trading with the Enemy Act, you wouldn't be able to send payments to Guoji Shudian. That's the firm in Peking from which I import Chinese publications. You would have to deposit funds owing in an account blocked by the US Treasury.' Since my eyes were blinking shut after an all-night bus ride, Margaret said tactfully, 'So we'll talk more tomorrow.'

After working for a week at Imported Publications and Products, I felt excited and depressed at the same time. How could we go into business with a zero-zero balance at the bank? But Margaret had avoided the subject. 'This is not only a commercial business, it's building a bridge of friendship between two great peoples,' she explained with pride. 'An opening of doors and windows which Joe McCarthy and his cronies thought they had shut for ever. The American people need to know more about the people of China. By beginning to shape their own history, the Chinese will take the Western world back to school and teach us how to refashion an economy and morality that put humans first, not dollars. The American people can in turn supply the Chinese with science and technique to speed up their material development and help them raise their terribly low living standard.' Then she asked me point-blank, 'Well, what will it be?'

'I'll have to be frank with you. We haven't a dime to invest.'

'You won't need it. You pay as you go. Every month you deposit what you owe to Guoji Shudian in a blocked account. You don't need capital.'

'But what about you? After all the time and energy you've put into it? Margaret, you'd better find somebody else. We don't have enough dough to buy a decent typewriter!'

'Now you've considered all the negatives, what about the political importance?'

'You sound like my wife,' I laughed.

'But seriously, you seem to have solved other problems in your life. Surely this is no more difficult than processing grievances, organizing Opera House meetings?'

'It's not the difficulty . . .' I began to object.

'I know. I'll be happy to give you every assistance, and there will be no exchange of money between us. You seem to be the kind of person who won't be in it for the money, with your interest in the Chinese people. There are half a dozen progressives here in New York who want the business, but they are concerned only with politics. If China's line should change or the USSR and China should follow different lines, they would jump ship and follow the Soviet line. The Chinese people deserve somebody like you.'

I was overwhelmed. I called Gertrude to explain. 'Margaret's made me an offer. How can I refuse?'

'You can't,' said Gertrude, with gung-ho enthusiasm. 'I've been thinking about it all week. Let's do it!'

Margaret Cowl was one of the few selfless people I have ever met. She transferred the whole import business of Chinese publications to us as promised and refused any remuneration with a curt, 'There's no bottom line between us!'

When I came back to Chicago with the news that a new import firm to be called China Books would soon supply Romaine's with its publications from China, Paul and Marguerite congratulated me with a three-sided embrace. Marguerite said, 'You're in on the ground floor', and Paul, 'You're lucky, while it's still a small business, to get your basic training. But make no mistake, this is just a beginning. Relations between the US and China are bound to open up ahead. There's already a firm basis of friendship between the Chinese people and ourselves – always has been. You'll find millions of Americans interested in the New China once you get rolling. In the meantime, come and work with us. We promised to show you the ropes – and we will. To begin with, you should read the latest arrivals. Here's Felix Greene's brochure on his 1957 trip to the PRC which City Lights in San Francisco has just published. Also, you should read Rewi Alley's *The People Have Strength* from New World Press in Peking – the best account so far of China's reconstruction after the Civil War. You'd better do your homework now, because once you get into the book business you'll have no time to read!'

As Paul climbed back up the stairs to his mezzanine office, Marguerite handed me a slim lemon-coloured book, *Red Flood Over China* by Agnes Smedley. 'A present for you to celebrate the opening of your new enterprise. Edgar Snow gets all the credit for publicizing the Chinese revolution, but a woman journalist beat him to the draw. Three years before *Red Star Over China* appeared, Smedley published her account of the setting up of the first Chinese Soviet Republic. It's rare. Treasure it, and may it bring you good luck!'

Six weeks later, we received a letter from Guoji Shudian offering to open commercial relations based on the strong recommendation of Margaret Cowl. Since our family budget made no provision for renting a store or office, we tacked up a small shingle on our front door and registered ourselves with the record office as China Books & Periodicals, CB&P.

Our next problem, serious though not crippling, was to deal with restrictions imposed by the US government under the Trading with the Enemy Act. Under the First Amendment of the Constitution, Americans were guaranteed the right to read even publications originating in a communist country. But all trade with China had been cut off in 1951 and import of publications was possible only under Treasury licence. The Treasury kept us on hold for several months before finally responding favourably to our application, but its conditions were onerous. Since we were forbidden to pay Guoji Shudian, we were required to deposit funds owing in a blocked account in a US bank.

When I went at bank opening time down La Salle Street into the canyon of the Midwest empire of banks, brokerage and insurance firms and asked for the foreign department at the Continental Illinois National Bank, which was then the most prestigious institution in Chicago dealing with foreign moneys, the young people in the department were amazed and delighted that a normally dull Monday morning could turn up such a unique problem, never faced by this bank before. 'Hmmm! Open a ... ?' After palaver back and forth that eventually went up to a vice-president on the fifth floor and an afternoon appointment, the young bankers and their secretaries went flocking off to lunch wishing me good luck. The senior vice-president of the Continental Illinois showed a deadpan, bloodless face with an abrupt, flat-backed skull, heavy shoulders mounted in opposition to new things, facing me across an acre of polished desk.

'*Open* a blocked account? It's impossible, a contradiction in terms.' Then he allowed his negative banker's logic full play: 'We can block or freeze assets already deposited under the Trading with the Enemy Act. But *open* a blocked account? It's impossible. Besides, I doubt if it is strictly legal.' That was it. He was dismissing me after five hours of futile negotiation that had reached the top and had nowhere else to go.

'Do you think', I asked heatedly, 'that the US Treasury would oblige me to do something that was not strictly legal?' He held his hands palms up. The interview was over.

I took my hot head over to Irv Steinberg's office on the run. Irv was about as cool and militant a lawyer as you could find in Chicago. 'You seem to be upset,' he said, to cool me down. 'So what if the Continental Illinois doesn't want your money!' He held his hand up, since further details were not of substance at the moment, as he dialled the Exchange National Bank. 'Mr Tinucci, please.... How are you, my friend? This is Irv Steinberg. I have a client here with a problem. Something new. He has a Treasury licence to import books from China. Yes, I said China – the People's Republic, not Taiwan. He is required to deposit funds owing in a US bank since he can't send them to China right now because of Treasury restrictions. So what we need is for you to open a blocked account for these funds.'

I couldn't hear Vice-President Tinucci's words, but gathered he was putting up the same kind of argument as the Continental Illinois. 'There's no time to worry about all the buts,' Irv reassured him. 'All you have to do is say "blocked by Tinucci" and the Treasury will back you up. After all, it's what *they* legally require.' So the blocked account was actually *opened* at the Exchange National Bank, a first for the City of Chicago.

In August, we were advised by the US Customs Department that they were holding a shipment of some two tons of books from 'Red China' and that we should make arrangements to clear them. I learned from Margaret Cowl that, with bonding, an importer could clear shipments without using the services of a broker and save about $200. I went to Customs and filled out three preliminary entry forms; then I went to the Hartford Insurance offices, put down $40 and got myself bonded.

The Customs House had ten floors. In the next three days I was shunted from one to another, up and down, back and forth. A lot of this was deliberate because superintendents and clerks had their own favourite brokers and were setting up stumbling blocks to force me to use their services. Finally, I cut or broke through all the red tape and shipment was released on condition that I would have Guoji Shudian fill out a special Customs declaration on official US stationery. The books came sacked, filled our two front rooms at 334 W. Schiller Street, and made the floor sag dangerously. We filled a hundred pear boxes, lining the walls with books title out, and opened store to the public. Three months later we received a letter from Guoji Shudian advising that it was not appropriate for their firm to fill out a US official Customs declaration. The implication was obvious: without diplomatic relations between our two countries, this would be a violation of protocol. The US Customs then retaliated by slapping a $1,200 fine on CB&P for failing to comply with US government regulations. By some standards this would not seem a large sum, but with sales running $200 the first month and $500 the second, it was more than punitive – it was ruinous.

Again I hotfooted it down to Irv Steinberg's office. Irv was imperturbable, as usual. After hearing my breathless laments, he picked up the phone and called Customs. 'You are asking my client to do something that's impossible. He has your notice . . . ' and Irv went into details, concluding, 'Since there are no diplomatic relations between our two countries, we cannot expect the Chinese to recognize or sign official US documents. You understand,' he added, in his best pacifying voice.

Silence, then a new proposal: 'They agree to reduce the fine from $1,200 to $12.' Irv held his hand over the mouthpiece. 'Do you agree?'

'No, why should I pay a cent?'

Irv commanded silence. 'My client agrees.' He put down the receiver before I could protest. 'Don't you see, we've won a victory? They've admitted it, but they have to save a little face. You can't be a hothead about these things. You've got to use diplomacy. You have to show willingness to abide by the letter of the law, even if you don't agree with it. You're not a civil rights organization, you're on your own. Remember, if things get rough, you are creating evidence of compliance in advance if we ever have to go to court. You need to bend over backwards to show how co-operative you've been.'

'I'm not very good at piety – never have been – but I'll try,' I assured him. 'The most serious problem now is the licence. I'm going batty with these reports to the Treasury. On every item I have to deposit 50 per cent of the sales price in the blocked account. It's insane!'

'You should go to Washington or, rather, New York, and talk to the Foreign Assets Control. You know, say you've given your full co-operation, but . . .'

'Margaret Cowl says to steer clear of the government,' I interrupted. 'I'll get worse, rather than better terms. Let sleeping bureaucrats lie.'

'Margaret Cowl may be right for herself but wrong for you, Professor. Just be straightforward and sincere.'

The next week, after another all-night ride on Greyhound, I was looking for the Federal Reserve Bank on Wall Street. The building itself was a substantial monument to American government and its financial operations.

Mr Greig, in the office of Foreign Assets Control, was a short, energetic, fussy type of bureaucrat in spats and stylish grey suit and tie. His face came to attention, then seemed to go back into itself, turtle-like, so that it was hard to know when and if he listened. He was indifferent to my request to simplify my licence until he found that I had been a professor of English. 'I lecture on economics myself to various groups, mainly business, in Manhattan,' he informed me, as if we were now in the same batting league. Then he batted questions in semantics at me, which I fielded to his satisfaction. For half an hour we compared notes on how best to keep an audience awake for an hour. Our dialogue was interrupted by Mrs Schwartz of the Treasury in Washington, calling to confer on a problem of foreign assets and then to exchange fried chicken recipes. Finally, Mr Greig put down the receiver, carefully filed the fried chicken recipes, then turned to me with a smile.

'What was it you wanted? Something about your licence? Oh yes, you find it unusually complex. Well, why don't you write me a letter saying you find it difficult to make a living and propose a simplification. I'll see you get it, don't worry.' Concerned now with my livelihood, he went to his file and pulled out the cards of three British firms that imported furniture and art objects from China. 'You can't make much of a living out of books. Why don't you open relations with these firms? There's a good sale for Chinese furniture, rugs and such – of course, imported before the embargo of 1951.'

Before I left New York, I wrote Mr Greig a proposal that we deposit the exact invoice price of items sold. This was not only a more viable formula, but also consonant with normal import–export transactions. By the end of the month CB&P had an amended licence valid until 1971, when licence restrictions were terminated and US funds could be transmitted to the People's Republic of China.

Our problems were not only with legal restrictions and regulations, however, but with political forces from right to left. Our preliminary base, inherited from Imported Publications and Products, consisted of the eight radical bookstores affiliated with the Communist Party. But one by one, these began to defect from supporting China to supporting the Soviet Union only. *Long Live Leninism* was actually the parting of the ways. Several articles, combined under this title, were featured in the *Peking Review* No. 17, 1960, which was the first publication we had received from China. We had hardly got over the excitement of opening the first packages, shipped airmail direct from Peking, when our phone started to ring. From left to right, callers wanted this issue. 'It's controversial, you know.' Why, I wasn't exactly sure at the time. It presented Lenin's well-known thesis on imperialism: that war was inevitable unless the peoples of the world were strong enough to prevent it, presumably through revolution. In supporting Lenin's thesis, the Chinese polemicists characterized the rearmament of Germany and Japan as US imperialism's way of breaking down the peace and laying the basis for a third world war.

Several weeks later an airmail shipment of *Long Live Leninism* arrived in book form, with a white linen cover and a red jacket with Lenin's portrait in black and white. It became our first bestseller and was sold out in a month. I heard from Margaret at this time that a top-ranking Party official in New

York was urging her not to handle the book because it was too controversial, besides being sectarian and damaging to the peace forces. When I asked, 'What is your reaction?' she replied, 'Who am I to decide between my Chinese and Soviet comrades?' Soon afterwards I had a call from the educational director of the Illinois State Communist Party, who said he wanted to bring a leading ideologist in his party out to the store. 'Fine,' I said, 'I'll be happy to show you both our books. But if he wants to discourage me from handling *Long Live Leninism*, please tell him he'll be wasting his time.' There was a hasty click at the other end of the line.

'Peace at almost any cost' seemed to be the new slogan of left-wing parties both in the United States and Europe. But Mao Tse-tung was telling the Chinese not to be intimidated. People made the atom bomb; people should agree never to use it, and then to destroy it once and for all. On the other hand, Khrushchev was saying that the atom bomb is not a toy for children, thereby justifying his refusal to share it with China and other fraternal countries and torpedoing the unity of the 'socialist world'.

The rift between China and the USSR widened through polemics that China first directed at the Central European communists and then at the USSR itself. Since the US Communist Party sided with what the Chinese called Soviet revisionism, the radical bookstores we served showed less and less interest in handling publications from China, and then open hostility. 'My people hate the Chinese,' one of their managers blurted out when he cancelled his orders for Chinese magazines. 'No, we don't want any more stuff from China!'

'Even the children's books?' I asked sarcastically. 'How can a professed Marxist–Leninist hate a whole people, especially as many as 800 million?'

Political splinter movements from the CPUSA – the Provisional Organizing Committee, Hammer and Steel and, later, Progressive Labor – supported the Chinese side of the polemics, but their influence was limited and they could not fill the gap in book sales left by the departure of the communist bookstores. It was time for us to enlarge our market, or close our doors.

In Chicago our clientele was small, confined mainly to teachers and students. I decided to travel the country by Greyhound and investigate other possibilities, particularly the West Coast. On a $99 ticket I could travel the whole country as long as I did not backtrack. I decided to concentrate on the periodicals, since they carried the latest information about China and would play an immediate role in ending the myth that it was the 'unknown'. In five weeks, I lined up forty-three newsstands in major American cities to handle *Peking Review*, *China Reconstructs*, and *China Pictorial*: in Denver, Seattle, Salt Lake City, St Louis, Los Angeles, Omaha, San Antonio, New Orleans, San Francisco of course and other cities.

I remember especially the bus trip across Kansas, all night pursued by an engulfing thunderstorm. Lawrence, Kansas appeared and disappeared between lightning flashes. At last clouds sorted themselves out in the predawn over Kansas City and areas of daylight began to show through. The bus splashed into the station through streets flooded from backed-up sewers. During the fifty-minute breakfast stop, I waded through the downtown area to the two news dealers who handled out-of-town and international newspapers. They could both see a chance of making an extra buck and agreed to try out the Chinese magazines, though they could hardly believe that material from China would be in English and that it could actually be imported into the United States. That was our problem, I assured them, and boarded the bus for St Louis. Two months later, Chinese magazines were on sale in both Kansas City and St Louis and in some forty other cities.

In San Francisco, Louis Swift of L-S Distributors had agreed to handle the Chinese periodicals for wholesale distribution. Louis, a victim of polio, was a living example of how a disadvantaged person could overcome a serious handicap and help others in the process. He sat at his desk in the front office and shouted orders that could be heard in the back stockroom, and even in the basement. On his wall was the golden key to the City of San Francisco, which Mayor Christopher had presented to him as one of the city's most distinguished citizens. Louis Swift had a winning smile

behind a rugged moustache and beard, grey hairs yielding
only in patches to white. 'San Francisco is the place for you,'
he advised, and at the same time commanded by inference
that we should transfer CB&P to the West Coast.

I needed no persuading: San Francisco was my first
American city. When the *Ecuador* docked there on 31
January 1919, we had stepped back on land after a violent
crossing from Hong Kong. It was with nostalgia and
admiration for this most beautiful of all cities in the United
States that I wandered around its harbour and streets in the
spring of 1963, forty-four years later. 'It is the only city in the
world', boasted a friendly bus driver, 'where you have winter,
summer, fall and spring all in the same day!' San Francisco is
also one of the most tolerant and progressive cities in the
United States and, facing the Far East, a city whose labour
unions and business enterprises favoured resuming trade with
China. The harbour had once been the Golden Gate to China,
and Louis Swift was confident that it was destined to become
so again.

His confidence was so infectious that it inspired me to call
home that night and surprise the family with a question,
'How about moving to California?'

One Million Little Red Books

When I left San Francisco on my $99 Greyhound ticket, we
had already decided by phone to move China Books &
Periodicals to the West Coast. Gertrude approved. Chris
thought it would be easier out West to work up into the big
leagues as first baseman. And Nicky had seen so many Errol
Flynn, Kirk Douglas and Roy Rogers films that she was sure
she could ride a horse to college.

We had scarcely set up shop in San Francisco when Herb
Caen, the best-known gossip columnist on the West Coast,
came strolling in to inspect us and our books. Two days later
we were given an official welcome in the Caenfetti Column of
the *Chronicle*, which described CB&P as 'Peking's foot in the
door' and a firm that had ambitions to expand rapidly. The
paper had only just hit the newsstands when we began to

receive calls from enterprising realtors offering us whole buildings with railroad sidings to help us expand. The owner of the corner café, however, rushed in to say we should sue Herb Caen for libel. 'Imagine calling you Peking's foot!' But Louis Swift, who had tipped him off about our arrival, called to say, 'Send Herb Caen a thank-you note. Now you are kosher!'

Our new location in the heart of San Francisco's Mission District on 24th Street was at the epicentre of the Bay Area, convenient by freeway and bridge to the Stanford and Berkeley crowd and more locally to the many San Franciscans – longshoremen, ex-members of the armed forces, overseas Chinese, students and teachers – who had a personal or academic interest in the People's Republic. We also received orders, chiefly on the telephone or by post, from merchants, bankers and civic leaders who favoured opening trade channels. Before World War II, 40 per cent of the docks in San Francisco Harbor serviced the China trade; a whole dockside area was still called the China Basin. Since the trade embargo of 1951 by presidential decree, many of these surplus docks were being turned into boutique complexes and amusement centres for tourists – or closed. Robert Gomperts, President of the World Trade Association, who dropped by our store to welcome us to San Francisco, estimated that 90 per cent of the businessmen on the West Coast were pressuring the President to end the embargo. We received calls from textile importers, paint and varnish exporters, wheat merchants, travel agents, all asking what our magic formula was for opening trade with China. They even offered us junior partnerships if we would give them a hand. Our reputation and clientele broadened out.

From 1964, the San Francisco Bay Area was the right place for us to be. It was a germinal period in American culture and we found ourselves at the centre of new movements fertilized by a confluence of intellectual and political cross-currents. Groups, as well as individuals, were interested in China's approach to socialism and many of them turned our store into a material resource centre, beginning with the free-speech movement. In Berkeley, Mario Savio and the 'free speechers' were demanding a complete restructuring of the multi-university and the society whose interests it served. People came first, he insisted, especially the young. One of the first quotations from Chairman Mao to become current in Berkeley, three years before the Little Red Book arrived from Peking, was his tribute to youth: 'The world is yours, as well as ours, but in the last analysis, it is yours. You young people, full of vigour and vitality, are in the bloom of life, like the sun at eight or nine in the morning.'

Why should students 'full of vigour and vitality' waste four years in classrooms with five hundred other auditors listening to a professor reading lectures from fifteen- and twenty-year-old notes? A new incentive to change the old academic world brought students from all over the Bay Area to browse at CB&P and find ideological support for their campaigns – even the extremists who found in Mao's attack on stereotyped writing a justification for launching a free-speech movement. 'We're fed up with academic euphemisms. Four-letter words are earthy, gutsy, full of the life of the streets' – so went the campaigns in the student press. 'We're going to use "fuck" in our papers whether the Board of Regents likes it or not.'

At about the same time a group of seven 'diggers', unbeknownst even to themselves, were launching the psychedelic movement which was soon to embrace and overpower the free-speech and four-letter-word campaigns and incite the nation's youth with incense, pot, hash, the Jefferson Airplane and much more. Taking their name from a communal and anti-Establishment group in England a century earlier, the San Francisco diggers adopted a three-principle philosophy. They advocated peace on earth and, more immediately, the end of the Vietnam War and the withdrawal of American 'advisers'. They were ultra-democratic in practising brotherhood and sisterhood of the Buddhist as distinct from the Christian orders, and they believed in smoking dope and baking brownies laced with marijuana. In their more sober moments they read books on the Chinese revolution, guerrilla warfare and communism, sitting in lotus positions on the floors of CB&P and the Psychedelic Shop on Haight Street near the intersection of Ashbury. Since they were always short of ready cash they felt no urge to buy, and as long as they didn't smoke dope or burn incense in our store, we let sitting diggers read. We, like them, were infected by the tolerant spirit of San Francisco's patron saint.

Peace, love, freedom, brotherhood and sisterhood were words put back into meaningful circulation. The media could only report their excesses. But new mimeographed handouts, New Age weeklies, poetry broadsides chanted in restaurants and distributed free on the streets, and rock music expressed the new way of life, the new Tao of freedom. If any section of the people was oppressed, how could any other section be truly free? Liberation – women's lib, sexual liberation, black and brown liberation – was a powerful wind blowing away old stenches and stereotypes.

In spring 1967 we received an airmail sample of the *Quotations from Chairman Mao Tse-tung*. We had no notion at the time that this Little Red Book was to give a powerful boost to all the young liberation movements and our sales a great leap upward. We thought we were taking a big chance in ordering a thousand copies, the largest order for a single title we had ever placed with Guoji Shudian. Two days after we received airmail shipment, all thousand were sold. The Little Red Book became a status symbol for anybody opposing bureaucratic authority. Waving it was evidence that whoever owned a copy was at least a rebel, if not a self-styled revolutionary. Our store was flooded with status-seekers from all over the country. We cabled Peking to loft 25,000 more *Quotations* to us by air freight. They were gone in a month. We ordered 100,000 more. It was our big break-through into the book world. We sent a postcard announcement to every bookstore in the United States and received over a thousand orders. By the end of 1968 we had distributed over 250,000 and in the following fifteen years we were to sell over one million.

The extravagances of the 'Great Proletarian Cultural Revolution' in China had already been served up by the media. The wild youth of China were shown night after night on prime news time in unruly mobs wielding the Little Red Book. Negative analysis on the radio and in the press, aimed by newscasters to discourage American youth from such outrageous behaviour, backfired. Mao Tse-tung was the only national leader at the time encouraging youth to have confidence in their power to change the world. 'Go ahead, bombard the headquarters of reaction,' he was urging. And young people around the world were responding, 'We hear you!'

It was a period of massive civil rights struggles in the South with sit-in strikes in drugstores, bus boycotts, the Supreme Court decision for equal rather than "separate but equal" education. Above all, however, it was a period of growing dissatisfaction with the war against the Vietnamese people and with the Establishment that waged it with the lives of young Americans. A disproportionate number of these, shipped home in flag-draped caskets, were black or brown. It was a period of peace marches, united fronts of diverse political and religious elements. It was a period when the Black Panther Party organized a new national movement which seemed to threaten the existing order of white supremacy with its programme for peace in Vietnam, socialism in the United States and diplomatic relations with the People's Republic of China.

By the end of the 1960s, CB&P had become a model people's bookstore. In a dozen major cities, similar movement bookstores had been opened to meet the reading demands of a generation which was organizing new political associations and setting compasses for new social horizons. They shared a conviction that wars of aggression and nine-to-five subservience to money-making were not the way of life, the Tao, which they wanted to travel.

※ 5 ※

Doors Begin to Open

The US Media Rediscover China

In summer 1970, President Nixon made an announcement
that took the media by surprise and caused a flood of
speculation: imports from Hong Kong, valued at not more
than $100, even though they contained material originating
in the People's Republic of China, would be passed by US
Customs. Was this an opener to a new trade policy with
China? Or new relations in general? For twenty years the US
government, under the Trading with the Enemy Act, had
banned all trade and forbidden export of money to the
People's Republic. China Books & Periodicals was exempted
from the general ban by a US Treasury licence, which
authorized import of publications, but payments to be held in
escrow in a US bank. We were the only importing firm
holding such a licence and therefore the immediate target for
the fact-starved media to aim at when the President's
announcement hit the copy desks.

In the previous ten years I remember only two interviews,
outside the left and student press, that were not set up to
badger us. The first was with an Associated Press reporter,
Jack Schreiber, who was strolling through the San Francisco
Mission District one Sunday afternoon and happened on our
store. 'What kind of outfit is this, anyway?' he asked, with
amazement rather than hostility. Our first thought was: here
is another of these John Birchers or Ku Klux Klanners, or

possibly a harmless patient from the psychotherapy ward of nearby San Francisco General Hospital. But our policy was always to try to give a serious answer to questions, foolish or otherwise.

'We import books and magazines from China.'

He screwed up his face as if in pain. 'You what? Unbelievable!' Schreiber's most incredulous smile radiated outwards at Gertrude and me, and for the next hour he pumped question after question in a high-pressure interview. 'My God,' he said, expelling air in an abrupt whistle of approval, 'you guys deserve the Nobel or at least the next Carnegie peace award. Imagine, from Red China!'

'The People's Republic, please,' I needled. 'Even the *Chicago Tribune* gives the New China its correct name. Why not the AP wire service?'

'About time too. Say, I'm going to put you in print if my news editor will pass it. Our wire service goes out to 260 US news channels, newspapers, radio stations. Around the world, of course, too. It's time people knew about you. Since McCarthy it's been like the Dark Ages. Now, I just want to get the facts straight about this Treasury licence of yours. That makes you *legit*, you see what I mean? It's an angle.'

The next morning we had a call from Charles Howe, Far Eastern correspondent for the *Chronicle*: 'About this AP wire, can we arrange an interview?' So the Associated Press news editor had approved!

'I've come by to see if you actually exist,' Howe began his interview as he strolled into our store that afternoon and glanced around curiously. 'I've always had an admiration for the foolhardy courage of the Chinese volunteers from the time I covered the Korean conflict. They kept coming in massive waves and blocked our troops from crossing the Yalu. Too bad we were on opposite sides. Well, that was years ago. Now things are changing – slowly – between China and ourselves. The AP release is a sign of better times ahead.'

Howe's article, printed next morning in the *Chronicle*, featured a 'unique import business in the heart of San Francisco's Mission District' – along with my missionary background, to make me 'legit'. Other reporters had ignored us altogether or made monsters of us, but Charles Howe put us back into the human race. And for the next ten years, people dropped into the store because they had read his article – especially after the Nixon visit to China, when they could at last feel 'legit' if they bought a book or periodical imported direct from the People's Republic.

Planned ignorance about 800 million Chinese, soon to exceed a billion, could not last for ever, however often and with however much misinformation the brains of a quarter of a billion Americans were sanitized by the US media. Now, recognizing the first straw aloft in a wind that might blow in a whole new policy towards China, they consulted us as the only commercial weather vane in the Bay Area to give new directions. At first the calls came from the press, radio and television stations in San Francisco, Berkeley, Oakland and San José; then from across country. We were interviewed, taped, photographed, questioned by one reporter after another all week. They were only too anxious, after the twenty-year freeze, to publicize our 'unique import business'. Where have you been all these years? was the question uppermost in my mind, which I tactfully refrained from asking.

By the end of the week we thought the media had run out of puff – but no. On Saturday morning Chris buzzed me from the store. 'Put on your collar and tie, Dad. CBS is here!'

The CBS reporter showed none of the old-time hostility of media personnel to us or to China. We were now celebrities. Or were we? CBS invited me cordially to appear on their Sunday-evening controversial half-hour radio programme, to be beamed out live through the Bay Area and beyond. We were concerned that CBS might turn the half-hour forum into an inquisition, yet most of the publicity that week on China Books & Periodicals had been either favourable or neutral, with only two minor snide attacks. In family council, the four of us debated the pros and cons over the weekend and decided to chance it. Maybe the thaw was for real.

We placed our terms squarely on the CBS table: 'I agree to participate in your controversial half-hour on two conditions: one, that the subject be, however you want to beef up the title, Publications Imported from the People's Republic of China; and two, that you will not make a controversial issue of my personal beliefs or politics. We are a commercial firm, not a political organization. We service a very broad section of the American reading public, and we intend to keep it that way.'

'We understand and agree,' was the cordial answer. 'Of course there will be stiff resistance to anything favourable you may have to say about China ...'

'Yes, and I'm sure much interest and support', I interrupted, 'by many of your listeners.'

'Because this is a controversial programme. Now, is there anybody you'd like to have join us on the air?'

We came up with two suggestions: Charles Howe and/or Jack Schreiber of the Associated Press Wire Service. Charles Howe was available and agreed to join us on the Sunday-evening programme. That made four, including the CBS moderator and the CBS expert on Far Eastern affairs whom, for the sake of station identification, we will call Bob.

CBS received us cordially, tested our voices and struck up a casual, relaxing conversation as we approached the seven o'clock zero hour. Our moderator, affable and silver-haired, warned us again that this was a controversial programme, therefore not to take offence if questions were sharp. 'Our radio audience likes a challenge,' he said affably.

'I do too,' I assured him, 'within the parameters of our agreement.'

'Of course,' he assured me in turn as the countdown reached zero.

After welcoming his radio listeners to the Sunday-evening controversial half-hour, our moderator characterized the featured guest of the evening as a unique businessman: 'He operates a unique business here in San Francisco. He imports books and magazines, in English and Chinese, from Communist China. Yes, I said Communist China. He operates under special dispensation from the US Treasury and runs the only business in the United States that currently has any dealings with Red China. Legally, I might add. We are expecting some fireworks here this evening, because our friend Bob, our CBS expert on Far Eastern affairs, has some questions to ask; in fact, some very pointed questions. We also have with us this evening Charles Howe, an expert on the

Far East, as I'm sure you all know from his feature articles in the *Chronicle*. He will give his own slant in what threatens to be a free-for-all. First, Bob . . .'

'How is it possible for you to import books from a communist country?' Bob delivered his question like a blow, preparing for a knockout. 'Can you do that with a clear conscience?'

'We have a US Treasury licence which makes it legally possible. I believe we are the only business in this country so entitled. The First Amendment of the US Constitution guarantees the right of Americans to read, and our customers are happy that we can supply them with publications imported direct from China, giving the unadulterated Chinese point of view. They are students, teachers, government officials, you name it. As to conscience, yes, I believe mine is an important business that supplies a needed service to people interested in US–China relations. It's a service to better future relations between two great peoples.'

'But do the Chinese bureaucrats allow their people to read. . . ?'

'Certainly, they're a literate people – since the revolution.'

'That's not what I meant.' Bob's features and voice were tensing up. At this point, Charles Howe intervened.

'We see the Little Red Book waved in both the US and China on TV, have for several years. How do you account for its popularity?' Charles Howe had an amiability that was more than surface-deep as he gave Bob and me a bland smile.

'Well, I guess you could compare Mao in a way to Moses leading his people across the Red Sea – rather, the Long March – on to a better life. They'd starved for five thousand years, many of them. Mao put weapons and tools in their hands. And they feel, I suppose, that the Little Red Book is a bit of both. Here in the US . . .'

'Yes, we've heard about the weapons,' Bob interrupted. 'How many millions did the communists kill in their rise to power?' CBS Bob thrust his face and his question at me with a sarcasm intended to obliterate.

'A revolution is not a garden party, according to Mao,' I quoted, somewhat glibly. 'When a tyrannical government is overthrown by the people, they have to do it with guns. The way we did in the American Revolutionary Wars. But after the defeat of the Kuomintang and the flight of Chiang Kai-shek to Taiwan, Mao said, "Let there be little killing, because it's easy enough to cut off heads, but hard to put them back on."'

At this point the moderator signalled that I had said all that was necessary in answer to Bob's question, but I persisted: 'The revolution provided the people in general with what they most wanted: food, shelter, warmth, education for their children and for themselves. And most important of all, perhaps, the right of self-government.'

'But you don't mean to say that your Mao Tse-tung . . .'

'Let me finish,' I insisted. On October 1st, from Tian An Men, Mao said, "The Chinese people have stood up." This was in the same square in front of the Imperial Palace where once the Chinese people had to kowtow to the Emperor's edicts.'

CBS Bob had tried to interrupt me several times, so I figured it was only fair to give him equal time. He used it angrily to overstep the limitations of our agreement and to punch me out. 'Are you a communist?' If he'd had a gun in his hand, I am sure he would have pointed it at me for emphasis.

For twenty years I had heard many an intimidated progressive on the air take the Fifth Amendment, which says I do not have to answer your questions, but Aristotle had taught me at the high-school debating stage that victory comes only if you stay on the offensive. 'Isn't that an old-fashioned question?' I taunted. 'Coming right out of the Joe McCarthy period? Because a person is interested in China, do you think he would have to be a communist? That would include all our senators, our whole State Department . . .'

'But are *you* a communist?' Bob insisted, in a voice reaching a new crescendo.

'I think I've given you the answer that your question deserves, haven't I?' I turned to the moderator with a frown of deep displeasure, in effect saying, 'We had an agreement. It's your job to enforce it.'

Bob was infuriated by what I had said, and also by the way

Charles Howe was coolly smiling at him. The moderator was too embarrassed to know how to cover up for Bob, and permitted him to blurt, 'What *are* you then, one of these so-called Marxist–Leninists?'

'Come on,' I chided him with a laugh, 'you'll really have to tell me and our audience what you mean by that.' It was no laughing matter, though, since he was trying to undermine the very free speech his controversial half-hour was supposed to advance. My hands were sweating from a tense grip on the arm of my chair. 'What next?' I asked, since the moderator failed to function.

At this opening, Howe intervened. 'I understand you also import books and magazines from Vietnam. Is there much interest in the US?'

'Yes, particularly in academic circles.' The half-hour was up before I had much time to compare Ho Chi Minh with Mao Tse-tung and the publications of the Foreign Languages Publishing House in Hanoi with those of the Foreign Languages Press in Peking. The moment we were off the air, CBS Bob stalked out. It was possibly the first time in CBS West Coast programming that a favourable report on the People's Republic of China went out over its sound waves. The moderator, with reassumed affability, shook hands and thanked me for participating. 'One of the most controversial,' he commented. 'I'm sure you gave our listeners a lot to think about. I'm almost certain China will continue to be a hot issue. Hope to have you back with us one of these Sundays.' So much for the media! CBS never invited me back.

At home the family had huddled round the radio. They were excited and critical of my performance, all in the same breath. 'Why didn't you talk more about China Books & Periodicals,' Gertrude wondered, 'with such a golden opportunity?' Nicky complained, 'You didn't have too much to say about Chinese women and children. How come?' Our baseball enthusiast, Chris, congratulated me for 'knocking that CBS foul ball out of play'.

But Nicky's father-in-law gave the appropriate summary, with due thought for the listening audience: 'If you'd said you were a communist, you would have lost half your customers. And if you'd said you were not, you would have lost the other half.'

New Relations between the United States and China

The controversial half-hour with CBS marked the beginning of new relations between the American reading public and China Books & Periodicals. Demand for Chinese publications broadened out from the academic and China expert clientele, and from the old and new left, to the curious and the underinformed in every state in the Union. The anti-China crowd was now on the defensive, powerless to counter the new interest in the People's Republic – China 'the unknown', as the media still characterized it – not only in its politics and socialist economy, but in its art, literature and music, in the daily life of a quarter of the world's population. We were barraged with questions by phone and post and from customers in our stores, such as: 'How come "women hold up half the sky" and what on earth does that mean?'

Our distribution went up 1200 per cent in the next seven years. We opened our store on Fifth Avenue in New York in 1971 and a few months later reopened a centre in Chicago. We set up a regionally orientated sales department and began to cover any bookstore in the country that would conceivably be interested in publications from the People's Republic. The chain bookstores found it profitable to handle not only the *Quotations* but books on history, art and literature from China, and our salespeople were no longer received like agents from another planet.

The encirclement of the right-wingers in the McCarthy period – the so-called Committee of One Million, whose actual head count was closer to one thousand – was shattered. Many countries around the world, England and Canada among others, had recognized the government of the People's Republic of China as the sole legitimate government, exchanged ambassadors, and downgraded their relations with Taiwan. The United States was hesitantly to follow in the 1970s, reluctantly seeing the People's Republic gain its seat in the United Nations and finally agreeing to exchange ambassadors at the end of the decade.

The American diehards – not dead yet, by any means – were more and more isolated and encircled by new attitudes developing towards China in the 1970s. The first great setback they suffered was in 1971, a watershed year in the relations between the American and Chinese peoples. Ping-pong opened a two-way door for negotiations between the governments of the United States and the People's Republic. Many other emissaries had served in the previous history of world diplomacy, but never before paddle-pushers! In a few days American and Chinese youth in friendly competition broke down barriers of ignorance and prejudice that had taken Joseph McCarthy and his ilk twenty years to raise. Latter-day McCarthyites were still directing their ideological wrath against the USSR with hate phrases like the 'red peril', but they were out of step with history, since the Soviet peril was no longer so red. Instead of trying to bury imperialism, the USSR had taken over its methods, still masking its policy behind the upfront faces of Marx and Lenin. Since the publication of *Long Live Leninism* in 1960 the Chinese had launched massive polemics, first against 'Soviet revisionism' and then against 'Soviet imperialism'. Khrushchev, later echoed by Brezhnev, made it plain by their encirclement of China that their enemy was not only US imperialism but also Chinese socialism.

In inviting the US table tennis team to Peking, Mao and Zhou were masterminding a new united front with the American people, since they regarded the USSR at that time as the major enemy. Zhou was astute in both the art and science of diplomacy – and an innovator. He was also familiar with media traps. When the reporters tried to trip him up with queries about the 'decadence' of American youth with their cloroxed jeans, long hair and rock 'n' roll, Zhou suavely answered: 'Youth shows its rebellious spirit in different ways in different countries. We have always been willing to unite with people of good will – it's the firm policy of our Chairman – and on the basis of the principles of coexistence.' Which, in a nutshell, meant mutual respect, co-operative trade and cultural exchanges, including table tennis, and above all settlement of differences not with guns pointed, but with frank discussions. In these areas Zhou was sure that the United States and China could find much common ground. There was no demand on China's part that the United States should become communist before any agreement would be possible, nor did Zhou encourage the United States to negotiate on the basis that China was about to return to the capitalist fold.

Even before engaging in ping-pong diplomacy, Zhou had made these points to the young Concerned Asian Scholars, the first American group to be invited to visit Peking at the beginning of the 1970s. Mao's interviews with Edgar Snow and Felix Greene's with Zhou, even earlier, had pointed up the willingness on China's part to tear down the 'curtain of ignorance', as Greene entitled one of his books on the misreporting of the US media over the years, long before the Department of State was prepared to listen or act. But by 1971, Kissinger's not-so-secret visits to Peking were already helping lay the groundwork for an American president's visit in February 1972.

We were, of course, immediately affected by this abrupt reversal of a policy which one year treated a quarter of the world's population as non-persons, the next as a billion potential mouths and bodies to be fed and outfitted by a sagging US export market. Ninety per cent of businesses and financial institutions in San Francisco had advocated trade with China for many years, since half the city's docks were empty, but the rest of the United States had been slow to follow until the climactic years, 1971 and 1972, in US–China relations.

China was now to be wooed back into the world economy, according to the US media's Far Eastern experts. Propaganda took an abrupt U-turn. Journalists turned their field glasses around to look through prisms that brought China closer to the United States. England and Japan had multi-billion-pound and -yen trade exchanges with the People's Republic. It was surely time for the United States to muscle in with the dollar.

Prime Time on NBC

In autumn 1971 the highest media honour for CB&P was yet to come: prime time on NBC's national news broadcast. Incredible as it may seem, this was due to a week's backpack trip I co-led around the Palisades in the High Sierra. On 1

September, as I was preparing to take off with the Sierra Club, an airmail letter from Peking arrived with an invitation to spend five weeks in China.

For eleven years we had done business with Guoji Shudian, whose representatives we had never met face to face. With goodwill on both sides, we still represented two very different systems and two different ways of doing business, and there were times when we had to walk tightrope or tread water because of political differences between our governments. On the economic level, even our book-keeping systems were so different that we rarely caught up with each other's figures in a zero-zero balance. Balancing accounts in earlier days was purely a formal matter in any case, since we were not authorized to pay bills direct to Guoji Shudian. But at about the time Kissinger began his *sub rosa* negotiations with Mao and Zhou, the President decided that the People's Republic of China no longer came under the Trading with the Enemy Act. As a result we were able to pay current bills to Guoji Shudian after May 1971, though the accumulated blocked accounts were not to be released by the US Treasury until 1980.

The invitation to visit China was in itself a harbinger of new relations which would profoundly affect our business and, I was sure, its rapid development. In the circumstances, could I afford to take five weeks off? The temptation was hard to resist.

The next morning Chris and I sat down to make a basic decision. He happens to be the tallest in the family – six foot eight, no less. He has an affable and easy-going nature, befitting a person whose size commands instant respect. In a father–son relationship we had worked together for a decade and developed a business partnership that had put distribution of books and magazines from China as a primary and occasional differences of approach as a secondary. Also, in the days before we were computerized, both Chris and I relied on his phenomenal memory.

'That letter kept me awake all night,' I began. 'I am tempted to go, of course. But we both know, I'm sure, that there are too many problems. Chris, it's up to you.'

A normal rather sleepy early-morning look in his eyes

suddenly dissipated. 'Wow, China! We always knew the day would come. But why do they specify "not before October 15th"?'

'You'll find out, but first I'm going to take off for a week in the Sierra. I promised Bill to co-lead. His usual second in command has to go back to school after Labor Day.'

'But, Dad, if you can take a week off, why not five? I'm sure they really want you, not me.'

'They only specify in their letter "a representative".' In a flippant bureaucratic manner I settled the problem. 'You've got a better memory for detail than I have, and a bigger appetite for Chinese food.'

On the last night of our Sierra Club hike, I found myself on the same clean-up crew as two journalists from Chicago, Mike and Sean, who worked for the National Broadcasting Corporation. It was my last chance to tell them about our 'unique import business'.

'Books from China – in English?' Mike couldn't believe it. I was expecting a bit of anti-China fallout. Quite the contrary – both Mike and Sean showed a keener interest than in anything I had said the whole trip. Then Mike's natural scepticism took over: 'You must be kidding?' It was a question, though, rather than a statement.

'No, we started our import business in 1960 under a US Treasury licence,' I assured him, 'and now that new relations are opening up, my son Chris has been invited to take a trip to China. As far as we know, he is the first American businessman to get an invitation.'

Mike began to interview me in brief, sharp questions, expecting brief, sharp answers. After a thousand and one questions, NBC style, he said, as the midnight hour approached and the coyotes had long ceased their yapping, 'I'll have to get in touch with our West Coast director, Frank Berkholtzer. He'll put your son on prime time. Imagine, going to China – the unknown!'

'Speak for yourself, Mike,' I laughed. 'We've known about China all along.'

'That's the difference between you and me, buddy!'

When Berkholtzer heard from Chicago Mike that we were sending a representative to China in October, he flew up to

San Francisco especially to interview Chris. The prospect of slides and film footage of modern Chinese life taken at first hand by a young American was as exciting to Berkholtzer as the trip was to Chris. He offered to supply NBC equipment and wanted to set up a contract. At that time of new and early developments, we were not sure what the official attitude in China would be to our filming for an American television network. We politely declined the offer and purchased our own equipment. Chris departed for the People's Republic in the second week of October loaded down with cameras and film, black and white, coloured and moving – all set for an unofficial, pioneering, diplomatic adventure.

He arrived in Canton three days later. It surprised him and all of us who subsequently travelled for CB&P that we were received at the border as VIPs with diplomatic immunity. Chris was even more impressed by his reception as it began to dawn on him why he had been invited to arrive by 15 October. Sleeping lightly on the first night in Canton from jetlag and excitement in a bed made for six-footers, he got up early and was invited to join a basketball game of local People's Liberation Army personnel in one of the hotel courts. The language of basketball, like that of ping-pong, was international and he found himself in immediate demand by both sides because of his height.

Friends from Guoji Shudian with whom we had corresponded for eleven years, but had never met face to face, joined Chris after breakfast to take him on a guided tour round my old home town. He was accompanied by Vice-Manager Zhong Hong, Jin Zhonglin from the European publications section, and interpreter Yang Aiwen. They visited bookstores, the Sun Yat-sen University, the Peasant Institute founded by Mao Tse-tung, and were hosted in the evening at the North Garden Restaurant by the Chinese Friendship Society with Foreign Countries. They finally wound up at a stadium filled with Chinese sports enthusiasts. The basketball match between two competing women's teams from local factories was stopped for a moment while the announcer introduced 'Our guest and long-time friend from the United States'. Chris was overwhelmed by the cheers that went up from players and spectators, happy enough to melt back into the crowd as play was resumed.

The next morning, 15 October, was the opening day of the Canton Trade Fair. Chris was met and escorted round the Fair by a 'leading member of the Revolutionary Committee'. When he asked if other American businessmen had been invited, he received the answer, 'Not yet.' Buyers from Macy's were invited the following spring; the president of the Bank of America and vice-presidents from Crocker National Bank and Bechtel Corporation were soon to follow. 'We know who our faithful friends are,' said Zhong Hong. 'They come first in our estimation. Under extreme difficulties, you have managed to distribute Chinese publications widely in your country, for which we thank you warmly. You are here, which means that the relations between our two peoples are improving.'

'It's about time,' Chris replied briefly. In the next five weeks, he visited Shanghai; Peking; Yenan, the old revolutionary headquarters of the Chinese revolution; then Sian, the ancient capital of China known centuries ago as Chang An. Here he wandered up to the central square without benefit of interpreter. A tall white stranger must have seemed an incredible phenomenon to Chinese workers returning home from the factories by bicycle and bus. They dismounted and poured out of buses in a spontaneous and curious reception committee. There were only two expressions in the crowd, Chris reported: one of amazement, with mouths hanging open; the other of cordial welcoming smiles. In a few minutes, the square filled with thousands of men and women in blue trousers and jackets and black cloth shoes. Chris took moving shots of the multitude, estimating they numbered at least five thousand. A local photographer offered to help, shooting Chris in the midst of smiling or amazed faces: an American given an all out welcome in China's Midwest. A goodwill demonstration from the grass roots!

These were the shots that appealed to NBC's Berkholtzer when he flew back up to San Francisco the week Chris returned from China. The media were eager to show China in a favourable light for the first time since 1949. Right-wing doomsters in the United States were predicting that if President Nixon went there he would never come out alive, but here on Chris's films thousands of Chinese were welcoming an American in the heartland of China in a great popular demonstration of friendship. And he came out very much alive! NBC presented the whole film sequence on its six o'clock, prime-time newscast two and a half months before Nixon flew to Peking.

You Can't Go Home Again

It was not until 1975 that I was able to follow Chris via the airways to Kowloon and on up to Canton by rail. The four intervening years were packed with new developments, new problems, and many new opportunities for a wider and wider distribution of books from China. Gradually our image as distributor of the Little Red Book enlarged and we became known as a resource centre for anybody interested in the Chinese language, Chinese art, literature, travel, medicine – acupuncture in particular – as well as the politics and economics of the People's Republic. Our staff increased from five to thirty, a 600 per cent growth in four years. It was difficult to keep up with the ever-changing relations, generally improving in this period, between the American and Chinese peoples, the changes taking place in both countries, and with the many problems of representing both in a commercial enterprise – some legal, some economic, some political. In addition, there were problems with the left splinter movements. One day they were friendly, with encomiums for the great work we were doing; the next they might be picketing our stores and plastering our plate glass with anti-Mao slogans – rarely, of course, settling their outstanding bills. So we had a number of tightropes to walk and fortunately succeeded in maintaining a balance between a hundred wobbling contradictions. It was not until 1975 that I felt the home fires would keep burning in my absence and could accept a long-standing invitation to revisit the land of my birth.

In the spring I took my usual three months' sales trip, returning through Ohio by the old family home in Seville. My father and mother were both deceased and, before them, all my great-aunts from the Civil War period. I now stood on the top rung of that ladder of generations constantly renewing themselves from below, but not recycling those at the top. 'You can't go home again,' I was sentimentalizing. The old elms were still swinging oriole nests in the breeze and a cardinal was flashing through top branches as I turned into the driveway. The white pioneer house had been resurfaced with beige shingle and remodelled almost beyond recognition. A carport had been built at the back. The old barn and strawstack were missing. In the house itself there was no longer a museum room with silk gowns and sandalwood fans from China, vases on teakwood stands, or the peach embroidered scroll presented to my Aunt Harriet after fifty years in China by the staff and students of Truelight Seminary. Attic rooms were no longer filled with bundles of old letters in trunks and century-old garments and shoes, or laid out with onions, apples, pears, and corn drying on old newspapers. No, I could not go back to the 'house on the hill' which I first visited in 1922 – or back further in the nineteenth-century family history to my great-grandfather Varnum, who stood six foot six in his stockinged feet, and my great-grandmother Lois, who could stand under his outstretched arm with her boots on. They had built this place and raised a family of nine here, including my grandfather.

In the economy of our twentieth century, my mother had sold the old home, out of necessity after my father's death, to a radar patroller. He had set up spyglass and electric timer in the corner attic room that overlooked the new highway in both directions. His job was to report speeders to the local patrol – this in a period before helicopters took over. He was happy to invite me in and showed me his equipment with pride. Was it for this, I asked myself melodramatically, that my ancestors had come from Massachusetts in 1832 – to set up a base for a spyglass?

'By the way,' volunteered the radar enthusiast, with a voice that shattered my reverie, 'since your folks used to live here, maybe you know who this old geezer was? This fell out of the wallpaper when we were redecorating.' He handed me a brown and stained daguerreotype of my grandfather as a young man, with a bristling black beard and eyes full of spirit for the China trip and whatever else lay ahead. Geezer? I could see my grandfather lying on his deathbed with his white beard floating above the sheet. What a transformation, what a life he had lived, a prophet without honour to be called a geezer in the house he was born in!

'Thanks,' I said in a faraway, frozen kind of voice. 'It was my grandfather. He was a sort of saint, chaplain in the Civil War and one of the early missionaries to China. Took him 109 days from New York to Hong Kong.'

'Guess they never drove a car, even a motorbike in those days,' said my host, with his eye furtively glancing up and down the road and his hand ready on the spyglass.

My heart was on low beat with the faces and voices of my great-aunts appearing vividly in memory, especially my Aunt Emily. The last time I had seen her just before leaving for England in 1936, when she was confined to a wheelchair, she had laughed as she said, 'You'll be a scholar just like Henry, your grandfather.' Her face was deeply grooved by her ninety years, but the spirit burned in her eyes like two tiny suns. Neither she nor my father could have fully understood how I did follow in my grandfather's footsteps. Perhaps my grandfather would have understood – he was a man of imagination – perhaps not: I was doing as valuable a job in the twentieth century as he thought he was doing in the nineteenth. Values change. He did a job for what he thought would change the world, distributing Bibles around South China, and I stayed at home to do a job for a new generation of 'unenlightened heathens'. Missionaries of two different generations, we were both earnestly concerned to make the world a better place to live in for both Americans and Chinese. Instead of proselytizing abroad, I felt that idolatry, love of money, misuse of power should be challenged at home. Perhaps Henry Varnum would have agreed if he had lived through this century of world wars and changing values. We were both iconoclasts with a mission, and I hoped mine would last as long as his – to the end of my time. What was missing in the twentieth century as it grew older was the sense of community, of people caring for each other on a world scale. The youth of the sixties had tried to restore this, but . . .

The sharp voice of my host abruptly put an end to my

daydreaming. 'Back to work,' he rasped as he dismissed me at the front door. 'Any time you want to come by again. . . .'

But I did not, and I knew I never would again. My Aunt Helen was the only survivor of my mother's and father's generation. She said on the phone when I called her from Seville that she would be happy to see me. She regretted that she could not put me up for the night, since she was living in a condominium for retired people. But her daughter Sue, who had a big house down the street, had plenty of room.

Wooster, my father's college town, had grown beyond recognition since the 1930s when I had last visited it with him. My aunt's condominium was on the outskirts in a newly developed area where the squares of sod had not yet grown together to form a smooth lawn. I was expecting to see a rather cheerful, sociable face with a frame of grey hair, looking a bit like my mother's, but when my Aunt Helen opened the door I saw a face white and emaciated, and a frame angular under a loose-fitting dress. 'Oh my God,' I thought, guessing that she was in the late stages of terminal cancer. Why hadn't anybody told me?

'Henry, it's just a treat to see you. Like I said on the phone, I'm really sorry I can't put you up, but Sue will be here later to take you over to her place.' Then she added, in a matter-of-fact way, 'I have cancer. The doctor gives me three or four months.' It was always like Aunt Helen to come straight to the point. She did not give me a chance to express sympathy. 'It's been a good life generally, with its ups and downs. I guess I'd do it again if I had the chance. Bill was a good husband to me. We worked together as a team. He worked himself to death, as you know. Ulcers. And now I'm fortunate in my children. Sue is in and out every day. I want for nothing.' Aunt Helen ran out of breath. She motioned me to sit down. There were homemade cookies at my elbow, made by my cousin Sue, I was sure.

'I've just come from Seville.' I tried to imitate Helen's matter-of-fact tone. 'Things are very different. You can't go home again, can you?'

An answer would have been irrelevant. Aunt Helen was studying my face as if for the last time. 'Yo do look a little like him. Your grandfather, I mean. You probably wouldn't remember his passing in 1914? You were a young child then.'

'I remember it very well. One of my earliest memories.' Words did not come easily. I could not help talking in a hollow voice. 'And my grandmother. I remember when she died years later. About the size of a doll at the end. In the Missionary Rest Home in Toronto. Still with that Irish sparkle and smile like the Cheshire Cat's.' I could not seem to get off the subject of death, nor could Aunt Helen.

'Strange,' she said, 'how old people shrink down almost to the size of a six-year-old. Some of them. Like Roe and Grace before they passed.'

'Yes, I remember the last time I stopped by Cayuga on a sales trip. Aunt Grace was such a large woman in the old days, so imposing with her Providence Rhode Island accent and her President of the University Women's Club manner. What a lot of suffering she must have gone through to shrink to the size of a six-year-old! Yet she was very sweet to me, manoeuvring her weight on the bar suspended above her bed. And Uncle Roe was pushing himself around in that aluminium frame. Imagine, he insisted on cooking breakfast for me before the housekeeper came!' Life never quits till it has to, I went on thinking to myself. Aunt Helen's face showed her determination to live it out to the end, whatever the suffering.

She went to the drawer of her desk. 'I wanted you to have something, Henry.' She handed me a small porcelain locket with a tiny photograph of my mother holding Billy and me in her arms. 'Mary sent this to me back in 1912 before Bill and I went out to China. Poor Mary,' she added, 'I hate to say this, but with all the suffering from erysipelas and everything, I was glad when it was all over for her.'

'I know what you mean. With my father it was different. He hardly knew what it was to be ill till the week he died. I thought you might like to see what I wrote at the time of his funeral.'

Aunt Helen scanned the Tribute I handed her. Then she read some of my words back to me: 'My father made the most of his eighty years – a traveller and a teacher. He spent his life with a purpose, used it up with an eagerness the way fire burns oak till nothing but the ash claimed by the wind is left with us. And now the wind blows and scatters into the endlessness of space and time the atoms that once his will mastered and gave voice to and articulation. His will to live was strong. He was too stubborn in the line of duty to say, "I quit!" So without his awareness or consent, sleep took him on his last journey.'

Aunt Helen finished reading and turned to me with a smile melting away the wrinkles in her face and seeming to flush her cheeks with new life. 'It's very beautiful, Henry. I'd like to keep it. Do you believe in immortality?'

'I believe our beloved ones live after in us as long as there is human life. I remember hearing the Dean of Canterbury saying that years ago in Chicago. Do you believe in personal immortality?'

'Well, we've talked a lot about life after death from college days on. With your mother, too. When Bill and I first went out to China, I guess we both had a sort of youthful faith. It seemed simple then to believe. Your grandfather was such a powerful persuader, you know? But now that the time is getting close for me – I'm not so sure.' She didn't seem to expect me to respond; instead she began to reread the Tribute as if it was strengthening, then folded it carefully and put it away in her desk drawer with her other valuables.

'You've had an interesting life, Henry. We both have. What's ahead for you?'

'I'm going back to Canton one of these days when I can get out from under all the problems . . .'

'Yes, it would be good to find out what's really happening there. From the books you've sent me, it seems like things are improving for the average person,' she said cautiously, 'but I don't understand all this waving of the Little Red Book.'

'Youthful enthusiasm,' I said, with a laugh. 'But seriously, I think things are improving for the people generally. Remember the foreign gunboats and the beggars along the riverfront? Anyway, I'll soon have the chance of finding out for myself.' I hesitated, then quickly added, 'I'll let you know all about it when I come back.'

But long before I took flight for China, I heard from Cousin Sue that Aunt Helen was dead, the last survivor of my mother's and father's generation, the last tie with childhood days in Canton.

✻ 6 ✻

China Again after Fifty-seven Years

*We Arrive in Guangzhou**

The opportunity came at last, in 1975, for me to return to China. It was a different homecoming from the nostalgic Seville experience, rather a celebration of new things: achievements rising out of the oppressions of the past, with its feudal traditions and imperialist domination, by a people determined to revolutionize old systems and themselves.

My hosts had arranged for me and the manager of our New York store, K.C. Foung, an itinerary that corresponded in the main with advance requests. In Shenzen we were met by Jin Zhonglin, assistant director in the European Department of Guoji Shudian, the export firm which had supplied us with Chinese publications since 1960; and in Guangzhou by Cao Jianfei, who was a vice-manager. Two more opposite types of dedicated socialists would have been difficult to pick out of a population pushing one billion. Cao was a sturdy individualist, rugged, gruff and explosive, a thousand per cent attentive to making our stay in China one of the best experiences in a lifetime. He told me from the outset, however, that my request to visit Tibet would have to wait for a later trip, since Tibet was too far. And as to swimming the Chang Jiang River, it was too cold. When I reminded him that Chairman

---

*In the following chapters I have used the modern spelling of Chinese names. See Glossary on p. 219 for old and new spellings.

Mao swam the Chang Jiang, Cao closed off discussion with 'Not in April!'

Jin, on the other hand, existed in an atmosphere of silence, speaking only when absolutely necessary in as quiet a voice as I heard anywhere in China in the five weeks of my visit. He had the facility of a genie to appear and disappear at appropriate moments with tickets and passports to assure that all arrangements for travel by air, land or water would proceed as smoothly as the train ride up from Shenzhen. No travelling bag or toothbrush ever went missing under his omniscient care. We called him our 'barefoot doctor', since at a mere sniffle he was ready to rush us off to the nearest hospital.

The first item on our Guangzhou agenda was a conference with the Chairman of the Central Planning Commission of the City of Guangzhou, who would brief us on the history of my natal city and bring me up to date with developments since 31 December 1918, when I was last there. Chairman Huang arranged to meet us in the famous Orchid Garden in one of those stone and teakwood pavilions that serve Chinese gardens as pivotal centres for paths, lagoons, stone bridges arched like the half moon, with orchid plants of every size and shape on display. In such a pavilion, Li Bai and Du Fu sipped wine of Tang vintage and wrote their famous odes a thousand years ago.

It was appropriate that Chairman Huang's narrative was an epic dealing with the past as prelude to a more glorious present and future. He spoke proudly of the resistance of the people of Guangzhou to the opium traders and the guns of foreign men-of-war, and armed opposition to the seizure of enclaves on the South China coast by Western armies and navies. Li Zicheng, leader of the Taiping Revolution, was born in or near Guangzhou and led the great revolt of peasant armies in the mid nineteenth century. Dr Sun Yat-sen himself was born not far from Guangzhou. It was not until the Revolution of 1911, led by Dr Sun and continued by Mao Zedong, that the people were able to set up a government strong enough to end foreign control and, finally, to drive back the Japanese invading armies in the 1940s. Guangzhou was famous for its Peasant Institute in the 1920s. Under

Mao's leadership, cadres were trained in the techniques of revolutionary warfare and dispatched to all parts of China to organize the millions of peasants who helped to overthrow the old order. Later, Chiang Kai-shek, with a remnant army, fled from the North to set up his last-stand government in Guangzhou before throwing in the sponge and taking flight for Taiwan in 1949. 'Guangzhou', Huang concluded, 'was a centre of pivotal importance for the revolution.'

On a personal note, Chairman Huang digressed with a comradely smile: 'I understand that we are compatriots, that you were born here in 1910, the last year of the Qing dynasty. Many changes have taken place since then, and many more are scheduled. Guangzhou was a consuming city until 1949. It had little industry, small craft shops, bad housing, narrow and uneven streets, no sewers for drainage or for run-off rain.' He went on to describe how the city had been transformed from a scene of wartime destruction into an industrial producing centre under central planning when the communists took over. The riverfront in particular was transformed according to plan. Boatpeople who had lived on cramped sampans all their lives had moved ashore into fireproof apartment buildings. The old filth and degradation of the waterfront had been wiped out. The transformation was possible because of Chairman Mao's mass line and the revolutionary spirit of the Chinese people.

'Men, women and children', Huang went on in his epic stride, 'volunteered to build sewers, ponds and reservoirs, new houses and parks. The Japanese had denuded the city and nearby White Cloud Mountain of all trees. In the reconstruction period after their defeat, brigades of women went out from the city to plant one billion trees in the devastated areas. It was the strength and energy of the people that accounted for the rapid development of Guangzhou into a modern city with sanitation, a clean water supply and flood control. In June, when the Zhujiang River usually floods, water is pumped out of the river back into overflow channels or reservoirs. The old destruction of floods carrying debris, corpses, snakes, dead pigs, is a thing of the past.'

No briefing in China during the Cultural Revolution was complete without a host of statistics, which Chairman Huang marshalled with routine enthusiasm. I learned that Guang-zhou had grown by 50 per cent since 1949. Housing space had been doubled in the same twenty-six years. Two bridges had been built across the Zhujiang River; 230 kilometres of sewer pipes laid; 150,000 square metres of new streets and roads; four recreation lakes and several new parks.

Rather than the absolute figures – which were impressive, though not too meaningful to me – I was much more interested in the socialist planning apparatus that made these improvements possible, so I fired a series of questions: 'How does city planning work? Who makes the decisions? At what levels? How is local planning integrated with national planning? What city, provincial and national agencies, bureaux and ministries are involved?'

'You ask a great many questions,' Mr Huang laughed as he shifted gears into his own area of expertise. 'Let's talk about the Chinese Export Commodities Fair as an example of how socialist planning works. In the first place, it was a great honour for Guangzhou to be chosen by Chairman Mao and the Central Planning Ministry in Beijing. It was necessary for our local commission, then, to plan a suitable window – or perhaps one should rather say *door* – to open on the whole world. It would have to be large and appropriate to represent the revolutionary spirit of the Chinese people. I can assure you that much time and thought were given by the people of Guangzhou, our city administration, the provincial government and the central planning bureau in Beijing.'

The first problem was to pick a site. The City Planning Commission chose a suburban area, which meant displacing the fewest number of residents. Notices were then posted, and people living in the area were invited to attend meetings to give their opinions. They had every opportunity at that stage to raise ifs, ands and buts – and did, according to Mr Huang. There were few objections and there was much support, since displaced persons were promised better housing than they actually lived in. 'Was the promise carried out?' I asked, with a dubious inflection. 'In the US such promises are often made, but not always fulfilled.'

'We have a people's government here,' said Huang, with veiled indignation. 'We carry out our promises. It is our principle to serve the people. You see, our people are highly politically motivated from the time they are children,' he added, to overwhelm the scepticism of a visitor from the outer imperialist world. He then went on to survey the transactions that took place between city, provincial and national commissions and ministries before the acquisition of the site could be approved and building actually begun. 'Of course, additional plans had to be made to accommodate our guests to the Trade Fair in the new hotel where you are staying, and for the great increase of visitors we expect in the years to come from your country.'

When I said I was much impressed by the changes that had been planned and carried out by his Commission, that a whole new city had risen out of the old Guangzhou of 1918 when I was last there, he countered, with the characteristic Chinese modesty, 'Many of the old crowded sections still exist. We must do better.' We understood from his smile and his question 'Do you have any criticisms?' that the interview was at an end.

After a last cup of tea, our host guided us back over flagstone walkways and half-moon bridges to the gate of the Orchid Garden. 'I regret that few orchids flower in April,' he said in parting. 'You must pay us a visit in the summer or autumn. There are some very special varieties you will see in bloom here, but nowhere else in the world.'

We Are Guests at the Chinese Export Commodities Fair

Our arrival in Guangzhou was planned to coincide with the opening of the Chinese Export Commodities Fair. Cao and Jin met us that evening in the grand foyer of our hotel. Visitors from all over the world were congregating to attend the official opening banquet. Although this was a formal state affair, with gowns and dinner jackets optional, the atmosphere was cordial and friendly. A mixed group of Arabs, Africans, Asians and Anglo-Saxons assembled at our table, introduced one another, and immediately set up a lively international exchange. Japanese businessmen and their wives outnumbered the rest of us.

Banquets in China usually begin with tea, conversation and speeches. The opening speech was delivered by the Minister of Foreign Trade from Beijing on the special new features of the Trade Fair for 1975. He gave a United Nations slant to the purposes of trade with foreign countries. The exchange of goods and commodities was not solely an economic affair, but rather a launching pad for peaceful coexistence and mutual assistance. The Export Commodities Fair was therefore a door to the rest of the world, a door that swung both in and out to promote friendship with the peoples of all nations.

I could see a general nodding in agreement by Third World representatives as the Minister elaborated. Ten per cent of China's machine-tool industry, he said, was orientated towards assistance for Third World countries to industrialize and to convert their own raw materials into finished consumer products. In that gathering of black, brown, yellow, red and white faces the Minister's phrase 'we must have a correct world outlook' was applauded as a slogan for the future, rather than mere rhetoric. The Minister illustrated his point with a reference to the Tanzan Railway: 'We assisted the people of Tanzania to build their railway not as charity, but to help develop the economy of another Third World country and so develop the world economy as a whole. And not only to help build the railway, but to assist Tanzanian workers to develop skills so that they might at the same time take over management and maintenance.'

In conclusion, the Minister stated that the Trade Fair was orientated not only to underdeveloped countries, but also to the advanced capitalist countries. He offered textiles, ceramics and art objects to balance out China's imports of mining and drilling equipment in the spirit of the five principles of coexistence between nations. He emphasized the need for equality among nations, peaceful negotiations and a respect for each other's sovereignty. These principles, advocated by the United Nations, could be the basis of a peaceful world in which friendship would come first and competition second.

Fortunately for sharpened appetites, speeches, including the Minister's, were short. Toasts were the only interruption to the flow of wine, food and lively conversation in a seven-course banquet. From the head table toasts were proposed to 'our international visitors' in maotai* and red, red wine. *Ganbei!* was the roar from the tables as counter-toasts were proposed to our hosts and the Chinese people for a world in which trade and friendship would replace war and conflict.

While we were still enjoying course number 7, a cool egg-white gelatin, our vice-director, Cao, suggested immediate departure for the people's concert, hosted and arranged by the Central Philharmonic Society. Buoyed up by a last gulp of maotai, we floated out of the smoke-filled banqueting hall into a balmy April evening. Subtropical moonlight splashed our path and strains from erhu and pippa and the more substantial notes of the sheng lured us along the path that serpentined through bamboos and flower beds to the music hall.

A polite, seemingly absolute attention was given by an overflow audience to the orchestral numbers by modern Chinese composers, also to folk songs and dances accompanied by traditional instruments. Choruses and dances were revved up beyond traditional tolerances to revolutionary pitch: no longer were the singsong arias in high falsetto style, as in the old days when I used to hear them from Guangzhou's crowded streets at night when I stayed with my Aunt Harriet at Truelight Seminary, or from the wine shop across the canal on hot nights in Fati. These were songs and dances from Yanan days and after, from the Modern Revolutionary Peking Operas, and poems of Chairman Mao rendered by chorus and symphony orchestra: 'Snow', 'Loushan Pass', and the 'Capture of Nanjing by the People's Liberation Army'.

Next to the flute songs entitled 'The Song Fest of Birds', the most popular number on the programme – also the most popular with Vice-Director Cao – was 'Battling the Typhoon', composed by Wang Changyuan. It was incredible to think that the soloist, Liu Shikun, could reproduce all the sound and fury of a typhoon on one grand piano, but he did, while Cao pounded his cane on the floor during the loudest crashes of thunder and windblasts to show his

---

*Maotai: a strong, colourless liquor distilled from sorghum.

appreciation. It had such a powerful effect on my ears that I woke up in the middle of the night from a dream that a typhoon was breaking over Guangzhou, and I stepped out on the moonlit balcony to end such nightmares.

Great red balloons with long streamers floated above the new Trade Fair buildings across the boulevard from the Dongfang Hotel. Character quotations in black on the red streamers welcomed foreign guests with slogans like 'People of the World Unite!' Great red characters topping the buildings offered a larger welcome and a new open-door policy to the nations of the world: no longer a policy dictated by the Western powers, but one expressing the new national identity of the Chinese people and their New Democracy.

'Books Are Ideological Weapons'

It was revealing to learn at the banquet that Third World countries now had access to some of the most advanced technical means of production through trade with China. Capitalist countries had reserved these for home industry and tended to export only machinery necessary for extracting raw materials. But the USSR in earlier days had broken through the gentlemen's agreement of the big Powers to set up a steel mill in India, and now China was supplying the under-developed countries with modern machines and loans at low interest or none. At the Trade Fair next morning, I had a chance to ask Chinese experts in the machine-tools exhibition, 'How can China export 10 per cent of the lathes, milling machines, grinders and other machine tools you produce – also, tractors and rice planters – when you need these for your own modernization programme?'

'China is a socialist country,' our informant explained. 'Chinese workers and peasants have strong ties with the Third World peoples. We are only too happy to supply them with machine tools and tractors, because it means helping them raise their standards of living. We do not export outmoded machinery to Third World countries like the imperialists [whom he tactfully refrained from mentioning], but only our best and most up-to-date, even though this means a certain sacrifice to our own developing industries. In the long run China, which is also a Third World country, will benefit from mutual aid.'

Briefings in the machinery, textile and ceramic divisions were speeded up at Cao's urging. Soon he conducted us back to the enormous book display at the entrance to the Fair. Here we were joined for a group conference by Mr Wu, who headed Xinhua Books in the Guangzhou area, and Mrs Xu, who was general manager of Waiwen Shudian. Xinhua Books was an immense, all-China network of a thousand or more stores, large and small, distributing books in Chinese in nearly thirty provinces and autonomous regions. Waiwen was a smaller enterprise which handled books in English, French, Japanese and other foreign languages in several of China's largest cities. Cao, Wu and Xu had pooled resources to set up one of the largest book exhibitions I have ever seen, a gigantic display that confronted every merchant and trader, concerned with books or not, as they entered the Fair. During the Cultural Revolution, books, ideas, politics came first. Red ribbons and red roses garlanded the works of Mao Zedong in Chinese and in some thirty foreign languages. In similar focus of stage lights were displayed a hundred works of Marx and Engels, Lenin and Stalin in Chinese, and some in English.

Wu and Xu gave us a guided tour through their respective sections. They showed us books on medicine, acupuncture and herbs; books on art and the latest archaeological finds from early dynasties; travel guides and pictorial albums of the cities and mountains of China and of people at work in the rice- and cottonfields, in mines, in steel factories and printing presses. One of the largest and most colourful sections was given over to the Modern Revolutionary Peking Operas, monopolizing the stage and screen at that time by order of Jiang Qing, Mao's wife. Opera heroes and heroines, known to every schoolchild, were shown with raised fists and red flags on book covers and posters. Yellow-uniformed KMT, or Japanese enemy officers, cringed before larger-than-life heroes of revolution. Books about children who carried messages through enemy lines and performed other patriotic duties in the Chinese civil wars rounded out the display. Politics came first, everything else second.

As we adjourned from the Fair to visit the bookstores managed by Wu and Xu, we glimpsed in passing our fellow-foreign guests who had come from all over the world in their national dress: togas from Africa, fezzes from the Middle East, business suits Miami-style and foulards and sheath-tight dresses from Saks Fifth Avenue or Paris designers, suits of new synthetic fabrics and silk kimonos from Tokyo, straw hats and coiled perfumed hair and a few open-necked, flowered shirts and blouses from Hong Kong and Polynesia. Like an animated flower garden they had taken over the Fair, arriving early on the first day to negotiate bargains while the warehouses of Guangzhou and Shanghai were still overflowing with saleable commodities. These included, of course, the famous Chinese rugs, baskets, jade and ivory carvings, mother-of-pearl three-dimensional goddesses, ceramics, silk shirts and pyjamas and dresses in hundreds of designs – all the exhibits we had glimpsed before we were rushed by official car to the centre of Guangzhou on one of the new main thoroughfares. General Manager Wu preceded us, arriving just in time to receive us at the kerbside in front of Guangzhou's largest bookstore.

Wu was short, earnest-eyed, in his late forties – a man of intense loyalties and convictions, his eyes lighting up with a glow of spirit every time he mentioned Chairman Mao. After a tour of the bookstore, which was a smaller model of the Xinhua stores we visited later in Shanghai and Beijing, Wu motioned us to chairs in his office and bowed to Cao to open a formal briefing on book distribution. Wu was only too ready to open up discussion when Cao gave him his cue.

'When a new work by Chairman Mao was announced in the days of paper shortage,' Wu began, 'people would line up the night before it was received at our bookstores in Guangzhou, wait all night in the cold and even the rain to be sure of getting a copy. Our staff would be inspired by the need of the people for books to learn the truth. The staff would serve them tea in the middle of the night.' Wu spoke with the rhythms and inflections of a poet inspired as he went on to define books as 'weapons in the hands of a revolutionary people and a powerful preparation in the pre-revolutionary period before 1949 for educating and uniting the masses. Books are no ordinary commodity, they are products of the human spirit.'

Cao was quick to elaborate on Wu's point: 'We do not regard book distribution as a matter of buying and selling. In our socialist society, we distribute books as ideological weapons in class struggle, scientific experiment and production.' As usual Cao spoke with force, as if to demolish a powerful opposition. I wondered if he was also formulating the correct political line for 1975 and that the word *spirit* was out of order. The Great Proletarian Cultural Revolution, prolonged by the Gang of Four for their own purposes, was still in the saddle and commanded a meticulous orthodoxy. In any case, Wu as well as Cao flooded the briefing with quotations from Mao's 'Talks at the Yenan Forum on Literature and Art' to prove that culture's function was to serve workers, soldiers and peasants and to raise the political consciousness of the masses.

Soon Cao terminated the briefing with a sharp tap or two of his cane. It was time to move on to Waiwen Shudian, where Xu Xiufang, a grey-haired woman in her fifties with a hearty smile and sense of humour, was waiting to receive us. Her store was open to the street, like Xinhua Books and many other stores in Guangzhou where the climate is subtropical. Students and teachers of foreign languages, and also learn-a-language customers, crowded the counters outside and in. They were leafing through books in French, Persian, Spanish, Arabic, Swahili, English and a dozen other foreign languages. 'Several million Chinese are now studying English,' said Mrs Xu, adding, with an impious smile, 'Russian used to be most popular foreign language before 1960, but now it's English. They will want to talk English with American friends on the streets. You will see!'

What impressed me most about the Waiwen and Xinhua bookshops was the number of readers who, according to Mrs Xu and Mr Wu, crowded them all day long: workers and cadres in their blue tunics and trousers, children in bright-coloured jackets, People's Liberation Army soldiers in green uniforms and red-starred caps – a great contrast in simplicity with the foreign visitors we had seen at the Trade Fair.

We Visit a People's Commune

After lunch and the usual have-a-rest hour, the China Friendship Association with Foreign Countries hosted us in the person of Mrs Li. Raised partly in Hong Kong, partly in Guangzhou, she had a perfect command of English-English and also of information foreign visitors were likely to request. 'The Chairman of the Revolutionary Committee of the Luogang Fruit Commune will be happy to receive American visitors,' she said, with a smile at K.C. and me. Like Jin, she was a person of few words.

The Luogang Fruit Commune was located at the base of White Cloud Mountain, the tallest rise on Guangzhou's skyline. Here in the woods, the guerrillas had set up a stronghold at the onslaught of Chiang Kai-shek's counter-revolution in 1927. It was here that students from my father's school had been detained for six months by the communists and given an orientation on the future of China as an independent nation, liberated from domestic warlords and foreign aggressors, before being returned to Pui Ying Middle School alive and well. It was here that the Japanese had cut down every tree, even bush, to further their war effort against the local people during their occupation of the Guangzhou area between 1937 and 1945. And it was here, after the setting up of the People's Republic in 1949, that volunteer women, according to Chairman Huang, had planted over a billion trees. These trees were now twenty feet high, lining the roads, as we drove to the commune centre.

On the way I kept thinking of China's ricebowl, which we had smoothly navigated by railway coach two days earlier. Extending as far as the eye could see, limited only by a remote range of blue mountains, some of the most fertile riceland in the world had flowed past the windows of our coach. Showers out of the unevenly clouded grey sky were pelting the countryside with April vigour, promising rapid growth and an overflowing ricebowl. The immense green plain was dotted with villages, brick kilns, and trees. In the fields, thousands of peasants in oilskins and broad-brimmed straw hats, umbrella size, were busy at a hundred tasks, some barefoot ploughing behind slow-motion water buffaloes. A few tractors, pulling loads of bricks or straw on the lanes, punctuated the landscape with vivid red. Draught animals, goats and a few sheep were tethered along streams or roads, some tended on halters by the very old or the very young. There were no fences, no dogs and no overseers' whips. The water towers no longer served the function of observation posts for landlords to oversee their peasants at work, as in the days back in the 1910s when we used to travel by riverboat from Guangzhou to Hong Kong.

As we turned into the gateway of the Luogang Commune, I remembered my father's description on one of those riverboat trips. When the peasants owned their land like Ohio farmers, he had said, they would be freed from landlord oppression. All China one day would develop brotherly relations as the old feudal system broke down under the impact of Western democracy and the Christian religion. His prophecy was not wrong in essence, but it was revolution, rather than conversion, that won a new life for Chinese peasants.

Picturesque impressions of the South China landscape were intensified as we drove through groves of orange, banana, bamboo, guava and lichee on the Luogang Commune, and between newly drained fields of rice ripening for early harvest. The commune supplied the Chinese consumer market with fresh fruit daily and the export market with canned lichees and mandarin oranges. We had seen cans of fruit with the Luogang label in the food display at the Trade Fair; some had won first and second prizes. Our host, Wang Shikun, was very proud of the awards. He received us at the door of commune headquarters with a muscular handshake. He was a short, sturdy peasant with an earnest manner, as if he accepted his duties as Chairman of the Luogang Revolutionary Committee with utter dedication. His task at the moment was to welcome us and spend the best part of the afternoon giving us a rounded view of commune life.

While Chairman Wang was giving us a detailed briefing, we were served jasmine tea and samples of fruit grown on the commune. We learned that the commune was populated by fifty thousand peasants forming twelve brigades, further divided into a hundred workteams. We were informed as to how many hectares were allotted to each type of fruit grown and given a hundred other statistical details, after which Wang accompanied us through pouring rain to the central school. 'Welcome to our American Friends!' was chalked neatly on the blackboard of the English class, and in unison the pupils stood up and chanted: 'Welcome to our American Friends', gleefully showing their mastery of a foreign language. They were as excited as we were in this exchange of friendship and clapped us a reluctant farewell after a further chorus of complimentary phrases in English and half a dozen Mao quotations. Unlike the teacher, our guide, and other adults on the commune, the children, particularly the girls, wore bright fabrics rather than the usual grey or faded blue. Their eyes were alive to new possibilities in life ahead and new relations with foreign peoples. The girls' red ribbons rippled like waves as we departed. 'Every child goes to school in our commune,' Wang said with pride. 'The aims of our school system are to motivate our children to serve the people, rather than their own self-interest, and to give educational opportunities to youngsters from poor peasant and working-class families. It is possible now for our best-qualified students to go on to the Sun Yat-sen University in Guangzhou.'

At the central commune hospital, we were received by both modern and traditional practitioners: surgeons and X-ray machine operators, and two barefoot doctors who were processing herbal medicines in a dispensary which boasted two thousand local items in neatly labelled bottles and packets. The hospital was primitive by Western standards, with tamped earth floors and ducks and chickens pecking at the entrances, but in comparison with pre-revolutionary days, medicine was now available to all the peasants. Before 1949, in a population of fifty thousand, there were two resident doctors who served only the landlords – so went the briefing. No peasant could afford a doctor's fee in those days. Now there were several hundred medical personnel serving the commune members with preventive as well as curative medicine. Wang told us with quiet pride how local medical teams had organized mass campaigns to eliminate schistoso-miasis carried by snails in the ricefields and streams – also tuberculosis and leprosy which, if not totally eliminated, were on the way out. Syphilis and smallpox, he said, were afflictions of a past age. Chances that a child would reach adulthood were 1000 per cent better than before 1949.

As we returned to visitors' headquarters late in the afternoon for a final cup of tea, Wang Shikun finished his briefing with a glow of enthusiasm: 'In spite of the rains, which have been unfortunately heavy today and made it impossible to show you our fish ponds, canning factory and orchards, we are no longer victims of flooding on the one hand, or drought on the other. We pump the excess water in wet seasons into reservoirs over the hills and reverse the process when it is dry. You have probably noticed,' he said at the gate, giving us a warm farewell handshake, 'that we have planted trees where there wasn't a single bush before!' Like all cadres who briefed us about 'new socialist things', Wang was an enthusiast in his own serious way, his eyes flashing with visions of the future. 'Come back again in a year or two and we will show you many improvements. We hope the weather will be better – but that's one thing we can't yet guarantee.' He marked out the limits of socialist planning with a laugh and a farewell wave.

Pui Ying Revisited

Time was running out on us. Our last full day in Guangzhou was agenda-packed as usual, beginning with an early breakfast on the top floor of the hotel. From this high point, we could survey a good part of Guangzhou in a 360-degree sweep. The suburban areas around the Trade Fair were newly green, the crowded areas of the old walled city grey under a rain mist through which the sun was beginning to filter.

With her usual quick smile, Mrs Li met us in the hotel lobby to review our agenda for the day, beginning with a stroll through Shamian, the former foreign concession; then a drive across the river to the Fati side to see what was left of Pui Ying Middle School, its main building now converted into the Marine Parts Factory; finally, an afternoon in the new Riverside Neighbourhood where the boatpeople, formerly a lower-caste group, were now housed in new fireproof apartments in a community of sixty thousand.

Our driver hooted and honked us through the downtown area and delivered us safely to the Shamian footbridge. Mrs Li led us into what had once been the foreign concession. No Chinese were permitted to own property on Shamian while the Westerners were in occupation, or even sleep on the island as guests. Servants were, of course, exempted! The island was no longer the stately white-mansion-palm-tree enclave of the Western Powers, where white-clothed, sunhatted officials strolled between consulates and dockside ships and gunboats. The old banyan trees that had once shaded tidy lawns were unkempt, whipped and truncated by typhoon violence since I had seen them early in the century. The elegant apartments where my Aunt Helen and Uncle Bill had once lived while he was a China agent for the Sloane Furniture Company were now workers' residences with blue jackets and trousers hanging at windows to dry. The foreign consulates – except for the Polish, which was still maintained -- had been converted into workers' quarters or warehouses and the flags of foreign Powers no longer dominated the island breezes.

Memory evoked a Shamian which had been the stage for pageants of the Western Powers – with foreign flags draped around children, my brother Bill included; young Western beauties (clothed to the neck, in deference to participating missionaries) dancing on carnival-decked platforms under spreading banyan trees; and foreign armies, navies and marine corps represented *en masse* around bandstands where British, French and American brass bands asserted their hegemony over the Republic of China – the Zhujiang River basin in particular and the South China Seas in general – eighty miles inland, defying Chinese sovereignty. Here on Shamian were once celebrated the Fourth of July, Quatorze Juillet and Queen Victoria's birthday. But now the book of history has closed on queens and kings and foreign gods as far as the People's Republic is concerned, and 1 May and 1 October are celebrated on Shamian as national holidays by the Chinese people themselves. Red flags with five gold stars have waved since 1949 in place of the Union Jack, the Stars and Stripes and the French Tricolour. And there were no more gunboats, even Chinese, at uneasy anchor in the river that April morning in 1975 when we strolled around Shamian.

Our driver was waiting at the bridge to project us at jet speed across the new Zhujiang Bridge to the Fati side of the river. 'The Westerners, with all their technology and engineering capacity, never saw fit to bridge the river,' Mrs Li explained as we slowed down in narrow streets scarcely wide enough for the Honqi, the Chinese luxury car, to navigate. 'It remained for Chairman Mao and the Chinese Communist Party to bridge the river, and eliminate the need for sampans and the drudgery of the boatpeople. Fati is still almost like the old China in appearance,' Mrs Li went on, 'except for the spirit and livelihood of the people. Now, of course, nobody dies of starvation or drowns in floods. The children are no longer pot-bellied urchins but are adequately clothed and fed, as you can see, and attend school.'

The former Presbyterian mission compound was barely recognizable. The gateway, with tiled roof upturned at the corners to loop evil spirits back up where they came from, still stood but were devoid of function, since the compound walls embedded with sharp glass fragments for lacerating hands or legs of unwary thieves were all gone, the bricks restructured in buildings that replaced the Henry house and the Spencer house. The pond between the two houses where we used to fish for shrimps with bent pins was filled in and built over. Only a quarter of the house I was born in still stood. The palms at the four corners and the pomelo tree shading the entrance, the lawns and the bamboo grove were all gone. Even the creek that once idled and bubbled with fermenting odours between compound and village was filled in, the space used as a lumber yard. The former school grounds, including the tennis court, were piled high with frames and castings, shafts and propellers and other marine parts. The main school building itself had been converted into the Marine Parts Factory. Instead of students chanting scripture in unison, the chorus of many machines was a chant of production in progress sounding through the open windows of what was once Severance Hall.

The name Severance, that of a Cleveland millionaire

philanthropist, had long been forgotten in Fati and as we entered the building I noted that the portraits of Chairman Mao and Marx, Engels, Lenin and Stalin replaced former Christian symbols above the platform that had once been furnished with altar and podium. In a flash of memory I could see my grandfather's coffin lying there back in 1914. Now the platform was occupied by several buffing machines powered by transmission belts.

Mrs Li introduced us to Li Kwok, Chairman of the Revolutionary Committee of the Marine Parts Factory, who came smiling a welcome down the main aisle to greet us. The lunch bell rang at the same time, a signal for the work staff to turn off their machines and make themselves comfortable on the floor with Thermos flasks and the contents of lunch boxes. In the confusion, Comrade Kwok relayed over the loudspeaker the information that Mrs Li had given him. He informed the lunching workers that I was a missionary's son who was born on the premises of the Marine Parts Factory in 1910, the last year of the Qing dynasty, and had come back from Meiguo, the beautiful country, to visit the place of my birth. He then welcomed me again with an official handshake, as if to demonstrate that not all missionary children were bad eggs.

The workers responded with an incredulous smile or stare which seemed to ask two questions: How could anybody have been born a hundred yards away in what was now the office building of their Marine Parts Factory? And how could that person be me? Seeing the expressions of scepticism and amazement, Li Kwok asked my interpreter to explain about missionaries and schools before liberation, which she did briefly. Gradually, the workers relaxed and looks of disbelief dissolved into friendly smiles. They listened with mouths full to the dialogue that developed between Li Kwok and myself on the way Chinese and American factories were operated.

'Who manages the Marine Parts Factory?' I asked.

'Our Revolutionary Committee,' he answered.

'As Chairman of the Committee, are you elected or appointed?'

'Elected.' Li nodded for confirmation to the workers he represented.

'Are you a member of the Communist Party?'

After a whispered consultation with Mrs Li, he said quietly, 'Yes.'

'What is the difference between your Communist Party and your Revolutionary Committee?'

'Chairman Mao and the Party are our guides,' he replied with enthusiasm. 'They inspire us to put politics first, to do a better job.' I was to find in the next five weeks, wherever I went in China, that the Communist Party was like the nerve centre of factories, communes, hospitals and neighbourhoods, the hub of the wheel extending outwards to keep the whole vehicle of socialism on the road.

'Then what is the function of your Revolutionary Committee?'

Li Kwok answered simply, 'We plan production and carry out the day-to-day work. We have a three-in-one combination here. Our Revolutionary Committee consists of the old, the young and the in between.'

'Are they elected at the shop level?'

Li nodded, but added, 'A list is prepared by the workers. The Party may add to this list, or raise objections to any name on it. Then a vote is taken.'

'Do you have a trade union?'

'No,' Li answered. 'This is a small enterprise, as you can see. We have a workforce of two hundred. Welfare and recreational activities are therefore handled by the Revolutionary Committee. In larger factories these are, of course, the tasks of the trade union.'

'I thought trade unions were mostly eliminated during the Cultural Revolution?'

'I don't think so,' he puzzled, 'but I am not well informed.'

'When I was on the negotiation committee of the International Association of Machinists in Chicago, we bargained for higher wages and better working conditions. Is that the case with unions in China?'

'Wages are set by the state,' Li Kwok answered.

'What about health care? Do you have a clinic here? Any barefoot doctors?'

Three hands shot up. 'These are barefoot doctors,' the Chairman confirmed.

'What are your tasks?' I was catching on to socialist idiom.

'Treat minor cuts and bruises, dispense medicine, gather herbs,' one of them replied. Her answer was direct, without quotations or political padding. 'Serious ones we take to the hospital. But headaches, muscular pains and so on we deal with here.' She pointed to a glassed-in dispensary at the corner of the hall with surgical table, equipment and acupuncture charts. Curiously, it was exactly where the students' clinic had been in the 1910s and I remembered the agony of being treated there for a dog bite with possible complications from rabies. The doctor had used a red-hot poker to cauterize the bite between thumb and forefinger.

While I was painfully reminiscing, another of the barefoot doctors, sounding like a Party member, pressed home a political point, as if her sister barefoot doctor had missed an opportunity to impress a foreign visitor: 'We try to be self-reliant and serve the people at their workplace. Chairman Mao directs us to use our own initiative and depend on professionals only when absolutely necessary.'

The post-lunch bell rang. Chairman Li held up his hand for silence. It was time to get back to production to meet the April quota. 'We thank our American friend for coming all the way from a foreign country to visit our small enterprise. We hope he will visit us again.' Then, turning to me as the workers went back to their benches and machines, he added, 'We have a small enterprise here. We have not done a very good job. Do you have any criticisms?'

I began to say, 'I don't know enough about your enterprise yet to make any criticism. . . .' But when I realized that he was genuinely disappointed with my reply, I said I would be glad to tour the shop and give him my reactions.

Immediately he took me by the arm and conducted me down the central aisle. 'This is a Russian machine, no good,' he said, wrinkling up his nose. 'This is an American machine. It still works. But we are replacing them with machines made in China. This lathe is an excellent machine made in the Shanghai Machine Tools Plant.'

'Will you be replacing the Russian and American machines with the new models I saw at the Trade Fair?' I asked.

'In the future,' he answered dubiously. 'There are perhaps

more important priorities than our little enterprise.'

After touring the shop we went out into the factory yard, once Pui Ying's volleyball court, stopping between castings and bins of finished propellers while Li repeated his question, 'Now, do you have any criticisms?'

'Yes, I do.' The Chairman seemed relieved that I was going to give him an honest answer. 'I can see your problem is to make the old serve the new – walk on two legs, as you say here in China. But I don't think you use enough safety precautions. Women workers with long hair should wear caps. With chips flying, workers at lathes and milling machines, even drill presses, should wear safety glasses, you know?' I went on speaking from the experience of a former shop steward. 'And most important, the power belts should have guards. That's where many a worker loses an arm or a leg.'

I was afraid I had offended Chairman Li, that he would think I had a poor opinion of the way he carried out his responsibilities. On the contrary, he smiled happily, clasped both my hands in his with a warm fraternal handshake and said, 'Thank you, thank you, thank you! We will try harder in the future and we will take up your suggestions at the next meeting of our Revolutionary Committee. Come back next year. You will see we have done much better.'

There are still many small factories in the United States operating with old equipment. Inflation and/or recession are driving most of these out of business. In China, it seems, an opposite trend is the rule. Their economy is still at the stage where the small develop into the large. Many of the factories I visited in 1975 had grown from just such a small beginning as the Marine Parts Factory. Large modern factories like the Shanghai Machine Tools Plant or the great new Xinhua Printing Press, covering four city blocks in Beijing, started as small enterprises and in a few years became eminent in their field, as up-to-date in plant equipment and layout as advanced enterprises in the West. The advantage to me in visiting the Marine Parts Factory before visiting the larger enterprises was that I could see the way production gets started in a socialist economy. Old machines were used to do new things and the enthusiasm and developing skills of the workers were powerful transforming forces, so that Chinese industry one day could pace the most advanced capitalist production. Chairman Li and his two hundred fellow-workers were preparing for that day by building one of the many thousand launching pads for China's modernization programme.

There was an additional reason for the feeling of elation I felt as I mounted our trusty Hongqi again. The workers at the Marine Parts Factory had apparently never received a foreign visitor before. Their attitudes and responses were fresh, obviously not warmed up as in the more sophisticated enterprises I visited later. Besides, they were probably the children and grandchildren of people I had passed in the streets and lanes of Fati and along the canal when I was a child. So my visit to the Marine Parts Factory was a real homecoming.

Boatpeople Ashore

Riding back through Fati in a Hongqi was like riding a modern dragon that snorted and bellowed its way through impossible roadblocks at the command of our magician driver. As we recrossed the river on the Zhujiang bridge, a flash of memory brought back a miraculous experience. 'I remember the first airplane that was ever seen in Guangzhou back in 1917.' I raised my voice to Mrs Li over the roar of bridge noises. 'It was a hydroplane. We saw it take off from the river like a gull. I remember the expression of amazement on the faces of the crowd because I felt the way they did that an unbelievable thing was happening. I was only seven then. When we left China at the end of 1918, 31 December to be exact, Guangzhou had only three automobiles!'

'It is very different today,' Mrs Li was proud to say. She was less doctrinaire than some of my guides during the Cultural Revolution and refrained from illustrating every achievement of the Chinese people with a quotation from Chairman Mao. 'We have more cars now than our streets have room for, and until we widen all our streets . . . .' A shoulder shrug and a smile finished her thought. We were blocked at that moment by every kind of vehicle known to man while only bicycles and motor cycles, at breakneck speed, were able to weave through the traffic.

After lunch and the usual have-a-good-rest interval on our agenda, we were driven back through the city to the riverfront, the old Bund. The Zhujiang River was still muddy but seemed cleaner than in the old days. Dilapidated wharfside structures were gone, replaced by concrete retaining walls and walkways between lawns and flowerbeds. The river itself, which had once flooded its banks every June and brought death and misery to countless thousands, was now like a tamed serpent gently winding towards the sea. It was and is one of the great rivers of the world, flowing down from its mountain headwaters in four provinces: Yunnan, Guizhou, Hunan and Jiangxi; and in one autonomous region, Guangxi Zhuang, draining the whole of South Central and South-East China through Guangzhou and the fan-shaped delta of Guangdong Province into the South China Sea. Barges and tugboats were busy hauling freight, battened down under tarpaulin, up and down this busy trafficway. There were few junks and no sampans to impede their rapid movement. The river was liberated from the old congestion and the stinking flotsam and jetsam – and also from the human misery that used to disgrace its banks.

There were no beggars holding out hands and cups to passers-by, begging for the right to survive. Only in memory could I see them squatting there. Elephantiasis had enormously inflated arms and legs. Syphilis had wasted away nose cartilages and melted down cheekbones. Every skin disease referred to by the great pharmacologist Li Shizhen in his *Compendium of Materia Medica* registered its devastation in yellow, orange or swamp green on the faces and bodies of these victims of poverty. Beggar women held children bony and skinny from rickets and pellagra to their milkless breasts. Older children with swollen bellies from worms held out hands for a mercy that doled down an occasional cash.* All the distress and pain I had seen in the 1910s, which as a child I had associated with Cary's illustrations of Dante's *Inferno* in

---

*Cash: a low-denomination coin with a hole in the centre.

a leather-bound volume in my father's study, had completely disappeared.

In the museum of the new Riverside Neighbourhood, the record of pre-liberation days was preserved for future generations. For a thousand years, generation after generation of boatpeople had lived as social outcasts on the river. In their frail and patched sampans they were at the mercy of storms and floods. Hundreds were drowned every year. But even worse was man's unkindness to man. The boatpeople were forced by the corrupt city government to pay thirty different taxes: wharf tax, police tax, anchorage tax, land fee and so on. In bad years some of them were forced to sell their children into slavery, or watch them die of slow starvation.

Our informant at the museum was Chen Rencheng, Vice-Chairman of the Revolutionary Committee of the Riverside Neighbourhood. He told us that a Chinese Neighbourhood elected its own committee, which then became the administrative organ of its thousands of residents with jurisdiction over elementary schools, recreation and small workshops and stores. 'This kind of local self-government was possible only after liberation,' Chen continued his briefing, 'when the boatpeople were permitted to move ashore. They were no longer considered an outcast group. When they were asked where they would like to live, they replied, "We have remained on the river for many generations, so now we would like to continue to live by the river." Fifteen housing projects were built along the banks of the Zhujiang River to accommodate sixty thousand boatpeople. Jobs were assigned to all over eighteen after they moved ashore. Some still preferred to work on the river as stevedores and pilots; others were given jobs in stores, factories, schools and hospitals. We never knew until liberation that life could be happy!'

In spite of typhoons that clobbered the South China coast, the boatpeople could now live securely. 'All we have to do now when the typhoons come is to close our windows,' said Chow Chen, a retired worker aged seventy-five, who received us in his family's apartment in the Riverside complex. 'Typhoons used to catch us unawares and whole families would be drowned in the river. In the old days we were just trampled underfoot. In many families, two or more members had to share a single pair of trousers and work at different times. Now we are guaranteed clothing, housing, food, medical care. My pension is sixty yuan a month. Some of us retired workers have study groups and always have something to think about and do. We look after our grandchildren, help neighbours when they are sick. We have a useful and happy life. Who would have thought it possible in the old days?' Chow Chen introduced us to the other members of his family; first to his mother, who was ninety-nine years of age, slight and smiling, with her feet curled up on the settee. His son, who worked on 'inland water transportation', was away at his job, but he introduced his daughter-in-law, who worked in a nearby garment factory and was active on her women's factory committee. As she was busy preparing a meal, Chow spoke for her: 'We are engaged in a mass campaign against Confucian tradition. We are getting rid of the mentality that woman is inferior to man and we no longer believe in the sole authority of the husband.' Chow had obviously been through the struggle himself. Wrinkles on his forehead showed as he went through it over again in his own mind and tried to make us understand the transformation in men–women relations which had taken place in China since 1949.

Chow's grandson, Chow Po, a truck driver on his day off, analysed the family economy for us. His mother and wife were at work, one making cigarette lighters in a neighbourhood workshop, the other in town at an insulating equipment factory. Their combined monthly income was 189 yuan. Rent, including water and utilities, was nineteen yuan. 'In the old days,' Chow interrupted, since he was afraid his grandson might forget to mention class privilege in the old society, 'only the rich had running water and electricity. Now we all have it!'

'The average cost of food per person', Chow Po resumed his analysis, 'is twelve or thirteen yuan. My cost is a little higher because, as a truck driver, I eat away from home a good deal and am therefore subsidized twenty-five fen per meal in addition to my sixty-five yuan per month.'

Chow Po's two children were playing happily on the floor,

unconcerned with economic problems or foreign visitors. What a contrast with the old family life aboard sampans a metre and a half wide and four metres long! The average family afloat, including grandparents and children, was seven or more. When we were ferried across the river from Fati in the old days, the man and woman in the family would oar us across while children and grandparents shrank into the stern or bow. I used to play with the children on the way and invite them to come back to our house to play with our toys. But it was always impossible, for reasons I could not then understand.

As we left the Riverside Neighbourhood to return to our hotel, I felt deeply impressed by the changes that had taken place since the revolution. The contrast in human relations and the spirit of the people between the 1910s and the 1970s was like a leap from an old world clean into a new. It was not that I thought then, or think now, that China has solved all her social and human problems, or eliminated all feudal hang-ups, or caught up with the West in technology. But she had taken the first steps along a new road, and the spirit of the people was infectious. Why should China ape the West? Maybe it was her destiny to introduce a new way, a new Tao, into human affairs.

I thought in a personal and somewhat nostalgic way of life in the old China with my parents and relatives. All, except two of my brothers, were gone: I could not go home again. But in a contradictory way, I was glad to come back to a new China where the essence of the change-over was a statement by Chow Chen as we were saying goodbye. When I asked him what he thought was the main difference between the old China and the new, he replied quite simply, '*Now* we care for one another.'

Pyrotechnics for a New Age

Wisdom said, go to bed. You've got a month's packed agenda ahead: business negotiations in Beijing and Shanghai, visits to communes and factories, neighbourhood centres, bookstores and publishing houses; also visits to Yanan, Xian, Zheng-

zhou, Shijiazhuang. Rest and sleep would be at a premium
for the next four weeks.

Still, I lingered on my balcony that last night in Guangzhou, reluctant to shut my eyes on the ancient city where I
was born. Here it was in legend that 2,800 years ago five rams,
mounted by five outer-space deities, descended from heaven
to found a city on the Zhujiang River delta, a century before
two wolves, nurturing Romulus and Remus, were to found
another 'eternal city' on the opposite side of the world. Here
history was still in the making. Over the old walled city rose
the aura of a new system of illumination. Electric street lights
were unknown when we left China at the end of 1918. In that
year, there were only three automobiles to serve a population
of two million. Now, ten storeys below, a dozen cars with
flashing headlights were turning into the oval drive to deliver
foreign visitors back to the hotel after a night on the town.
The Dongfang Hotel itself was so new that a whole wing was
still under construction and, from drawings in the lobby, its
landscaped gardens could only be imagined with their
grottoes, lotus ponds, flagstone walkways and half-moon
bridges yet to be. Here the old and the new were creating a
complex symphony: old-time melodies from sheng and erhu
floated up from the lobby to orchestrate with new-time
cacophonies from the picks, shovels and pneumatic drills of
night-shift workers in knee-high rubber boots laying pipes in
trenches under floodlights. The new was visibly transforming
the old.

In the process, I wondered, would the Chinese people
succeed in transforming themselves? Would they, where
others had failed, build a new collective society? A classless
society in which differences between town and country,
workers and peasants would actually be resolved, hand and
brain reunited in a new phase of human evolution? In
practice, would one billion people, on an upward spiral of
history, actually learn to care for one another?

It was a night to believe that such social miracles were
possible: a magic full moon had risen over the new Trade Fair
buildings and suddenly, above them, a burst and scattering of
gold and silver, of green and red sparks flashed through the

clouds and filled the sky. As flares died out in puffs of smoke, new exploding marvels zoomed into upper space. Rainbows and umbrellas of fire, creations of one of the oldest of Chinese arts, gave promise of a new age.

✳ 7 ✳

'Serve the People'

We Meet Our Chinese Book Exporters Face to Face

Beijing at last! Dropping through mists that blanketed the capital, we saw ground lights up close channelling our plane to a safe landing. I was expecting a warm welcome from friends at Guoji Shudian with whom we had corresponded for years, but was surprised to be met by the whole senior leadership – face to face at last.

Jin Zhonglin, who had accompanied us on our flight from Guangzhou, solemnly introduced us to Shao Gongwen, General Manager, a senior citizen in his early sixties with a fresh complexion and a sparkle of good humour behind his glasses. There was a simple graciousness in his manner that was surprising in an important official, the director of the China Information Centre which supplied publications and handicrafts to 147 foreign countries. 'You are most welcome,' he said, as he gave me one of those warm handshakes reserved for special friends in China. 'We have been looking forward to your visit for many years.'

In the massive airport terminal, with its slogans in black characters on gold or red – 'Serve the People', 'Peoples of the World Unite!', and so on – passengers and crews were crisscrossing in a noisy effort to reach departing planes, ticket booths, or seats in the vast waiting room. Jin had to raise his normally quiet voice to introduce Zhong Hong, Vice-General Manager of Guoji Shudian. Zhong, in his late fifties, thin in body and face, had deep-set eyes that scrutinized me as if to say, 'I want to know who you are we've been dealing with all these years.' There was a gentleness in his eyes, but the strength of steel in his hands as he took mine in his and said, 'You are no stranger to China. We are happy to welcome you back to the land of your birth.'

Next in line was Wang Hongshen, a round-faced cadre in his early forties with a ruddy complexion and a semi-permanent smile which he beamed at me as he said, 'I have conducted your son, your daughter and your wife to the Great Wall – and now I hope to have the honour of conducting the last of the Noyes family....'

'Don't be too sure,' I smiled back. 'I have three grandchildren.' Wang's manner was more formal than Shao's or Hong's. He seemed constantly to be aware of his own important role, which he defined in negotiations as 'the Party representative'.

The only woman in the line, who had already served as interpreter, was Yang Aiwen. 'Chris sends his very best wishes. He has told me how you wrestled with his Americanisms for five weeks when he was here in 1971.' Yang's serious expression relaxed for a moment, but her forehead again puckered with worry wrinkles as she wrestled to turn my Americanisms into correct Putonghua (Mandarin). Translating Shao Gongwen's Chinese into the English she had learned at the Shanghai Teachers' College, however, was plain sailing for her. I was soon to learn that she was much more than an interpreter, rather a leader in her own right with an understanding of the politics and economics of Guoji Shudian which she shared with me at critical moments.

Finally Jin introduced me to Chen Tingsun and Yao Yinsheng, who were to be my constant guides and companions in Beijing to evening entertainment: basketball matches, films, concerts and circuses. Chen, in his early thirties, was full of bounding energy, darting here, there, then gone to make last-minute arrangements and gather our luggage into one heap. Yao, opposite in temperament, was a solid, ex-People's Liberation Army type in his late twenties, solid in body, face and mind; at the same time, modest and unassuming – an observer. Chen, who had graduated from a

Shanghai business college, understood English far better than
he would admit. His face was as expressive as an actor's. He
acted out huge enjoyments and monstrous worries, while Yao
looked on with the unconcern of a bystander. Chen and Yao
were perfect foils for each other, like a twosome on the old
vaudeville stage. When we visited the Great Wall on a Sunday
the three of us raced up the steep side, and of course Yao and
Chen won. I was wearing a pair of lugged hiking boots, so
challenged them on the downhill run. They slithered and
slipped in their smooth-soled shoes and easily lost the race.
From then on, they no longer called me Lao (Old) Noyes.

On evenings and weekends, which Yang Aiwen spent with
her family, Zhang Huijuan joined us as an interpreter. She
was a hearty-voiced woman in her late twenties, a graduate of
Beijing University. She described herself as an intellectual
who had been sent to a May 7th Cadre School to reform her
bourgeois tendencies. There she had been instructed how to
combine mental and manual labour and to remould herself.
The whole staff of Guoji Shudian, including Shao Gongwen,
had been sent at one time or another to the nearby
countryside to remould themselves through physical labour –
with the exception of the workers in the packing and shipping
departments. The proletariat, according to the theory of the
Cultural Revolution, did not need remoulding. They were
already socialist men and women.

In the large oval drive in front of the airport, two Hongqis,
assigned to Guoji Shudian, were waiting for us and our
luggage. The drivers were Lao Tze and Yang. Lao Tze, who
had driven Chris everywhere in Beijing in 1971, was a veteran
of the Long March, bald as Yul Brynner and stout from his
fondness for Qingtao beer. Yang was a younger man in his late
thirties with cool nerves and a broad sunny smile, facially
resembling Zhou Enlai. We put our lives into the hands of
these two drivers, who were responsible not only to us but to
the state to ensure that we would survive Beijing traffic, its
two million plus bicycles, honking buses, army trucks,
tractors and all that moved on wheels, including donkey carts
and vegetable barrows pushed or pulled.

Down the aisle of road from the airport between poplars
we drove through an enchanted countryside, among tree
shadows cast by a moon that appeared and disappeared

through dissolving mists. Our driver, in semi-darkness, turned up headlights only when passing bicycles which had no lights at all. Soon, poplars gave way to half-lit streets and grey walls with tiled gateways.

Shao Gongwen was in a responsive mood when I said, 'We have known each other by correspondence for a long time, ever since 1960. Many things have changed since then, especially in the foreign policy of our countries. Your government no longer regards the US as the major enemy....' Shao held up his hand to give Yang Aiwen a chance to translate. This also gave me a chance to think out my next statement or question. At the same time I felt I was making a speech, instead of engaging in dialogue, and this feeling persisted during the whole five-week period I was in China.

'Imperialism is the enemy,' Shao responded. 'In the earlier days, the Soviet Union was our friend. But in 1960 it withdrew its support, blueprints and technicians. This created severe problems at a time when we also had some natural disasters. So we had to change our mind about who were our friends and who were our enemies.'

'Yes, we've handled the documents of the PRC, as you know, and have followed these changes from year to year. Even before ping-pong diplomacy, we began to notice a change in your policy towards the US and the American people.' Yang Aiwen held up her hand. It was her turn.

Then Shao responded, 'We think of the American people as a great people leading the world at one time in the advance guard of democracy. But it is the practice of governments that we judge in forming our opinions – whether they oppress other peoples or not. For example, the Vietnamese people. Now that your government is withdrawing its forces there is a better basis for mutual agreements, even though our economic systems are very different. These are my personal opinions,' he added, with characteristic deference to an invisible higher authority. Shao's glasses gleamed in the semi-dark as we turned into the half-moon drive in front of a multistorey building. 'This is the new wing of the Beijing Hotel, where you will stay.' He held my hands in a warm clasp as we parted and Yang Aiwen translated, with a note of finality: 'The future is bright!'

From the balcony outside our hotel room, under the moon

to the west, the roof of the Museum of Chinese History was visible and beyond, for the first time, I saw the Great Hall of the People across Tian An Men Square.

Our negotiations began in earnest the next morning at the headquarters of Guoji Shudian, in the north-west suburban area of Beijing. We were received at the main entrance by General Manager Shao Gongwen and other leading members of the staff we had met at the airport. 'Welcome to our American Friends' was chalked on a blackboard on a chair at the entrance. The word *Welcome* was surrounded with multicoloured chalk flowers.

In the meeting room upstairs, which was furnished in the frugal style of the Cultural Revolution, brief introductions were made to heads of departments: the European and the American, subscription, finance, political, warehousing, packing and shipping – an impressive leadership group who had been responsible for the past fifteen years for supplying us with Chinese publications. 'You have been our faithful friends for many years' was the way Shao Gongwen opened negotiations. 'Chairman Mao's line makes it possible for us to meet here today. The role of Guoji Shudian is to distribute works, particularly of Chairman Mao, to give peoples of the world an understanding of socialist society by promoting cultural exchange and friendly intercourse with books and periodicals. We are a worldwide headquarters.'

Although detailed statistics are now made available in China in most areas of production, in the mid 1970s it was customary to give generalizations. Shao reported that 'many millions' of books were distributed abroad by Guoji Shudian; or that 'many thousands' of subscriptions to Chinese periodicals were serviced every year; or that 'over a hundred thousand' letters were received every year from readers in foreign countries. He specified that *Quotations from Chairman Mao* had been distributed in thirty-nine foreign languages 'in the millions'. 'In China last year, 3,300,500,000 publications in the Han and minority languages were distributed through 100,000 selling places.

'Bookstores are inseparable from the revolutionary movement,' he went on to generalize. 'With the revolutionary movement's growth, they must also grow. Supply can hardly meet demand in a socialist society. But in the old Guomindang days, distribution of progressive literature involved very acute, even violent struggle. We will talk more about those days at lunch. In the meantime we should discuss an agenda for our negotiations.'

Discussion of our agenda was cut short by the noon bell and a strident cry from downstairs which was interpreted by Yang Aiwen to mean 'tug-of-war'. Between five hundred and six hundred staff members were assembling in the courtyard to cheer their team. The contest was between the African and European departments. The white handkerchief knotted at the centre of the rope seesawed for five minutes, causing alternating cheers and groans, but fully and finally went over the line to the African side. In conformity with China's concept of friendship first, competition second, winners and losers cheered each other and the bystanders joined in the raucous chorus.

'It was appropriate' – Wang Hongshen made a political summary typical of the Cultural Revolution – 'that the Third World should win! It is our considered theory of the Three Worlds that they will surround the imperialist centres the way Chinese guerrillas did the cities in our Civil War, and that the peoples of the world will be victorious. Shall we join General Manager Shao Gongwen for lunch and finalize our agenda?'

The Xinhua Printing Press

In our agenda-packed ten days in Beijing, mornings were reserved for negotiations; evenings for entertainment; and afternoons, in the phrase of Shao Gongwen, 'for enlarging our understanding of China' through visits to factories, neighbourhood centres, the Palace Museum (formerly the Forbidden City), the Temple of Heaven (surely ranking with the Taj Mahal as one of the most beautiful buildings in the world), the Summer Palace, the Sun Yat-sen Memorial Park and the Xinhua Printing Press.

The Press, which occupied at least four standard city blocks, was impressive, not only for its size but for the quality of the books and periodicals it produced. We were met at the gates by the 'Leading Comrade at Head of Production', Ke Pingyao, who welcomed us with a hearty laugh and a powerful handshake. He introduced us to the directors of the rotary press and the photo-engraving workshops, Liu Shushun and Sheng Yusheng, who also came out to greet us. We realized that we were being specially honoured as Ke Pingyao boomed, in a voice of a calibre to outdo the decibels of a dozen presses in operation, 'A warm welcome to our American friends who distribute Chinese publications abroad that we print in our workshops.'

'Many thanks for your warm welcome,' I responded, as he waved us into the administration office with a hand twice the size of mine. 'We learned at lunch from the general manager of Guoji Shudian that your press was burned to the ground in 1949 by the Guomindang. That's hard to believe when we see your enormous enterprise in operation – big as a city.'

Ke motioned us to a table in the reception room. 'Have a cup of tea. Yes, that happened. The Chiang Kai-shek reactionaries destroyed our press before we were able to drive them out of the city. All they knew was how to destroy. But Chinese workers know how to rebuild, so it took us only a short time to get back into production.' Ke Pingyao's enthusiasm was infectious as he described the growth of Xinhua Press after the revolution. 'Since then, we have modernized from year to year, as my colleagues will show you. We have eight large workshops occupying 24,000 square metres and a workforce of 3,700, of whom 42 per cent are women. We print *China Pictorial*, which you distribute in your country: a total run of 1,200,000 copies every month in sixteen different languages, including English and Chinese. We also print *Minzu Huabao*, the nationalities monthly, in five minority languages: Korean, Kazakh, Mongolian, Uighur and Tibetan, as well as in Chinese – 150,000 each issue. Every week we print 2,400,000 copies of *Hongqi*, which is, as you know, the official theoretical journal of the Chinese Communist Party. Perhaps you have some questions?'

'Yes, what changes have taken place here', I asked, 'since the beginning of the Cultural Revolution?'

Instant explanations were at Ke's command: 'Before 1966,

we were not clear about the correct line. Whom do we serve, the bourgeoisie or the proletariat? Under the revisionist line before the Cultural Revolution, we published few works of Marxism–Leninism. We printed candy wrappers . . .' – Ke paused long enough for us to laugh at the incongruity of an enterprise occupying 24,000 square metres and a staff of 3,700 printing candy wrappers before he added – '. . . instead of the works of Chairman Mao. But the criticism of the masses and discussions with them gave us a better understanding of our socialist task. In the five years before the Cultural Revolution we printed only 10 million copies of Chairman Mao's works.' Ke Pingyao's tone was downbeat, then rose in triumph as he began to drum on the table with his fist and make the teacups dance and clink, 'But after 1966, with a correct proletarian line, we produced several hundred millions in the five years that followed.'

An emergency call came through for Ke, so he turned us over to Liu Shushun and Sheng Yusheng, to 'enlarge our understanding of China'. In the photo-engraving department there was comparative quiet, which gave us an opportunity for multiple questions and answers on colour separations, but in the rotary press workshop Liu's explanations were drowned out by the Niagara-like roar of enormous machines rolling out the newsprint at top speed. Despite the boom and rattle of the presses and the soporific heat they generated, there was an air of relaxation, as in other Chinese factories we visited. Operators were intent on their tasks, but off-duty workers were having a snack over tea or fruit drinks, a few reading books or magazines. Women were employed in seemingly every job classification, but leadership roles were still mainly performed by men. There was no shortage of labour. Trainees at many machines outnumbered the operators.

When we returned to the reception room for a final cup of tea, Ke Pingyao gave us as hearty a welcome as if we had just arrived. 'Do you have any criticisms?' he asked in his jovial manner. 'I am sure we can do better.'

'It's been an education for us to see all the processes that are involved in the production of *China Pictorial*, for example,' I replied, 'but it would be good to know more about the management of such a large enterprise. I understand you have a labour-management system that somewhat corresponds to what we had in the US during World War II.'

'Perhaps,' he said doubtfully. 'In our system, since the beginning of the Cultural Revolution, cadres are obliged to work at least one day a week in the shop at physical labour. On the other hand, most shop workers participate in management.' I am not sure exactly how, since Ke did not go into explanations. He went on to describe the raising of the workers' consciousness through study and group discussions. To lessen the differences between town and country, workers from Xinhua volunteered to work on nearby communes in the busy harvest season, and in the slack winter season on the communes, many peasants came to visit the Xinhua Printing Press to keep in touch with the technological advances of their country. 'The unity of workers and peasants is essential,' Ke summed up, 'if we are to travel the socialist road.'

'Another question. In 1971 a delegation of Concerned Asian Scholars from the US, invited by Premier Zhou Enlai to visit China, reported back that Beijing workers went out to Qinghua University in the early days of the Cultural Revolution to calm the students down and convince them that armed struggle – firing homemade cannons at each other, for instance – was an incorrect way to handle contradictions....'

Ke Pingyao smiled wryly. 'Yes, we sent part of our workforce up there to "calm them down", as you say. That was a difficult time for the student factions to understand that they were not enemies, that under socialism their contradictions were among the people. Several of our staff members are still part of the Workers' Propaganda Team at Qinghua. You see, students are sometimes vacillating and it's important for them to learn discipline from the workers. The situation at Qinghua is in relatively good shape now. How are things with the students in your country?'

'Many American students played a progressive role during the Vietnam War and the new Kampuchea phase of it. Many of them waved the Little Red Book on campuses and peace demonstrations. But now that the Vietnam War is winding down, most of them are turning away from radical politics. We are in what is rapidly becoming a swing to the right.'

After a pause, since Ke did not choose to comment on American politics, he said, with his usual enthusiasm, 'You must come back next year. You will see a lot of improvements.' Accompanying us back to the gate, he gave us another warm handshake.

It was a relief to the ears to return to the parking lot, where driver Yang was waiting with the Guoji Shudian car and his usual smile. The roar of the rotary presses grew weaker as we drove back into the stream of Beijing traffic, but I could still hear their hum when I went to bed that night – like the roar of the ocean after a day at the beach.

Negotiations in Earnest

Our event-packed week in Beijing came to a climax on the Friday morning when we negotiated the only item on our agenda which we had carefully skirted: the role of CB&P as national US distributor. The problem arose because of changing conditions in the American book market and the theory of Guoji Shudian, implied rather than expressed, that there was a much larger potential sale of Chinese publications than CB&P was able to develop.

Through new relations rapidly maturing during the 1970s, China had broken out of an economic encirclement which the United States had tried to impose, and resumed her rightful place in the United Nations. It was obvious, after President Nixon's visit and the Shanghai Agreement, that normalization between our two countries would take place in due time. One of the encouraging developments in US–China relations as a result of the Shanghai Agreement was the cultural exchanges that began small and then enlarged. Wang, the editor of *Beijing Review*, had come to the United States on one of the early exchanges, with a delegation of Chinese journalists on behalf of the National Committee on US-China Relations and the American Society of Newspaper Editors, and had visited our New York store. A much larger cultural event took shape in 1974. After successfully exhibiting some of their finest historical relics and archaeologicial finds in London and Paris, the Chinese agreed to send the collection to the United States.

The beautiful flying horse, poised on the wings of a swallow, marine blue in antique bronze, became the symbol of the Archaeological Finds Exhibition. It opened at the National Art Gallery in late 1974, came to the Nelson-Atkins Memorial Museum in Kansas City in early 1975, and was due to open in June in San Francisco at the Asian Art Museum in Golden Gate Park.

Our promotion and advertising were geared the previous year for an expansion in the art and archaeological field that would surpass the concentration on politics in the 1960s. We expected to reach thousands of new customers through the art books from Guoji Shudian which we had already stocked in large quantities. But a situation developed beyond our control which threatened to destroy fifteen years of hard labour and a price structure that supported a widening distribution of Chinese publications.

In his opening remarks on that Friday morning, Wang Hongshen referred to a sheaf of our correspondence which he had laid with meticulous care on the table in front of him: 'There is no need to review our whole exchange of opinions on the question of national distributor, but we realize that there are misunderstandings to be cleared up and solutions to be reached.' He buttressed his generalizations with a paraphrase from 'On the Correct Handling of Contradictions among the People': 'Chairman Mao says that we should deal with contradictions in order to arrive at correct decisions and then move on to a higher level where, of course, new contradictions will arise.' With a pontifical manner and his usual smile, he asked me, 'What are your proposals?'

K.C. Foung and I had stayed up half the previous night to formulate these. At first, we had decided to be very diplomatic in handling a ticklish problem. But as I pointed out to K.C. later that night, CB&P had had only fifteen years' experience in diplomacy, and rather than beat about the diplomatic bush with negotiators who had a tradition of five thousand years or more behind them and a model like Zhou Enlai up front, we should not pull our punches but, according to the current slogan, be 'open and above board'.

'In the past week,' I responded to Wang Hongshen, 'we have cleared up a number of misunderstandings which arose because we do business six thousand miles apart and under two different economic systems. This would have been impossible without the goodwill that exists between us. I am sure that in the same spirit we can find a solution to the contradiction, as Wang Hongshen calls it, that is more basic than the others, since it involves our position in the US book market, which we have worked for fifteen years to develop.

'With the enthusiasm of your Cultural Revolution, you seem to have a concept that the US market offers an unlimited sale for Chinese publications. It follows that you conclude: the more distribution agencies you recognize in our country, the larger will be the circulation of information from China to the US reading public and the stronger will be the friendship between our two peoples. Also, you may be anxious that in our "dog-eat-dog" economy, as we say, a sole distributor might go bankrupt or out of business for other reasons. But in practice, what has happened? You have exported tens of thousands of books to an inexperienced student group calling themselves the Phoenix Corporation. Your reasons were legitimate in theory. Phoenix, you advised us, would deal with the US student market in mail order and probe other areas that you think we have not yet reached. In practice, however, they operated in an opposite way. Lacking experience in book distribution, they violated the agreements you advised them to make with our firm, which were: to maintain current prices; to seek new outlets, not duplicate ours; and to work out a partnership with our firm, rather than a competitive relationship.

'There were no contracts or even written agreements on these matters. "Between friends, there is no need" was the way you put it, but Phoenix failed to follow your guidelines. With the tremendous opportunities for expansion during the period of the Archaeological Finds Exhibition in Washington, DC and Kansas City, soon to open at the Asian Art Museum in San Francisco, Phoenix set up cut-throat competition, reducing by half the fair market price we had established over the years and offering even further discounts to many of our best trade accounts. How Phoenix expected to pay their bills, you perhaps know better than we do. And to make matters worse, just before I left to come to China, the head of

Phoenix Corporation came out to San Francisco. We had already made arrangements to serve the Exhibition through the Museum bookstore, but the manager cancelled his very large order with us abruptly, just as the Nelson-Atkins Art Gallery had done in Kansas City. We do not need to go into all the details over again, as you say. You have reports on why our price structure is necessary to support our promotion through catalogues, advertising and so on; also, to maintain our wholesale discounts, our sales people in the field and our exhibits at the American Booksellers' Association, the American Library Association, the Association for Asian Studies, and the US-China Peoples' Friendship Association. Instead of providing wider distribution of your publications at a time when, in your phrase, the door is opening, the practices of Phoenix are narrowing down these new possibilities, since neither their firm nor ours will long survive with the giveaway prices they have instituted. I can't emphasize this too strongly. It is the matter of our surviving as your national US distributor – or withdrawing into three local bookstores in San Francisco, New York and Chicago and ceasing to perform the nationwide role we assumed was agreed between your firm and ours. The decision is really up to you.' After a silence which seemed to last an hour, I added quietly, 'I hope you will reconsider.'

A few quiet words were exchanged in Chinese by the top leadership. Then Wang proposed a fifteen-minute recess, at the end of which he said solemnly, with the slightest flicker of a smile, 'We will give the matter our serious consideration. In the meantime, Vice-Director Zhong would like to invite you to visit Tianjin, his native city, and possibly the Dagang Oilfields, which are near by. We will meet again here Monday morning.'

Zhong Hong gave us his deep look of understanding as he said, 'You will be the first from your country to visit Dagang. I am sure we can arrange it.' Shao Gongwen gave us a warm handshake and a reassuring smile as we left.

Back at the Beijing Hotel, packing for the weekend, I asked K.C., 'Why do you think they arranged so abruptly to send us to Tianjin? It wasn't on our schedule.'

'They probably need more time to discuss our criticism. It was pretty sharp.'

'Would you have softened it?'

'Perhaps in emphasis. Still, it is a question of our survival, as you said.'

'How do you think they'll respond?'

'We'll find out Monday morning.'

The First Visitors from the United States to Spend a Day at the Dagang Oilfields

In negotiations Zhong Hong had played a reserved role, often giving us encouragement with a smile that said, 'We'll work things out. Don't worry!' On the train ride to Tianjin that evening, he shed all reserve to sing guerrilla songs he had learned in the 1930s and to tell us stories about book distribution in the days of the Japanese occupation.

'I was only seventeen when I started distributing revolutionary papers in Tianjin. I used to throw a daily paper over the wall of the Japanese garrison, until one day the soldier at the gate caught me at it. I thought that was the end, but that it was good to die for the revolution. Imagine my surprise when the soldier said, "You're only wasting your paper. The officers burn it. But if you give it to me, I will see it circulates among the rank and file." It was a lesson in history for me. Before that time, I could only think of all Japanese as enemies.'

In the park across from our hotel in Tianjin, I was surprised to see young couples strolling arm in arm in the twilight, almond trees flowering above their heads. With all the emphasis on politics and physical sublimation during the Cultural Revolution, love was not altogether forgotten. In the morning, where lovers had strolled at dusk, t'ai chi enthusiasts of all ages were practising one of the oldest physical fitness exercises in the world, with yin–yang movements that could advance or retreat at the threat of an invisible enemy in a complete 360-degree circle. The grace and poise, particularly of some of the elders, was a delight to watch.

Hunger and the day's programme, however, summoned us back from the park to a Western breakfast of bacon and eggs with toasted slices of a compact white bread. In the hotel dining room, we sat next to a table of eight Canadian nurses who had just visited the Bethune Memorial Hospital in Shijiazhuang. They were on a special mission there to study the new splint method the Chinese were innovating to knit broken bones in half the time the traditional casts required. In cross-table conversation they told us proudly that they had never known that Dr Bethune was such a great person until they came to China. 'He gave his life operating on the front lines of the People's Liberation Army,' the group leader explained. 'The Chinese love him. And he was a Canadian!'

After breakfast Zhong Hong and our interpreter, Zhang Huijuan, hustled us into waiting cars and we set off to the Dagang Oilfields in a drizzle blowing in from the Bohai Sea. Within a giant enterprise operating in an area of many square miles of sand dune and sea, crude oil was gushing up from a mile and a half under our feet. Offshore operations, invisible behind a rain mist, were described by our hostess and guide, a woman in her forties who had spent her life on oilfields, first at Yumen in the north-west, then at the famous model field at Daqing, and finally here at Dagang on the Bohai Sea across from Korea and Japan. She was a warm-hearted person with a round, weather-beaten face, always ready to smile or seriously to describe how problems were overcome in turning a sandy waste into a vital base for China's industrial programme. She slipped her own oilskin round my shoulders when we stepped from cars to buildings in the rain, attending to me as though I needed the most careful preserving. In China a great deal of care is taken by people who are younger for people who are older, and since we were the first American guests to visit Dagang, she made us especially welcome. Her companion, a young oil worker with ruddy complexion and a shock of unruly black hair, was our technical consultant to explain the dynamics of oil drilling. Like many of the younger workers and peasants we had met in the factories and on the communes, he showed a deep devotion to his task and treated us as old friends.

Dagang was typical of socialist enterprises, centrally

planned, radiating from a town centre that appeared unexpectedly out of a vast sandy waste with a few dozen green fields spaced at wide intervals. The new red-brick buildings of the centre housed forty thousand workers and their families. Schools, co-operative stores – even a Xinhua bookstore – surrounded the town square, which was being landscaped as a miniature park. Out from the centre we toured the 'field' to see, emerging from rain mists, giant oil rigs, pumping stations and the great pipes at the docks where tankers were loading oil for domestic ports and also for export to Japan. We saw a burst of oil from a well not yet capped rising like a geyser above the rig. We watched oil crews at work in yellow oilskins: women and men working together at jobs that are considered men's work in the United States. We visited the main pumping and distribution station operated by the 'Iron Twelve'. These were a dozen young women engineers who shared one of the most responsible jobs at Dagang: control of the oil flow from the wells to the loading docks and to the city of Tianjin. The group leader on duty told us proudly, 'This is how we hold up our half of the sky!'

As we returned to the cars which were soon to take us to Tianjin railway station on our return trip to Beijing, our guide pointed the lesson of the Iron Twelve: 'Women are now taking up tasks they never did before. Male domination and female inferiority are now things of the past. Before the Cultural Revolution women could not join construction teams, or be given positions of authority, or become engineers. The reactionaries said that if a woman was a member of a drilling team, they would hit a dry spot; or if on a construction job, the roof would collapse; or if working on a boat, it would sink. But mechanization requires skill, not so much strength, so physical inequalities are not so important and women are now promoted to leading positions that only men held previously, like pumping, watering and machine repairs.' Her enthusiasm was infectious as she waved goodbye. Her last words were, expectedly, 'Come back next year and you will see many new improvements.' She and forty thousand others had the will to triumph over wind and waves and the depths of the earth to create a new technological society in which oil was already playing a major role. But was equality between women and men, in reality, so fully established? I wondered.

Back in Beijing on Monday morning, our negotiations were resumed. In the opening pleasantries I gave thanks for the visit to Dagang, in particular directing my remarks to Zhong Hong: 'We were impressed not only by the tremendous undertaking of bringing oil up from the bottom of the sea but also by the small workshops where mothers, who have young children, and elders can work close to their homes in the electric-light-bulb factory, the adjoining glass-blowing enterprise, and the state-run stores. We didn't see too much, though, of Zhong Hong's home town.'

'That will have to wait until your next visit,' said Zhong.

With an emphatic clearing of his throat, Wang Hongshen brought us back to our main problem. I was amazed to hear him say, after a brief summary of our Friday discussion, 'We think lack of experience was responsible for the inability of the Phoenix Corporation to solve the contradictions in the US book market that you have brought to our attention. We tried an experiment, but it didn't work. We still think there is a much larger demand for our publications in your country than we are collectively able to satisfy at this time. We will finalize the matter after our trip to Yanan. I will be happy to accompany you, and Yang Aiwen will be our interpreter. K.C. will leave us as planned at Zhengzhou and return to Hong Kong. We will go on to visit the Chiliying Commune.'

Finalization of our negotiations took place on the last day I spent in China. A representative from the Phoenix Corporation agreed to withdraw from wholesale distribution of publications and concentrate on the import of artefacts. CB&P would continue to be the main distributor of Chinese books and magazines in English in the United States.

A Day at the Qiliying Commune

Our first stop in the western regions was Yanan, the former revolutionary centre about which I had first read in *Red Star Over China* by Edgar Snow back in 1937. Since Yanan had been Chairman Mao's base for the decisive years of the

Chinese Civil War and Wang Hongshen had defined himself in negotiations as the Party representative, it seemed appropriate to ask him what exactly he meant by Mao Zedong Thought, since he had used the phrase several times on our flight from Beijing.

Wang was happy to explain: 'Mao Zedong Thought is not a dogma, it is a method of analysing contradictions in nature and society. On the one hand it is a simple analysis of class struggle of the Chinese workers and peasants. On the other it is complex – responding to all the contradictions in China and in the modern world. It is the thinking of Marx and Engels that the hand is divided from the brain in capitalist society, that the brains of the few exploit the hands of the many. It is the thought and action of Lenin that those who do the work should seize political and economic power through revolution led by a party of the of the working class. Mao Zedong Thought is the application of these principles to the concrete situation in China.' For the rest of our trip, Wang was happy to give me an extramural course in the application of Mao Zedong Thought to the current realities of Chinese society.

From Yanan we went over the mountains to Nanniwan to visit the Cadre Reform School, where mayors and vice-mayors of cities were baking bread and engineers were operating primitive lathes. Those we interviewed were eloquent in describing how they were overcoming bourgeois tendencies in the hard life of a mountain village and learning how to serve the people with bread and machine parts.

On our whirlwind tour we spent a day in Luoyang, the morning at a ballbearing plant closed shortly after our visit by 'Gang of Four Sabotage', the afternoon at the Longmen Caves where thousands of stonecutters during the Tang dynasty (618–907) had sculpted over a hundred thousand buddhas and bodhisattvas. Local vandals down the centuries, in co-operation with agents from foreign countries, had hacked off heads, limbs, even torsos of some of the sculptures. Bronze plaques indicated in which European or American museums some of these were at present housed. 'We hope one day they will be returned,' our local guide said wistfully, 'since they are national treasures which were created here.'

From archaeology to modern agriculture was an abrupt change as we took off the next morning from Zhengzhou, crossing the Huang He to spend the day at the Qiliying Commune. Our road wound, like a serpent, twenty-five miles along the Victory Canal, through wheat- and cotton-growing country. Its construction had involved the labour of twenty thousand peasants for three years to bring water to fields which otherwise would have remained gravelly desert. It was here at Qiliying in 1958 that the peasants spliced together a group of advanced co-operatives into one central organization which they decided to call a 'People's Commune.' When Chairman Mao visited Qiliying later in the year, he said, 'That's a good name: People's Commune!' Our informant in 1975, Lu Shumou, was an elderly peasant who had been Mao's guide around the Qiliying Commune in 1958. '"Dig tunnels deep, store grain everywhere" was the slogan from that time on,' Lu explained. 'We have done our best to carry out Chairman Mao's directive.' His weather-beaten face, deeply wrinkled, showed the deep feeling of affection that all the peasant leaders we met had for the Chairman.

'Have you seen him since 1958?'

'Yes, once in Beijing,' he said with a proud smile, but seemed genuinely embarrassed when our host, Secretary Zhang Xinwen of the Revolutionary Committee, explained, 'Comrade Lu is our representative to the National People's Congress.'

'Your Congress must be very different from ours,' I said to Lu. 'In the US our representatives are mostly lawyers – few, if any, farmers. It is an honour to meet you.' On that sunlit afternoon, with the vast expanse of wheat and seedling cotton in the Huang He Valley and hundreds of the 55,000 peasant members of the commune working the fields, it was hard to believe Secretary Zhang's statistics that 'between 1940 and 1943, 2,700 people died of starvation in an area that now comprised the Qiliying Commune; 25,000 peasants moved out of the area in search of food; and 2,200 sold their children to keep them from starving.'

These figures were repeated later by Liu Chuan, Party Secretary and head of the Revolutionary Committee of the Shuzhuang Brigade, who invited us into his home. He was delighted at our surprise when he and his wife served us ice cream. 'This is socialism,' he remarked with a grin. 'In the old days we never had ice cream.' At the end of the main living room were two simple chairs stationed on either side of a brown lacquerwork table with gold-leaf decorations. Liu motioned me to one chair while he took the other. As his wife and family came in to socialize with us they sat on benches against the wall, with Yang Aiwen and Wang Hongshen.

As usual, we took a verbal trip backwards to the days before liberation. But Liu's was more than a standard briefing. It was a drama which he and older members of the family were re-enacting for our benefit, and also for the instruction of the younger generation. Statistics of how many people died of starvation in the Old China were common knowledge. I was familiar with the data that 10 million people had died in a single year from famine, that 37,000 people dropped dead annually on the streets of Shanghai in an average year from starvation, that the Red Cross could not give relief because Chinese famines were 'endemic, not epidemic, and of such proportions we cannot help'. But to sit in the same room with a man who told how his own father and mother had both died of starvation in 1942, and hear his wife say that her mother had died of hunger and her younger sister was sold into slavery so that she would have food to eat, was a very different matter – while the landowners' granaries were still stuffed with grain!

'In the old days, we had to suffer the triple devastation of first flood, then locusts, and finally drought.' Liu went on to explain that it was not until the vast new conservation and irrigation projects of the People's Government began to be implemented at Qiliying, and a gravelly, infertile soil irrigated, fertilized and cultivated by thousands of peasants over a twenty-five year period, that the people had anything resembling security. Lie's wife, Lian Fengyin, nodded agreement with what her husband said.

The gloom of the past was lifted by thoughts of happier days in the present. 'What is your task?' I asked Lien Fengyin.

'I work at home. We have a son who is a tractor driver, my daughter here, and these two young children. They keep me busy!' There was no hesitation on her part to speak out. She had a direct, friendly way of looking at me as if she was as much interested in my experiences as I in hers.

'She is also active in the Women's Federation,' said Liu, with obvious pride that his wife was more than a stay-at-home. 'She is one of the vice-directors.'

'In addition to production team committees, I understand you also have family household committees. Are these elected?' I asked.

'Yes,' said Lien Fengyin, with a warm smile at her husband, 'the man used to be the head of the household, and women were expected to obey. But now we are smashing the old obeys. In this brigade, women are 50 per cent of the Party and Youth League members.'

The children smiled for the first time as they were clued into the discussion, then sobered immediately. They seemed to think it was wrong to be too expressive in the presence of strangers, particularly since one of them was from a foreign country and did not speak their language. The tiny red ribbons on the plaits of the two girls fluttered a little, and the elder put her face into her hands in embarrassment. The youngest, a boy with a round, healthy face and probing eyes, was trying to puzzle out the meaning of adult conversation. How could people have starved, he seemed to be asking, in a world of such abundance as Chiliying?

'Now we elect the head of the household', Lien Fengyin continued, 'once a year. It could be any one of us,' she added with a note of finality, as if that settled the question of equality between the sexes once and for all.

'Who is the head of this household?' I persisted.

'My wife is,' said Liu, with a residual male dominance that insisted on his being spokesman for the family. 'I didn't do a good enough job.'

On the ride back to Zhengzhou, I asked trip leader Wang, 'How come, though the woman is elected head of the household, the man still sits in the seat of honour?'

Wang first replied, 'These are matters the peasants themselves will have to struggle out.' But suddenly his smile of enlightenment beamed across at me as he said, 'Perhaps it's like this. The man is the family's minister of foreign affairs!'

Farewell to China and the Cultural Revolution

My last night in China I hardly slept. The experiences of the preceding five weeks kept flashing back like a video sequence. The three-day trip to Shanghai with Shao Gongwen and Yang Aiwen, particularly our visit to Steel Mill No. 5, came back in vivid images. I could even hear the roar of the rolling mills and turn my eyes again from the too brilliant pour of molten metal from the furnaces controlled by white-clothed workers bathed in flame. The most far-fetched of all Cultural Revolution campaigns had been launched here at Mill No. 5 against Lin Biao and Confucius.

Once heir apparent of Mao as Chairman of the Chinese Communist Party, Lin Biao was denounced as a counter-revolutionary for having a Confucian scroll in his back room with the caption 'Conform to the Rites!' The more serious charge by young Comrade Xin, leading member of the plant's research committee, was that Lin Biao had tried to assassinate Chairman Mao and had therefore been meted his just deserts in a fatal plane crash over Outer Mongolia.

Comrade Xin extended his attack on counter-revolution to include Soviet Social Imperialism: 'As the Soviet satellites go up, their red flag falls to the ground.' His index finger pointing first at the ceiling, then at the floor, he took a hearty delight in his role as prosecutor. 'Khrushchev and Brezhnev have shot down the red star from the Kremlin!' Xin's final eloquence was waged against defenders of 'bourgeois right' – a theory which Marx had introduced in his *Critique of the Gotha Programme*, involving the elimination of money and the commodity market.

This subject was being hotly debated at the time in the Chinese press and also in the Capital Hospital in Beijing, where I visited Joshua Horn. Dr Horn, from earlier days in England an ardent supporter of socialist medicine, had spent fifteen years of his life as a surgeon in the Beijing hospital. During the Cultural Revolution, he set out for the country-side on his donkey with surgical kit to serve the peasants and help set up training centres for barefoot doctors. His *Away with All Pests* is a classic account of Chinese medical developments in the late 1960s and early 1970s. In bringing medicine to the people, he had a number of unique experiences. Once, after performing a hernia operation on a peasant, he was asked to perform a similar operation on the peasant's donkey. Horn, no veterinary surgeon, laughed at the idea, but the peasant insisted that he was serious: the donkey was his means of livelihood. So the doctor stopped laughing and performed the operation, sealing up the incision on his four-footed patient with a patch from the inner tube of a bicycle tyre.

From his bed in the Capital Hospital, Joshua Horn flashed his usual roguish smile at me. For a man with only a part of his heart still functioning, he gave me a robust welcome and, when I told him I had just had a briefing on 'bourgeois right' at Shanghai Steel Mill No. 5, he smiled as if the young researchers were taking up the campaign from the wrong angle. 'It was like this . . .' I began.

Israel Epstein and his wife, Elizabeth Chomeley, arrived at the moment and joined our discussion. They had been interned for several years during the Cultural Revolution and only recently released at the direction of Premier Zhou Enlai, with his apologies for the excesses of the Red Guards.

'First, you tone down inequalities of rank and wage,' I reported, happy to be at the giving rather than the receiving end of a briefing for a change, 'and then you try to eliminate departmentalism. According to one young steel worker on the research committee, the furnace teams had already eliminated rank. Each of the six members of each team was trained to be group leader on successive days.'

'Very plausible,' Horn laughed, 'but egalitarianism is something Chairman Mao has always warned against. Marx also. What's the rest?'

'The leading comrade from the maintenance department, a woman in her forties, short but tough, testified that her department was travelling the correct proletarian path. "We found ourselves overburdened from many breakdowns of old equipment. So we started discussions, criticizing departmentalism. In a socialist society, why should each person sweep the front gate of her own house, but not that of others? After discussing the problem with other departments and raising their political consciousness, the comrades agreed they should all share the heavy tasks and work with the repair shop. This has resulted in better relations between the workers and in the breaking down of departmentalism. With a correct theory, we are now able to develop a correct practice and speed up production."'

'Exactly,' said Horn. 'Proves my point that the theory is just the means of getting more work done.'

'Why shouldn't they speed up production?' asked Epstein. 'It's for the collective good.'

The doctor countered, 'You think breaking down departmentalism – which, let's face it, is a form of anarchism – and equalizing wages at the present stage will actually speed up production?' He answered his own question with a playful aside: 'It could have the reverse effect.'

'If they rush it, of course,' Epstein agreed, 'and the advocates of the current campaign seem to be doing that full steam ahead. Marx's concept was that bourgeois right could be restricted, but not eliminated under socialism. Mao said basically the same thing: that wage differences, money, commodity production and so on were bourgeois hangovers that could be eliminated completely only in a communist society.'

As John and Carolyn Service came in at that moment to greet an old friend, discussion of bourgeois right was suspended. It was time for me to say goodbye.

'My very warm greetings to Gertrude and the family,' said Horn, with a surprisingly strong farewell handshake. 'I will never forget her kindness in helping to arrange my American tour.'

'Nor we your tour,' I assured him. 'You were like the Johnny Appleseed of people's medicine.'

'And who was Johnny Appleseed?' Horn asked.

'A legendary public benefactor who planted appleseeds all over the US to benefit the people with the fruits of their new land. You planted a lot of seeds, my friend, that are bearing fruit in the medical field wherever you lectured in the US. Also in the Chinese countryside, when you set up barefoot doctors' clinics.'

'Thanks for including me in your American legend.' Waving a cheerful goodbye, he urged me to come back and visit him again, but that was the last time I was ever to see him.

Memories! Memories! Of May Day – a workers' holiday that originated in Chicago – in Beijing, featuring a morning visit to the Vietnamese Embassy and exchange of information about our distribution of publications imported under US Treasury licence from Xunhasaba in Hanoi. There was a sense of suppressed excitement over a cup of espresso coffee and pastries in French-Vietnamese style. That afternoon we were to hear the news that Saigon was liberated. The American press reported that Saigon had fallen.

Under the balloons and banners celebrating International Workers' Day in Sun Yat-sen Memorial Park, we witnessed a meeting of American and Vietnamese women. Hugs and tears between them, rather than words, were the communication they all understood. The holiday crowd grew silent in respect for grief shared and the knowledge that this was a historical moment long awaited, ending the carnage in which fifty thousand young Americans lost their lives and over a million Vietnamese, young and old alike, perished. That evening fireworks burst in umbrellas and rockets of sparks over the Great Hall of the People as Beijing celebrated the end of the Vietnam War.

Sleep was slow to close off such memories and give priority to dreams on my last night in China, and the last of these trooping memories before consciousness gave out was of the Bethune Memorial Hospital at Shijiazhuang. For Mao Zedong, Norman Bethune had 'the spirit of internationalism and absolute selflessness'. He came thousands of miles from Canada 'to adopt the cause of the Chinese people's liberation as his own'. As a surgeon in the front lines of the People's Liberation Army, he performed miracles with his scalpel and the assistance of a Chinese medical crew. He died in the line of battle from septicaemia contracted while operating on one of 'my wounded', as he called them. The spirit of Dr Bethune has been honoured with statues, museums and memorial centres in a number of Chinese cities. In his former headquarters, Shijiazhuang, south-west of Beijing in Hebei Province, his letters, manuscripts, pens, typewriters and photographs are preserved under glass for the thousands of visitors, many of them schoolchildren, who make a pilgrimage to the Memorial Hospital every year.

The head of the Revolutionary Committee at the hospital, a veteran of the Long March and an officer in the People's Liberation Army, received us with a welcoming embrace and recruited his foreign affairs committee, five exceedingly eager-eyed young guides, to show us the works. In the acupuncture ward, some thirty patients were receiving punctures and pressures to relieve muscular pains and aches, migraine headaches and other ailments corrected by the insertion of acupuncture needles on one or more points of twelve meridians. Moxibustion was also applied in smouldering cups over needles to burn out deep-seated pain more or less painlessly. We went on into the next ward – famous in China and abroad – which the Canadian nurses we had met in Tianjin had come eight thousand miles to investigate. This was the splint ward where, instead of cumbersome plaster-of-Paris casts, splints were used to draw fractured bones together in half the time it took the traditional casts. On charts clipped at the foot of patients' beds, we could see from weekly X-rays of badly fractured bones how rapidly they knitted together with the use of the splint method. Some patients smiled at us, others were too absorbed in the unique healing process to note our coming and going. Our five guides answered our questions in scientific detail – with the expectation, no doubt, that the information we requested would travel back around the world to prove to foreigners that China was at the cutting edge of modern, as well as traditional, medicine. Before the final conference over a cup of jasmine tea in the visitors' reception room, we were guided through a maze of paths in the herb garden where more than two hundred varieties of herbs were grown to supplement acupuncture and splint healing.

In the reception room, our PLA host greeted us with the customary question, 'Do you have any criticisms?'

'Not about your medical procedures, which I am not competent to judge. But yes, I do have a very serious criticism.' My host and all five members of his foreign affairs committee smiled at me in relief. They obviously wanted criticism, not praise. 'You have received me with the five young members of your foreign affairs committee. They have given informative answers to all my questions and shown great patience with my ignorance about medical matters. But – I hate to say it – they are the wrong committee. I am not a foreigner.' Amazement was registered in six faces while Wang and Yang began to smile. 'I am an Overseas Chinese.' Incredulous reaction to a verbal bomb! 'Yes, I was born in Guangzhou in the last year of the Qing dynasty, before any of you present in this room arrived in China.'

There was an unsuppressed roar of laughter. My host seized the bowl of peanuts grown in the memorial herb garden and poured them into my knapsack. 'Take these back to America with you in memory of Dr Bethune. And be assured that the next time you come to Shijiazhuang we will receive you with the correct committee!'

As his face faded out, and consciousness with it, I slept at last for a few moments only before Chen was ringing my telephone at 5 a.m. I could barely summon voice enough to croak, 'OK, I hear you. Thanks.' It was Chen's official task to get me to the airport on time. I lay in bed an extra five minutes with the taste of maotai and Peking duck and chives still thick on my tongue, wishing I could miss my plane.

At the airport I was met by the same reception committee that had welcomed me, now the send-off committee: Shao Gongwen, with his cheerful, rosy smile in spite of the early hour; Zhong Hong, with his deep friendly eyes saying, 'Now we know each other'; Wang Hongshen, with his immaculate tunic and cap and his perpetual smile; Yang Aiwen, with her serious look as if good times were about to end; Chen, darting around to attend to tickets and baggage, and Yao assisting him with a shy grin in my direction. What an imposition and honour to get all these friends and busy executives of Guoji Shudian early out of bed when only eight hours previously, over maotai and Peking duck, we had already made our eloquent farewells! But that was the Chinese way: friendship first, self last!

Crossing the open airport to my waiting plane, I felt very much alone for the first time in five weeks. I waved a farewell from the top of the boarding ramp with the nostalgic feeling that I was saying goodbye not only to friends and business associates but to members of a new international family.

As the plane circled up, the buildings of Beijing airport shrank to toy size. Yellow mustard fields and green rectangles of wheat were like postage stamps as we soared over the Chinese countryside. Clouds cast early-morning shadows over villages and peasants, like clustered dots, already at work in the fields and on the roads. With a red sun rolling up over the skyline, I watched the green and fertile land unfold its shining rivers and canals beneath us. I had no inkling at that time what tremendous conflicts were seething in the cities and towns, villages and countryside that disappeared under clouds that early May morning. They would break out into the open the following year, after Chairman Mao's death.

✳ 8 ✳

China Modernizes

We Arrive in Shanghai at Two Hours Past Midnight

In the summer of 1976, the Tangshan earthquake was followed by a political upheaval whose shock waves circled the globe with the news of Chairman Mao's death on 9 September. It took five years to rebuild Tangshan and the same half a decade for Mao's successors to reconstruct a shambled economy and create new laws and order. Jiang Qing, Mao's wife, with a suspended death sentence, was sequestered from contact with her three male co-conspirators and forced to abandon her dream of becoming the Empress of China in the image of the Old Dragon, Ci Xi.

What was going on in China? Was order actually being restored after Red Guard rampages? Could we believe, from a reading of the Chinese magazines we were distributing, that Deng Xiaoping and his four co-leaders had opened a new freeway to socialism? Or, after the brief tenure of Hua Guofeng, had they made a U-turn back to capitalism?

The radical movements in the United States, which had looked to *Quotations from Chairman Mao Zedong* to guide them along a revolutionary path, splintered, their clout dissipated, and most of their members went on to adopt reformist roles in an American society that was growing increasingly conservative. Rather than peace demonstrations, the largest popular rallies in the country were assemblies of born-again Christians preaching Armageddon. Signs of the times were Jonestown and the forced suicide of hundreds of devotees by cyanide; and the election of a messianic president determined to reverse the popular advances the American people had made in the previous fifty years.

In China, after ten years of Cultural Revolution which made the McCarthy inquisitions in the United States pale by comparison, the mood was upbeat. As the People's Republic emerged into the 1980s, with representation in the United Nations and an embassy in Washington, American tourists were able to visit the former Forbidden City and see the treasures of ancient China with their own eyes. Business people from the five continents were invited to set up joint enterprises in China, their investments and profits protected by new laws. Coastal cities were opened to foreign trade. Central authority was shared with provinces and municipalities to speed up the process of modernization. The clenched fist of revolution was opening into a welcoming hand to the West.

Our opportunity to see for ourselves the many changes that had taken place in China since the Cultural Revolution came in 1984 when we were invited to celebrate the thirty-fifth anniversary of Guoji Shudian – renamed, in the period of the Four Modernizations,* China International Book Trading Corporation – CIBTC for short. Our itinerary included a four-week tour to begin in Shanghai, continue on to Suzhou, Nanjing and Guangzhou, and end with a week's anniversary celebrations in Beijing.

When our CAAC flight touched down at Shanghai airport on the last day of October at two hours past midnight, our favourite interpreter, Yang Aiwen, was there to meet us with Cai Huiling, wife of the vice-director of the Shanghai branch of CIBTC. 'You must be very tired!' Cai Huiling took Gertrude's arm and guided us all across planks and through a forest of steel rods in what was becoming an extension of new airport facilities, including movable boarding ramps.

'Your modernization seems to be in full swing,' I said, while Yang Aiwen and I gave each other a friendly scrutiny.

'You haven't changed,' she said with a smile of relief, as if

---

* Of agriculture, industry, national defence, and science and technology.

she half expected me to arrive in a wheelchair. 'But many things have changed since your last trip.'

'True enough,' I agreed. 'US-China relations have taken a great leap forward, beginning with the Archaeological Finds Exhibition which opened in San Francisco shortly after I got back from China in 1975.' We were now whizzing through the almost empty streets of Shanghai, the tyres of the CIBTC van sizzling on wet pavement on our zigzag route to the Jinjiang Hotel. 'We were happy to supply the Asian Art Museum with books from CIBTC . . .'

'By the truckload,' said Gertrude. 'Thousands of them. Americans were anxious to see the relics of the past, but also to learn everything they could about modern China.'

'We were glad', I generalized, 'to be part of a rapidly developing movement that pushed the old anti-China crowd from front stage to the wings.'

'Several million people altogether', Gertrude continued, 'attended the exhibition in Washington, DC, Kansas City and San Francisco.'

Not to be outdone by Gertrude's enthusiasm, I added: 'The exhibition had the kind of impact in the cultural field that Nixon's visit had in the political arena. And then Deng Xiaoping's state visit to the US was a sort of clincher that put the PRC on the international map for good and all. Now in the 1980s, there have been so many cultural and scientific exchanges it's hard to keep track of them all. There was the trade exhibition, scientific exhibitions and conferences, student exchanges. Then tours back and forth. Our plane was filled with doctors and scientists returning from conventions in the US, students in physics and chemistry on the way home from two years' study at the California and Massachusetts Institutes of Technology, and a few in the humanities.'

As we drew up in the courtyard of the Jinjiang Hotel three hours past midnight, our driver, who was one of the younger workers at CIBTC, insisted on carrying all four of our bags into the lobby. 'Sorry to have kept you up all night,' I apologized.

'That's my job,' he said, with a cheery nod. During the Cultural Revolution, he would have said 'my political task'.

'Many things have changed at the Jinjiang Hotel, including

this new wing,' said Aiwen as she accompanied us upstairs to our room, furnished in modern Hong Kong style. She and Huiling carefully inspected chairs, beds and cupboards. Then, pulling back the curtains, Aiwen explained our whereabouts: 'The guest house in the middle of the courtyard was where your President stayed when he was negotiating the Shanghai Agreement of 1972 with our Premier Zhou Enlai. And the tall building beyond was where you, General Manager Shao Gongwen, and I stayed when we were here in 1975.'

'And where David, former manager of our Chicago store, and I stayed in 1974,' said Gertrude. 'So we'll all feel at home.'

'Particularly as this is your own home town, Aiwen,' I added. 'Gertrude and I are supposed to be retired, but here we are commissioned by our successors at CB&P to discuss joint publishing projects in China and to help celebrate your thirty-fifth anniversary.'

'And to have the best vacation in your lives,' Aiwen insisted. 'For tomorrow we have made no arrangements for your programme, expecting that you would want to have a rest after your long flight. Is that all right?'

'Sounds wonderful,' said Gertrude sleepily, giving Aiwen an impulsive embrace. 'Also to have you as our travelling companion.'

A Day in Shanghai

The rumble of traffic and the cadences of ships blowing their horns at a distance in the Huangpu River woke us up at midday with the blissful realization that we were actually back in the People's Republic. After a late lunch we ambled through the former French Concession where, under plane trees shedding their yellow leaves in a Chinese Indian summer haze, we watched senior citizens crouched on their heels feeding their caged songbirds or playing chequers along the Changle Lu, so intent on their game that they scarcely noticed our passing. We strolled along the Shaanxi Road to visit the former residences of Sun Yat-sen and Zhou Enlai. When we lost our way in spite of guidebooks and maps, we found self-appointed guides to practise their English on us. One was a young machine-shop worker who was studying in a technical school; another a retired chemist who complained as he guided us that under the new early-retirement plan he had nothing else to do; and a third a student who defined himself as a Christian and asked if we would like to attend his church on Sunday, and how could he get to the United States?

On our way back to our hotel, we stopped at the *China Daily* office on Maoming Beilu to check out the latest news posted in English. In the Cultural Revolution, the Chinese media had glossed over such problems as juvenile delinquency, unemployment, embezzlement and other crimes. But 'opening to the West' meant that the bulletin board of *China Daily* was free to share such problems with foreigners passing in the street and to seek common solutions in the international social arena.

The dining room at the Jinjiang was crowded with business people and engineers from the five continents who were in China to negotiate trade agreements or set up joint projects. An engineer from Japan, representing a bridge-building company, smilingly invited us to share his table. He informed us, with an ingenious command of English, that China was the freest country in Asia for people to speak their minds. 'I am knowing,' he claimed, 'because I make the bridge contracts with India, the Philippines, Pakistan and Malaysia for my company. And I talk with all peoples.'

'Freer than Japan?' I asked.

He nodded. 'In my country we must speak wearing slippers.'

'Is it true that China is setting up Peking duck – or should I say Beijing duck? – restaurants in Tokyo?' Gertrude asked.

'Yes, true. My country keeps the control with 51 per cent yen value. In Shanghai it's the same, only backwards. China keeps 51 per cent yuan value in joint enterprises.'

When our Japanese bridge-builder rushed off to an appointment, we were surprised to recognize David Chow, an old friend from San Francisco, at the next table. 'What brings you here?' he asked.

'To use the current jargon,' I laughed, 'we are here to help foreign-language publishers modernize. And you?'

'My line is computers.' David passed his card with his title, IBM Far Eastern Representative. 'I am here to set up offices in Shanghai and Beijing.'

'Yes, we've read about computer development in China in a UN Report earlier this year,' I volunteered. The report had outlined the assistance given to China in the current 'electronic revolution'. With UN help, a Centre for International Economic Information had been set up in Beijing; also the Institute of Computing Technology, and the Computer Institute of People's University. 'It's a good time for IBM to open up the market?' I queried.

'We've already opened the market, my friends. With the funding of the UN Development Programme, our computers were set up in every province of China to tally the census of 1982. That's how the PRC knew with certainty that the population had just passed the billion mark.'

'I can see China needs you more than she needs us,' I said as David, in turn, rushed off to an evening appointment. Everybody at the Jinjiang was in a hurry to 'open up the market'!

A grey-haired senior citizen, sitting at David's table, invited us over to share a cup of tea – and a few gripes about the Four Modernizations. She had a preserved English accent, and when she told us her name we found she was also a Gertrude.

'Everybody's in such a hurry these days,' Gertrude II sounded off after defining herself as a teacher of the Queen's English at the Shanghai Foreign Languages Institute. 'With their 5,000-year-old civilization, the Chinese used to take their time, but now they've got to do everything before the end of the century. My students expect to learn a language in a week – they've got your American instant "craze" – so things are in an awful mess in education from top to bottom. Wonderful people, though. Grateful for the slightest favour you do for them, and generous! But still so hampered by the unit system. Everybody belongs to a unit, like a closed circuit, and they're scaredy-cats about stepping out of line. So it's my considered opinion that modernization will be more of a myth than a reality – in any case, slower in the cultural field than in science and industry,' she added, with a kind of pervasive discontent. Then, with a cheerful lift in her voice, she summed up her two years' observations in a positive way: 'Things are getting straightened out, though, but slowly. More tolerance, fewer slogans. They've stopped blaming the Gang of Four for everything that goes wrong. People can go to church on Sunday just like back home in England, or pray at the mosques and temples, all of them recently rebuilt at the expense of the government. Socialist spiritual culture is not just a phrase!'

CIBTC, Shanghai Centre

'Shen Renqing and the staff of China International Book Trading Corporation would like to meet you this morning, and in the afternoon two of the younger staff members would like to accompany us on a cruise down the Huangpu. How does that sound to you?' Yang Aiwen was indeed determined to make this the best vacation of our lives, and the most informative, as she came to our room after breakfast next morning. 'The van will be here to pick us up in about half an hour.'

Achieving the goals of the Four Modernizations through book and magazine distribution was the main theme of the briefing given that morning by Vice-Directors Shen Ronqing and Peng Fei at an assembled staff meeting in the CIBTC offices. Shen took the lead: 'We set up the Shanghai branch of CIBTC four years and three months ago to assist our main office in Beijing in distribution to foreign countries. Shanghai is second only to Beijing in numbers of books and periodicals published, so our task is great for a staff of only seventeen. In expanding, we plan to handle also publications from Central and South China, including the provinces of Guangdong, Yunnan and Sichuan, and in minority-nationality languages from the Guangxi Zhuang Autonomous Region.' Shen was a thin man in his late forties with the obligations of managing the distribution of millions of books and magazines deeply imprinted in worry wrinkles on his forehead.

'Are these publications you distribute mainly in Chinese or foreign languages?' I asked.

'In both,' explained Peng Fei. She was an elderly woman

with glasses, radiating a friendly smile, with a zeal in her voice that equalled Shen's. 'We supply the internal market, as well as export to foreign countries. With the growing demand for information in every field, particularly in trade and finance, science and technology, we have an important role in the whole modernization programme.' Then she asked hopefully, 'Do you see many changes since you were here last in the period of the so-called Cultural Revolution?'

'Yes. From the immense amount of construction going up everywhere, the free markets supplying fast food and bright-coloured clothes, the streets more crowded with trucks and buses than in 1975, it seems your slogan now is "put economics first".'

'Our strategy now', Shen countered, 'is to restore the balance between economics and politics.'

'Our politics and economics are more deeply involved in serving our people, their real needs,' Peng explained. 'We no longer wave the Quotations or wear Mao badges.'

'You see, during the so-called Cultural Revolution,' Shen went on, 'we neglected the production forces in favour of political slogans which didn't guarantee our advance on the road to socialism, or even guarantee the people's livelihood. It is necessary to raise our living standards, or people will ask, "What is the good of socialism?" We no longer idealize poverty and frugality but are doing everything possible to eliminate them, and so give our people a richer life.'

'Do you feel the modernization programme is working?' I asked.

'You will be able to see for yourselves', Shen replied, 'when we visit the Jiading County Headquarters tomorrow. Since 80 per cent of our people are still rural, it was important to begin the reform in the countryside.'

'But what about the cities?'

'Our general principles are similar,' was Shen's reply. 'But it is more complex than the responsibility system in the rural areas. It involves changes in every field of human activities.' He went on to explain that the urban reforms would require not only the restructuring of institutions, including the army and production for defence, but the whole concept of state power – a shifting of many decisions still made in Beijing to the provinces and the localities to encourage individual initiative and self-reliance. At the same time he added a cautious rider that it was essential to preserve the core of socialist planning in the main industries and to encourage collective enterprise in the economy as a whole. He saw that we were puzzled by the contradiction. 'Remember,' he explained, '87 per cent of our production and distribution are state financed.'

'Yes, I've read the documents in *Beijing Review*. You seem confident that they're going to work. In the US many of the former progressives fear you are going back to capitalism, and the former conservatives and reactionaries are happy at the prospect.'

'That will never happen,' said Shen with an upward glance, as if the heavens were on the side of the modernizations and of the new emphasis on seeking truth from facts and applying Marxism as a guide, rather than a dogma, to China's socialist future. 'There will be some pollution, as Deng Xiaoping points out, but we are sure we can deal with it.' At this point Shen was glancing round the room at his staff to be sure they understood the importance of their work as he summed up, for their benefit as well as ours: 'And, of course, in distributing information in every field of human production, our work will be of major importance in achieving our national plan.'

As the staff members went back to their work in the warehouse and packing and shipping departments, Shen ushered us into the vice-directors' office. 'Make yourselves at home and have another cup of tea. If you are not too tired,' – he nodded at Peng Fei and Cai Huiling to join us – 'we would like to hear more about your undertakings. We have talked so far mainly about our own operations and problems.'

'We have plenty of our own,' I laughed. 'But so far we've been able to survive.'

'With all the changes in China . . .' Shen paused.

'And in the US, too,' I went on. 'With your open-door policies, CIBTC no longer had a monopoly of exports and CB&P no longer a monopoly, by default, of imports. The new situation makes it imperative for us to publish as well as import, in order to maintain our position as the China

Information Centre in the US book trade. As a result we have published about twenty-five books under our own byline, the latest being *Two Years in the Melting Pot* by Liu Zongren, which has already become a bestseller. The author, as you may know, is on the staff of *China Reconstructs*. He spent two years as a visiting journalist in the US gathering material for his very lively in-depth comparison of American and Chinese lifestyles.

'In addition to publishing books, we have been trusted, as you know, by the editors of *Renmin Ribao* [People's Daily] and *China Reconstructs* to print and distribute their North American editions. These are economic lifelines for us in a period of many new contradictions, but more important, they are essential means of developing US–China relations in the information field.'

'We must not tire our visitors,' Cai Huiling suggested. It was time for an early lunch and a rest before our afternoon boat ride.

'I think it's Aiwen who must be tired,' said Gertrude. 'She's had twice as much work as the rest of us.'

The Jiading County Centre

Our day in the country began shortly after sunrise in the CIBTC van weaving through traffic along the riverfront. Here, free-market pop and toy stands were already opening to early tourists. T'ai chi experts and amateurs were skilfully or awkwardly fanning their limbs against a background of ten-thousand-ton freighters and ten-ton junks afloat on one of the busiest waterways in the world. River traffic reminded Shen to ask us how we had enjoyed the previous afternoon on the Huangpu. Had we seen the new container loading docks with the giant cranes? Had we noticed that the new factories were discharging little smoke because carbon exhausts were being recycled?

'Your young people didn't miss a trick,' I replied. 'They told us all about the new, new age in science and industry, and also in the youth movement. Not so much *yiwu lao dong* [volunteer labor] as in the Cultural Revolution, but freedom of choice for high school graduates to choose their jobs.'

'Within limits,' cautioned Shen. 'For example, the two youths who accompanied you yesterday were interested in book distribution when they graduated from middle school, and asked to be assigned to CIBTC. Fortunately, we are expanding and had openings for them. But others may not be so fortunate and have to take second or third choices.'

'Even that's different from the 1970s,' I noted. 'Then, all the educated youths we talked to – a highly selected group, no doubt – said they were glad to be assigned by the state wherever the need was greatest. I wondered at the time how many of them were sincere.'

'The state still assigns university students,' said Shen, 'but the new system does allow more choice.' Another puzzling contradiction for us!

'I would think in the long run more choice would be essential in a socialist society, even university students deciding where they could make the best contribution to China's modernization. They will do the best job, in my opinion, if they can choose for themselves.'

There was unanimity on that point as we crossed the Suzhou Creek and headed off north-west. Shanghai was like a giant wheel with spokes radiating in all directions – roads, creeks, canals veining the landscape as we passed through concentric rings of factories, workers' houses, green belts, and on through a surburban string of villages and towns. It was startling to see ocean-going freighters cruising on invisible waterways across a landscape in which cement factories, brick kilns and canneries alternated with wheatfields and market gardens. Instead of massive workteams clustered on the commune fields of the 1970s we saw groups of half a dozen farmers cultivating their family plots under the new responsibility system, too busy to pay attention to passing cars.

'You will notice differences, I am sure, from your earlier trips,' said Shen. 'In the past, peasants – we call them farmers now – living in the countryside were likely to envy those living in cities; now it is just the opposite. Villages have become towns, towns cities. Industry absorbs half the rural population in these counties, and sidelines like mushroom-growing and fish-raising another 15 per cent.'

At the Jiading County headquarters we were received by Chen Fuming, who had the impressive title Secretary of the Office of the People's Government of Jiading County. Chen was a keen-eyed senior citizen, shortly to retire, in the meantime helping to train in a new generation to administer the affairs of the county. Instead of giving us the exhaustive type of briefing we were all too familiar with during the Cultural Revolution, his remarks were concise and he soon asked us, 'What would you like to know about Jiading County?'

'I expect the communes have disbanded in your county, as in most of China. Do you think the responsibility system is an improvement?' I asked.

Chen gave me a direct answer. 'In our experience the combining of political and economic power at the commune level did not work too well. Besides, the iron-ricebowl concept – everybody eating out of the same bowl, whether they did a good job or not – discouraged initiative. So what we have now is a new structure of government at the county level. The communes in most areas have been converted into what we call townships. These are economic, rather than political units. They have decision-making power to assign plots of land and sideline occupations to family groups. These are obliged to grow quotas of grain and other produce for sale to the state. They are then free to sell surplus on the open market. The county, on the other hand, is the central administrative body elected by the townships. It has charge of the courts, the schools, security, the militia. It is also the body which elects representatives to the Shanghai People's Congress, which in turn elects representatives to the National People's Congress in Beijing.'

'Jiading County is part of Shanghai?'

'Yes, Shanghai has the status, like Beijing, of a province. It includes ten counties, of which Jiading is one, and about two hundred townships. Enough crops are grown in these counties to feed the whole population of greater Shanghai and supply many of the factories with raw materials, even to ship some products abroad.'

At that moment Chen's wife was placing a bowl of large, amber-coloured grapes on the table between us. 'Help yourselves, please,' she urged. 'These are the Jiading grapes, for which our county is famous.' And Chen added, 'They are grown under our new responsibility system by specialized households.'

'Is the family responsibility system actually more productive than the old commune system?' Gertrude asked. She still wanted to be convinced.

'No question about it,' Chen answered, with a persuasive smile. 'Agricultural production has more than doubled in the past four years. Surplus labour would actually be a problem now if it wasn't for the rapid development of industry and sidelines. In driving to our county centre, you have no doubt seen new cement and garment factories, and new construction along the road. Villages of ten years ago are now cities. We have, for example, nineteen new industrial cities employing half our population, formerly rural.'

'That answers a question I was going to ask you', I said, 'about unemployment. When I was in China back in 1975, I wondered how you were going to solve this problem with the mechanization of agriculture. In the US a century ago half the population were farmers, now less than 5 per cent. If only 5 per cent of your 800 million farmers were able to support your whole population through technological revolution, that would require only 40 million. I wondered what you would do with the surplus 760 million.'

Chen just laughed. 'Perhaps you would like to find the answer to your question in a stroll through our Jiading County headquarters, with its factories and shops and free market. Then we can visit several of the townships whose sidelines include fisheries and mushroom cultivation. Mushrooms are an important sideline which we process and export; likewise the raising of long-haired rabbits, which are also a speciality of Jiading County. But first we shall have lunch and you will taste some of our products at first hand!'

A bountiful meal was served for us and our driver in the dining room of the county centre by a matron who took care to see that our table was overloaded from the moment we sat down, first with Jiading hors d'oeuvres including spicy mushrooms, duck, chicken, and rabbit, a delicious herb soup with shredded pork, and finally Jiading grapes.

After lunch we visited an electric-light-bulb factory and a 'knitting mill' in the county centre. Both were new collective enterprises, Chen explained, which were absorbing surplus labour and preventing the drift of population to Shanghai. We were introduced to mushroom-growing both in its collective method in sheds, state owned and financed, and in darkened rooms or basements of farming families. These families had also been assigned contract plots of land for growing vegetables, raising pigs, chickens and ducks. Each house had its own well and a covered pit producing methane from fermenting garbage piped to back-yard stoves. Round the houses and along the edges of footpaths and the road, rice sheaves from the autumn harvest were piled high.

'It was a good harvest this year,' Chen said, with much personal satisfaction. Before we left Jiading, he urged us to visit the County Museum down the road, housed in an old Buddhist monastery – dilapidated, but undergoing 'modernization'. Then he waved farewell with the sun setting at his back and outlining his silhouetted figure with gold – an old-time revolutionary soon to retire, as he said, to make room for a new generation.

Goodbye, Shanghai!

Our happiest vacation in Shanghai ended, it seemed, as soon as it began. We had seen a magician balance three eggs, then five chairs on his forehead to the delight of hundreds of youngsters and oldsters at the Children's Palace. Later, we listened to a youth orchestra playing modern tunes on eight accordions and watched a group of older children, with the help of an instructor, programming computer software. At the Shanghai Gymnasium, we had seen a live lion riding tandem on a motor-cycle and grinning in a comradely way at his trainer at the controls. Security-minded stage hands had lowered a cable net between lion and audience in case jungle instincts dating back to prehistoric times should prove stronger than the restraints of a five-thousand-year-old civilization.

We had visited the Waiwen and Xinhua state-run bookstores, surprised this time to see recent titles in English and American literature, as well as the latest in rocketry, satellite transmission, cybernetics and business management. Back in 1975, the most recent book from the United States I had seen in the Waiwen library was Jack London's *Iron Heel*. We had also crossed the 'bridge of nine turnings' into the Yu Garden in old Shanghai and encountered an ancient dragon, stretched a hundred feet or more along the top of a tiled wall. He had gazed down on us with a fierce benevolence. His eyes and teeth glistened as he seemed to roar mildly, almost with a smile, 'I am now a modern dragon, no longer servant of an emperor's wrath, but symbol of the power of the people.'

Finally we had taken a pleasure cruise down the Huangpu on the *Pujing*, 'the largest twin-hulled boat in China' according to the brochure of the Sight-Seeing Service of Shanghai. Where the Huangpu meets the Changjiang, freighters from all over the world were awaiting their call to dock in Shanghai's overcrowded port. It was here at the Wusong Entrance that our good ship the *Ecuador*, nine-thousand-ton displacement, a week out from Hong Kong, had anchored on 8 January 1919, to take on cargo and passengers before steaming off with my mother, three brothers and myself to Tokyo, Honolulu and San Francisco.

On our last morning in Shanghai, before boarding the afternoon train for Suzhou, Aiwen and Gertrude set off on a shopping spree with two new suitcases, which were soon full to bursting point with presents for friends and relatives back home: teapots, silk scarves, Shanghai-I-love-you T-shirts. In the meantime, I had wandered off to the Nanjing Road where in 1975 I had seen Red Guards in massive parades waving Little Red Books and Mao portraits. The glassed-in photo-graph gallery along the wall of the People's Park now showed scenes from the Olympic Games at Los Angeles. Featured were the Chinese women's basketball and volleyball teams, divers who had won gold and silver medals, gymnast Li Ning, who had won three gold medals, and weightlifting gold medallists Zeng Guoqiang and Yao Jinguan. Crowds admir-ing the athletes were so dense that I had to peer between heads and shoulders for a glimpse of the champions. Chinese people are great sport lovers, and happy in recent years to be represented and successful in world contests.

On impulse, I stopped in at the Puppet Theatre to see if the Shanghai puppeteers were back yet from their trip to California. In early October they had spent an afternoon at our store in San Francisco entertaining our customers, young and old, with an abbreviated version of *Monkey Fights the White Bone Demon Thrice*. The Demon's attempts to block the quest of Pigsy, Tripitaka and the Sha Monk for the True Scriptures were frustrated by folk hero Monkey, who slew three incarnations of the Demon to expedite his protégés' Journey to the West. The invisible string-pullers had staged the ancient folk tale with fantastic verve at the Chinese Cultural Centre, to sell-out crowds, and when they came to our store they showed the same kind of animation in person that they had infused into puppet life. Straight away they recruited the three tiers of children – seated, crouched, and kneeling in a semicircle – to become puppeteers, showing them with thumb and finger how to tell stories with one hand. And for weeks afterwards, kids in the neighbourhood were playing Pigsy and Monkey and slaying the White Bone Demon.

As I climbed the first flight of stairs at the Shanghai Puppet Centre, Pigsy (his human name was Dong Yongjian) came flying down from above to give me a big hug, then mustered the whole troupe for an 11 a.m. wine-and-tea party to celebrate their safe return and my safe arrival from San Francisco. After our celebration, Troupe Leader Zhao Ge-lou gave me an official send-off with a toast: 'A long, long life to our old friend! Come back to Shanghai soon!'

Suzhou, the Garden City: A Purple and Gold Nunnery

Liao Jinbo, Senior Member of the Foreign Affairs Office, met us at the railway station in Suzhou with a smile, a warm handshake and an apology. He regretted that because of meetings and other obligations he could not be our personal guide during our three-day visit, but he was happy to introduce Fang Lisheng, a member of his office staff, whom he had appointed to be our hostess and constant companion.

Spotting Gertrude, Aiwen and me struggling down the crowded platform, pushing, pulling and kicking two or three bags apiece, Fang had come racing to meet her new 'charges'. She hardly waited to be introduced before she picked up our two heaviest bags with surprising ease and piloted us all through the station.

Fang Lisheng was a slender woman in her late twenties with a grace and beauty equalled by an unusual strength, which she told us later was due to her three-year assignment as an educated youth to work on a commune. In the three days during which she hosted us in her 'garden city', the most beautiful of all Chinese cities, we began to think of her as the embodiment of its special beauty. Suzhou, city of canals and watergates, known to the West through Marco Polo's memoirs as the Venice of the East; Suzhou, famous for its sandalwood fans, its craftspeople, its Golden Gate, its black-tiled roofs and whitewashed walls, known around the world in print and artefact; Suzhou, an ancient one-storey, two-storey gem of a city whose architects and city fathers and mothers opposed high rises and wide boulevards in their birthplace, which was soon to celebrate its 2,500th birthday. No, we would never forget the spirit of Suzhou embodied in Fang Lisheng as she guided us through silk and sandalwood fan factories and introduced us lovingly to painters, weavers and craftspeople whom she knew as personal friends; also to seamstresses in the double-embroidery department who were stitching an exact duplicate of cats and flowers on both sides of the frame. Lisheng told us that silk threads one-fifty-sixth the diameter of a human hair were used for the most delicate parts and that the embroiderers and other craft workers took three years' apprentice training before being entrusted with the finer detail. 'Our standards here are very high,' she said, 'and the health of our workers is a priority. Because of the danger of eyestrain, they have a fifteen-minute break every two hours to do special eye exercises. Over here', she directed our attention, 'you will see one of our finest miniature arts.'

'Just fantastic,' I said in a tone of unbelief as I looked through a powerful magnifying glass to see miniature paintings on a single human hair!

In the afternoon of our first full day in Suzhou, Lisheng

took us on a jaunt up and down the Grand Canal. As our boat began to steam past coal and grain barges – some self-propelled, others linked behind sturdy towboats – she gave us statistics on the tonnage of cargoes transported on the Canal annually and said that the waterways of China were as important as the railways in supplying the population with basic necessities. Then she told stories about life on the Grand Canal to equal Mark Twain's yarns in *Life on the Mississippi*: 'The barge people spend the whole year on the water. To get an education, their school-age children have to live ashore with grandmas and grandpas.' Blue and grey workclothes were strung out to dry on lines rigged from stem to stern of barges, and from cabins at the rear smoke spiralled up from cooking stoves. Young toddlers, playing on deck, waved to us as if we were a floating exhibition set up for their entertainment.

Through Suzhou we chugged along past whitewashed houses with black-tiled roofs and small square windows, the subject of many a woodblock reproduction we had sold in our stores in the United States. The woodblocks had idealized the scene, however, omitting the women washing clothes on the canal walkways and hanging them out to dry on poles projecting from windowsills.

'Very picturesque,' we said, to encourage Lisheng to tell us more.

'Yes, picturesque. But people find it hard, especially young people with notions of modernization, to live in these old houses without proper plumbing or even adequate toilets. So the planners who want to preserve the old buildings – and our office, of course, favours them – are building a whole new extension of Suzhou to accommodate the general population and the million or more visitors who come here every year. But there are still enough residents who put up with inconveniences because they love the old Suzhou the way it is.'

The next day Lisheng's focus was on flowers, gardens and pagodas. She guided us along the walkways, through the keyhole gates and the pavilions and across the half-moon bridges of four world-famous gardens: the Fisherman's, the Humble Administrator's, the Linger-Here, and the Lion's

Grove. In Shanghai we had been impressed by the beauty of the Yuyuan Garden and its magnificent, ivory-toothed dragon; later we were to admire Nanjing's Temple Garden and the Orchid Garden in Guangzhou.

What was most impressive about these islands of retreat in the midst of traffic-flooded Chinese cities was the sense of remoteness in place and time; also, the multifaceted artistry which integrated natural beauty with the artefacts of a 5,000-year-old civilization. Each window in each pavilion looked out on a miniature mountain or a single peach tree in a tiled courtyard or a willowed island in a lake that reflected blue sky and bamboo-lined shores. In the pavilions were displayed enormous cloisonné vases in blue, gold and magenta; also, furniture crafted in the Ming and Qing dynasties. Autumn flowers, chrysanthemums and daisies, were trained to grow with artful naturalness out of rocks from Taihu Lake. The rocks had been fretted by water erosion through thousands of years until they looked like the creation of monstrous coral insects. Lion Grove Garden had the most spectacular-shaped rocks, such accurate resemblances to lions that they seemed to menace human life.

After the day spent in the gardens of Suzhou, we set off early next morning across the flat landscape of the Chang-jiang plain which gradualy billowed up into the hilly, then mountainous region of Lake Taihu. There was plenty of time on the way for personal talk. Gertrude opened up with a compliment for Lisheng: 'You seem to know everybody in Suzhou.'

'It's my job,' she laughed. 'I had to learn how to get on with all kinds of people during the Cultural Revolution: workers, peasants, officials. Besides, I like people. Most people, anyway.'

'What happened to you in those days?'

'I was one of the lucky ones. When I was what we used to call an "educated youth", I was sent for labour reform to a nearby commune where my grandparents lived. The author-ities made my parents welcome at New Year and on other festival occasions. I did learn a lot from the peasants – how to get along with people of different backgrounds. I wrote letters for them and we developed warm friendships. But several of my schoolmates were not so lucky. They were sent out to Qinghai Province, where conditions were very hard. At that time it was most difficult for intellectuals and cultural workers. One of our best-known authors today in Suzhou, Lu Wenfu, was assigned to hard labour in a machine shop, denied the use of pen and paper, and forbidden to communicate with other writers.'

'That seems to have been the lot of many of China's most promising younger writers,' I added. 'Liu Zongren, whose first book we have just published in the US, was imprisoned on a labour reform farm in Hebei Province and was assigned to digging irrigation ditches in mid-winter – knee deep in freezing water.'

'But most of them', Gertrude interjected, 'say they deepened their understanding of ordinary people, can deal with life in a more profound way as a result of their personal experiences, and don't regard those days as a complete waste.' Lisheng and Aiwen were silent, so that Gertrude felt obliged to change the subject abruptly: 'Do you have a family, Lisheng?'

'Fortunately my parents and grandparents are still living and in good health. My husband works in the Foreign Relations Bureau.'

'And children?'

'No. . . .' Lisheng hesitated. 'Not yet.'

Our road wound through a valley with steep terraced slopes planted out with orange trees, the fruit shining like gold in a jade setting. Abruptly round a sharp curve, Lake Taihu appeared beneath us half concealed in a blue morning mist. As far as we could see, the mountainous shores were terraced with mandarin-orange groves. It was harvest season for pickers and packers of all ages, whole families with ladders and baskets. Sweating and joking, they lined the roadside with loaded baskets and crates which they dumped on family trucks, army trucks or mule carts as these drove up. Even bicycles with carriers front and rear had been pressed into service, slowing traffic to many a standstill. The fruit-pickers were in holiday mood, shouting from tree to tree, as if happy to have turned this once forest-covered mountainside into terraces for golden harvests. For miles as we drove along the narrow, crowded mountain road, the sun glinted on deep green orchards and highlighted little golden suns like offspring bringing new light into the world. Below, the waters of Lake Taihu, lapping against its odd-shaped rocks as they had for millennia, were still half veiled by mist from the bustle of life on the terraces and roads – a lake of dreams to disappear between blue mountains as we turned back towards Suzhou.

On the drive back, we made a detour into a side valley on a road that seemed to come to a dead end. However, ahead in a fold between mountains, the tile roofs of what Lisheng named as the Purple and Gold Nunnery surfaced above treetops. Lisheng was not sure how these buildings had escaped the profanations of Red Guards a decade earlier – perhaps because the nunnery was off the beaten track, or possibly because the People's Liberation Army had protected it as a national cultural monument.

The path from the parking lot to the shrine was lined with fruit-sellers, mainly grannies and children, offering mandarin oranges in baskets of all shapes woven, as Lisheng informed us, of reeds from the margins of Lake Taihu. The serious expressions of the older women seemed to mean that their next meal depended on emptying their baskets.

'We will buy some on the way down,' said Lisheng. 'The Purple and Gold Nunnery is a famous Buddhist shrine dating from the Song dynasty – a thousand years old or more. It is being repaired by the state, as you can see from the workers tiling part of the roof. Religion is now respected, and many of the old temples are being restored. Besides, there are a number of very famous sculptures here of the Buddha, the Goddess of Mercy and the arhats. In the Buddhist religion, as you may know, arhats are monks who have achieved nirvana.'

Although this was a nunnery, the first of the sculptures to face us as we entered the temple was a masculine Buddha who reigned supreme in the main hall with a dozen male arhats of lesser size at a respectful distance in the side galleries. The Buddha's eyes were watching us wherever we moved. It would have taken an optometrist to explain why. The arhats were sculpted with characteristic features and stances that presented virtues to be imitated. Wisdom was bearded and benevolent. Learning was earnestly studying an ancient scroll. Courage was a dragon-slayer with sword drawn and muscles tense. The contest seemed unequally balanced between a mini-dragon – or was it a tiger? – affixed high up on a stone pillar, and Courage, who was ten times as large. The Buddha, combining all virtues, was naturally more impressive than any of the arhats, with his benevolent semi-smile and his mesmerizing eyes. For Aiwen, Lisheng and ourselves, the effect was one of surprising beauty of form and colour, but for some of the Chinese and Japanese visitors it was a religious experience. They bowed, prayed and meditated with the assurance of a constitution now enforced that they were free to express their beliefs in public.

The most impressive sculpture – 'idol' my grandfather would have called her – was the magnificent patroness of ancient nuns and women in general: Guanyin, Goddess of Mercy, surrounded by heaven-bound bodhisattvas. A temple wall divided her from the Buddha, back to back down through the centuries, invisible to each other. With her reserved, mournful eyes, the Goddess reflected the hard lot of women in the old days and the hope for a mercy they rarely had meted out to them in feudal times, but which she now had the power, symbolically at least, to grant.

On the way out I took photographs of workmen repairing the roof over the seminary. They waved and laughed at me as if foreigners were always wasting films. The path leading down to the parking lot was more crowded than ever with new busloads of visitors. As if performing a necessary ritual saluting the fertility of Mother Nature and the merciful Goddess Guanyin, we carried down bagfuls of mandarin oranges, waxy to the touch and sweet flavoured to the taste. And we were glad to see the smiles of the children and their grannies when we didn't bargain but paid the asking price.

'Religion is back?' I said to Lisheng, in more of a question than a statement.

'Yes, for those who believe. Our Constitution grants them the right which was violated in the Cultural Revolution, so the state provides funds where needed to rebuild what was vandalized during that period. We understand better that persuasion is the socialist way, not coercion.'

'Persuasion, not coercion.' Lisheng's phrase stuck in my mind on the drive back to Suzhou. It seemed to express the new spirit of China. Freedom of worship was no longer denied. Freedom for believers, as well as for atheists. Also, freedom of families to sell their mandarin oranges on the approach to the Purple and Gold Nunnery.

'Here we are at Suzhou's Golden Gate!' Lisheng startled me out of my reflections. 'You wanted to take a photo back to San Francisco to show your folks. Our Golden Gate', she laughed, 'is perhaps a few centuries older than yours.'

'Not to be competitive,' I laughed back, 'but our Golden Gate – not the bridge – is a few million years older. It's the entrance to San Francisco Harbor!'

Two years later we received a letter from Fang Lisheng reminding us of our good times together in November 1984 and inviting Gertrude and me to come back to celebrate the 2,500th anniversary of the founding of Suzhou. In a postscript she added: 'My first child, a girl, was born six months after your visit.'

Nanjing, City of Martyrs

Our days in Nanjing were like a refresher course in Chinese history from the early dynasties. Our instructor and host, Wang Yongbiao, Vice-Director of the Office of the Jiangsu Province General Publishing House, was a former revolutionary with a profound love of the mother country and a deep understanding of its history, which he communicated as he accompanied us up the 392 steps to the Sun Yat-sen Mausoleum or through the Museum of the Taiping Heavenly Kingdom. His assistant and our driver, Cui Bucheng, was a youth who spent every moment in parking lots boning up for his college entrance examinations while waiting to deliver us to the next point of historical interest. Wang, in his fifties, was experienced in the intricate unfolding of history from the Shang dynasty to the latest information on the Four Modernizations; while Cui, in his late teens or early twenties, was out to make history afresh in a period of new opportunities for young intellectuals.

We learned from Wang – whose briefings were literally brief, given in flashes in response to our questions – that Nanjing was a populated centre from at least twenty-six centuries in the long-ago of the Spring and Autumn Period, with a history one hundred years longer than Suzhou's. Nanjing was China's capital during the period of the Six Dynasties, AD 220 to 589. The city, a flourishing cultural centre in the Tang dynasty, was famous for its scholars, painters and poets, notably Li Bai. The first Ming Emperor, Zhu Yuanzhang, made Nanjing his capital in 1368 and from then to the present day it has been an important centre for politics and religion; for handicrafts, especially weaving; and for shipbuilding. Its ancient astronomical instruments on the Purple Gold Mountain and its magnificent bridge across the Changjiang, which Western contractors had long regarded as impractical if not impossible, testify to the inventiveness of Chinese ancient astronomers and modern engineers.

The humiliating Treaty of Nanjing, signed here in 1842, opened five treaty ports to the West and enclaves which were granted extraterritorial rights. Foreigners were soon to control China's trade, her customs, and even to print her postage stamps. For a brief decade from 1853 to the early 1860s Nanjing became the capital of the Taiping Heavenly Kingdom, the great peasant revolutionary movement which originated in the South and at its peak controlled four-fifths of China, almost up to the gates of Beijing.

'My grandfather was much impressed by the Taiping,' I said to Wang as he guided us through the Museum of the Heavenly Kingdom. 'His decision to come to China as a Presbyterian missionary was inspired by their leader, Hong Xiuquan, and his attempt to relive the Gospels in his own day.' If it hadn't been for the Taiping, I went on thinking about the zigzags of history, I wouldn't have been in Nanjing at that moment.

'It was tragic,' Wang summed up. 'The plains of the Changjiang delta after the collapse of the Taiping armies are said to have been whitened by the bones of the Heavenly Warriors and the peasants who supported them, twenty million or more. Not one is said to have begged for mercy! Our Communist Party learned many of the lessons of revolution from the Taiping strategies and tactics in warfare which were put to good use in eventually defeating the Japanese, the foreign interventionists and the KMT reactionaries. Nanjing was like a pivotal centre of revolution and counter-revolution. After the Revolution of 1911 when the child Emperor, Pu Yi, was deposed, Sun Yat-sen set up the first republican government, based on his Three Principles of People's Democracy. But Chiang Kai-shek betrayed these principles shortly after Dr Sun's death. Between 1927 and 1949, Chiang used the Rain Flower Terrace – formerly a sacred place for Buddhist pilgrims – to execute an estimated hundred thousand revolutionaries before he was finally forced to abandon Nanjing, set up a temporary capital in Guangzhou, and then flee to Taiwan. Before 1949 and the triumph of our revolution Nanjing had a most bloody history, especially in the period of Japanese occupation when some 300,000 Chinese were brutally slaughtered. Their rape of our city is one of the darkest pages in our 2,600-year history.'

In the five days that Gertrude, Aiwen and I spent in the 'Southern Capital', these and many other lessons in Chinese history were passed on to us by Wang Yongbiao in his quiet, unemphatic way. We still cherish the stones he selected for us on the Rain Flower Terrace – stained red with the blood of China's martyrs.

Bishop and Mrs Ting and the Three-Self New Christian Movement

Early on our second morning in Nanjing we heard the cheery voice of Siu May Kuo, wife of Bishop K.H. Ting, welcoming us to Nanjing and inviting us to a family-style dinner that evening. 'K.H. is coming back from Beijing especially to be with us. As you may know, he is a member of the National People's Congress, which is in session.'

'It's an honour. I hope he's not putting himself out for our sake?'

'No, no,' Siu May assured me. 'He has other reasons for returning a day early. He will call for you at your hotel at six, if that is convenient.'

Promptly at six, a tall, grey-haired, grey-tunic'd dignitary in his sixties appeared in our hotel lobby. With his serious, fatherly expression and eyes that sparkled with friendliness and good humour, Bishop Ting was unmistakably a man of religion. His white collar merely confirmed our impression. There was a simplicity and goodwill in his smile that immediately put us at ease. He spoke in a fluent English that he had acquired as a graduate student of the Union Theological Seminary in New York and then as secretary of the Student Christian Movement in Toronto. Back home in China in 1955 he was appointed bishop, subsequently President of the Nanjing Theological Seminary. He has recently been elected President of the Christian Council of the Three-Self Patriotic Movement of the Protestant Churches of China. In *Chinese Christians Speak Out*, published by New World Press, Beijing, K.H. Ting is the major spokesman of the new Chinese Christian Church, which unites Protestants under a single wide umbrella. Ecumenical unity is the focus, rather than former sectarian differences of doctrine, in developing a church governed and supported by Chinese and self-propagating without foreign assistance or control.

On the ride out to the Ting residence on Mo Chu Road, the Bishop described how religion was suppressed by Red Guard rampages. 'But religion is now very much alive and is growing. Each day in China a new church is being opened. During the so-called Cultural Revolution, we met in people's houses in small family groups like the early Christians. The Red Guard took over our seminary for their headquarters, so my wife and I and other staff members and students had to move. We had little freedom in those days and little to do, so we spent our time composing an English–Chinese dictionary which was later published in Hong Kong.'

'Yes, we know,' I said. 'It is still used by many American teachers and students.'

'My wife was an English teacher, still is,' the Bishop explained, 'but she is hampered by rheumatoid arthritis. Now, graduate students come to classes in our home. We have reopened our seminary, as you will see, and now have 180 mainly young people, studying for the Protestant ministry.'

'What do you call this period? One of religious restoration or liberation?'

'We have had our revolution, which has liberated us from feudal restrictions and Western control. The Latin American peoples talk about "liberation theology" because they are at a different stage. But in the stage of developing a native Chinese church as part of the Universal Church of Christ, we regard this as a period of reconciliation.'

'Is reconciliation between Christianity and communism possible, in your opinion?' I probed.

The Bishop answered in a roundabout way: 'Through direct contact with revolutionaries, we found them on the whole to be very different from Chiang Kai-shek's Guomindang officials, and far from the caricature made of them by some missionaries and Chinese church leaders. They were certainly not the monsters and rascals they were said to be, but quite normal human beings with idealism, serious theoretical interests and high ethical commitment. For the liberation of their compatriots, many of them sacrificed their all.'

'But they were, and are, atheists . . . '

'Yes, they reject God because the God they have been told about is nothing better than a defender of the status quo, an opponent of all revolutions in structures and values, a protector of all moribund and unjust social orders. Unhappily, many Christians all over the world stood on the side of Chiang Kai-shek, the enemy of the Chinese people; and in 1949, when the People's Liberation Army was about to cross the Changjiang in pursuit of Chiang Kai-shek's forces, some missionaries and their Chinese colleagues led Christians in praying that the soldiers of the People's Liberation Army would drown in the river.'

'Not to mention the hundred thousand martyrs', Gertrude added, 'who were executed by the KMT on Rain Flower Hill. Mr Wang Yongbiao has told us their story.'

Our driver had turned into Mo Chu Road, a wide boulevard whose residences were shielded by gates and walls and hidden behind century-old shade trees. The Ting home, like many in Nanjing, was sombre on the outside, but warm and inviting within. A cheery fire in the grate lit up the face of

Siu May as she gave us a laughing welcome from her wheelchair. She drew Gertrude over to sit beside her and talk about family and mutual friends while her son Heping came in to set the table for supper. He was a graduate student in the Physics Department, expecting an early appointment to the staff of Nanjing University. As Ting introduced us, I remembered meeting Heping's older brother Stephen in San Francisco. 'At the time, about two years ago,' I said, 'we talked about "socialist spiritual civilization". In the US we were frankly surprised at the new concept presented at the Twelfth National Congress of the Communist Party of China in 1982 and wondered if the word "spiritual" had a supernatural connotation?'

'Cultural, rather,' explained Ting.

'That was Stephen's interpretation. Some of the New Age people in America were assuming that spiritual meant transcendental.'

Later, Bishop Ting showed us artwork, painting, embroidery and the score of original musical compositions by seminary students. 'This is what we mean by a spiritual civilization, devoted to creation of beauty. Money should be a means, not a purpose.'

At dinner, while Heping set course after course in front of us until we could eat no more, we talked further about the role of the Three-Self Movement. Bishop Ting explained how reconciliation between the Christian Church and the Chinese Communist Party had developed in the post-Mao period. Since the Church had been an institution largely financed and controlled from abroad by foreign missions, it had served the interests of the West and become isolated from the mainstream of the Chinese movement for independence. The new Church emerging was non-sectarian: Episcopalians, Presbyterians, Methodists and other Protestant denominations were united in one association of believers. 'You will find a fuller answer to these questions in copies of sermons and speeches I will pass on to you, including my article "Theological Voices of Christians in China", a re-evaluation of the work of foreign missionaries. Since the Church structures were completely broken to pieces in the Cultural Revolution, we are now occupied with gathering Chinese

Christendom into a community of Christians who are joined together by their common experience and their newly gained unity. We don't ask foreign missionaries to come to China. It is our declared desire that no foreign group or individual undertake evangelistic work in China without the explicit approval of the Chinese Church, which has responsibility and jurisdiction in this province. We can't rely on foreigners for the proclamation of the Gospel and for the building of the Church among the Chinese people. The Church today should nurture its roots in Chinese soil so that it can blossom tomorrow and bear fruit.'

'Coming from a missionary family myself,' I responded, 'I fully understand. It's hard, though, not to be subjective. My grandfather set up Pui Ying Middle School in Guangzhou and my Great-Aunt Harriet the Truelight Seminary. My Great-Aunt Martha and her husband, Dr Kerr, founded the first institution for the blind and mentally disturbed in South China. Although conversion was their objective and Bible study a must, none the less they brought Western science and medicine, mathematics, geography and history to students who otherwise would have studied only the Confucian classics. Many of their students became part of the liberal movement that supported Dr Sun Yat-sen in the 1911 revolution. Perhaps "missionaries and gunboats" is too one-sided an indictment.'

'We no longer need to revive those relationships between the Cross and the Flag,' Bishop Ting responded. 'Certainly, what you say is true. Our present thoughts about opening to the West are how to do it without being controlled from abroad, to make our own contribution to the Universal Christian Church with our own Chinese characteristics.'

At this point Siu May saw her opportunity to redirect the dialogue between her husband and me to the role that women had played in Christian education. She had been Co-chairperson of the Women's Federation of Jiangsu Province for many years. 'I have heard of Harriet Noyes and Truelight. Your great-aunt was a courageous woman to set up a girls' school – when was it?'

'About a hundred years ago,' Gertrude answered.

'Girls were nobodies in those days,' Siu May added.

I felt obliged to say frankly, 'But my Great-Aunt Harriet, like most of the early missionaries, had some very reactionary ideas. So did my grandfather, even though both were strong supporters of Dr Sun Yat-sen. When French nuns were murdered in Tianjin in 1870, she endorsed a letter calling upon the US and British governments to organize an Anglo-Saxon invasion of China. And my grandfather, pious Christian though he was, praised the British for replacing one Chinese viceroy in Guangzhou with their own candidate "to restore law and order".'

'But your great-aunt did perform a service for Chinese women,' Siu May insisted. 'That you should not forget. There is a contradiction between politics and culture.'

Bishop Ting was solicitous of his wife's endurance, and after a last cup of tea, which she served from her wheelchair, he suggested a tour of the seminary. Siu May, lively as ever, waved us a loving farewell. And since then at Christmas time, she has sent us Ting family bulletins. She is as solicitous of her husband's welfare as he of hers. Affectionately she writes, in her 1985 round robin letter: 'K.H.'s main mark of ageing is his forgetfulness. He seems to lose more and more things as he travels about. Sometimes he writes and writes, then, at noon, suddenly discovers he hasn't shaved yet. But otherwise, he is the same K.H., unperturbed by odds of all kinds.'

Siu May writes in impeccable English, every comma in its appropriate location. She adds about herself, 'I've been thinking of embarking on something having to do with the literary appreciation of the English Bible. I know it is rather ambitious for this poor ant to nibble at such a gigantic bone. Do pray for me.'

South to Guangzhou: We Visit the Luogang Township

Mrs Xu Xiufang, General Manager of Waiwen Shudian, was our hostess for our ten-day visit to the South. She was the heartiest woman we met on our whole trip. She could hardly wait until we cleared the barrier at the airport to give Gertrude a big hug and shake my hand with a welcome back to my old home town. It was like a family reunion, since she had been a gracious friend to Gertrude on her visit to Guangzhou in 1974, and to me in 1975.

The next morning we had just returned to our room in the Dongfang Hotel after breakfast and a stroll around the garden court when Mrs Xu and Aiwen came in to present us with a ten-day agenda as full as the Cantonese banquets we would enjoy during our stay. 'For today,' Aiwen concluded, 'Xu Xiufang thought you would enjoy a visit to the countryside, so she's made arrangements for us to go to the Luogang Township. Since you have both visited Luogang when it was a commune, we thought you might like to make comparisons.'

Gertrude and I said 'Fine!' and 'Great!' at the same time; and soon we were speeding through Flower County on country roads lined with poplars. At Luogang Township headquarters we were received by Wang Shikun, who had been our host in 1974 and 1975. He was happy to respond to Mrs Xu's suggestion to contrast the old days with the new: 'You see we have a new reception centre. Production with the new family incentive system has risen steadily. We have developed new enterprises and sidelines to keep our surplus population from flooding Guangzhou. We will show you our new olive-canning factory. We have doubled our supply of dried fruits for export to many foreign countries. Perhaps you saw our exhibit at the Trade Fair?'

'No, unfortunately we arrived too late. But I did see your display back in 1975.'

'We supply Guangzhou', Wang continued, 'with 16,000 pounds of vegetables, bananas and oranges daily. We also have a thriving fish sideline here, many new ponds, greatly increased since you were here ten years ago. Do you have any questions before we have lunch in our new dining hall?'

'Yes. Friends in the US are concerned that the kind of intensive farming under the responsibility system, with the use of chemical fertilizers, is going to impoverish your soil and that erosion will become a greater problem. I remember you told us in 1975, quoting Mao Zedong, that each pig was a little manure factory and organic fertilizer had enriched your soil for five thousand years. Do you still quote Chairman Mao?' I asked, with a smile.

'Not so often,' Wang replied, 'but we are cautious with chemical fertilizers and still use mainly organic.'

'Another problem they raise', I continued, 'is the effect on education, with the new family system. A teacher friend of mine from a rural community near Kaifeng wrote that one spring she had forty-five children in her class. The next autumn, after the responsibility system was implemented, only eleven showed up.'

'We try experiments,' Wang generalized, with a faraway gaze, 'and not all of them work out well at the beginning. But we correct our errors and find new ways of solving problems. Children must now complete a required number of hours each week at school, for which they get a certificate. This permits them to do family work in their spare time.'

'Do families respect this procedure?' Gertrude asked.

'If they don't, they will be prosecuted by law, but this is rarely necessary. Parents want their children to get a good education, to do better than they themselves have done. So there's not too much of a problem any more.'

'Do you still have barefoot doctors?' Gertrude asked.

'Yes, but we call them paramedics now, and they are better trained.' Wang Shikun fielded our further questions over lunch. When I asked if the family responsibility system was an improvement over the commune system, he laughed: 'Yes, fewer meetings! Seriously, without the political responsibility which has been taken over by the county, we now have more time to devote to scientific farming.'

'Are you moving towards, or away from, your socialist goal?'

Wang took time to consider. 'You see,' he said slowly, 'the land is owned collectively and according to our socialist principle, "to each according to his work", fields are contracted out to individual households. These are required to meet a certain quota set by the county. What's left over is for their own use or disposal. This system preserves our socialist type of ownership and planning. At the same time, it rewards initiative and hard work.'

'Does it pan out according to theory?'

'Production has more than doubled here at Luogang since the family system was set up.'

'What about the use of large-scale machinery, tractors, combines?'

'That is not our problem here. Farmers can pool the use of small tractors at Luogang. In the North and West that is a bigger problem, but it is being solved. As machinery replaces human labour, farm workers turn to sidelines: fish culture, forestry, construction and so on. Besides, many of the youths find jobs at the county centres, which are rapidly becoming cities to absorb the working masses. Now, shall we take a tour?'

Wang, who had not lost his quiet enthusiasm for his public-relations job, guided us through a vineyard and then the Luogang canning factory, pointing out improvements made since the Cultural Revolution. His manner was still that of a peasant, son of the local soil, as he waved farewell and invited us to come back in ten years: 'You will be reassured that we are much further along the road to socialism.'

As we drove back through Luogang Village, it was a stop-and-go proposition for our driver. Stalls and barrows of the free market crowded the streets with displays of Western-style blue jeans; balloons, kites and toys; vegetables and fruit grown locally; and live fish in tanks. Teenagers on their way home from middle school were slow to make way for vehicles. Even cyclists were pushing their bicycles, rather than trying to ride through the village. People were livelier and more prosperous than they had been ten years previously.

On the road back to Guangzhou, after circling White Cloud Mountain, we stopped beside a large rectangular fish pond about the size of a football field to ask about the way sidelines were integrated into the township economy. A small crowd of children and parents gathered round, eager to answer our questions, which Aiwen had to translate into Putonghua and Mrs Xu into Cantonese. One middle-aged woman with two young children hanging on to her coat invited us into her house, which fronted on to the pond, to see for ourselves how prosperous peasant families had become under the responsibility system. Downstairs in her two-storey, whitewashed country house were kitchen and comfortable dining and living space with a television, and upstairs bedrooms, all very tidy with the afternoon sun slanting in through ample windows. Our hostess was proud to tell us that her new house had been built in the spring by her husband, sons and neighbours; also to explain how her family had contracted with the township committee to take charge of the pond and deliver fish to the local market according to demand.

'And do you keep fish for your own table?' Gertrude asked.

She looked at us curiously, as if we were accusing her of dishonesty. 'We buy at the fish market like everybody else,' she answered. 'We raise pigs for ourselves and also some of the geese you see here, and we have our own garden plot, but those are rights we all share.'

The Zhujiang Delta. Zhongshan and Foshan

Our next excursion to the countryside was to be a two-day affair. By previous arrangement, Li Rongsan appeared at our door early to pick up our overnight bags. He was a handsome, ex-People's Liberation Army stalwart: trouble-shooter and problem-solver for Waiwen Shudian, also our constant companion. His smile and easy-going manner showed that the five elements and the yins and yangs in his life were in harmony and that, like Xu Xiufang, he enjoyed every minute of time passing. The indefatigable Mrs Xu met us at the kerbside in front of the hotel, and in two taxis our party was whisked off on a rapid trip through the Zhujiang Delta area. The landscape was as flat as a prairie, interlaced with canals and creeks. Since harvest season was over by late November, there were few farmers working their family plots. That autumn the rice crop had been so plentiful that unthreshed sheaves were still stacked along the road – unguarded.

Near Zhongshan, we visited the house in which Sun Yat-sen and family had once lived. It was now a national shrine. A steady stream of visitors was filing through the rooms which China's first president had once occupied and paying their respects to his memory. In the 1980s there was far more concern in China for the contribution that Dr Sun had made to China's liberation than during the Cultural Revolution.

In Zhongshan City we were received by both the manager and trade-union representative in a new five-storey radio factory, built and operated by Chinese labour and financed by Hong Kong capital. Young women between eighteen and twenty, on their first industrial jobs, were assembling tape recorders in the department we visited on the fifth floor. Wages were low, but good working conditions were assured by trade unionist Li Haozhao. Profits for needed foreign exchange were assured by manager Ms Cheng. She explained that Hong Kong entrepreneurs received 20 per cent of the profit, and in her vocabulary *entrepreneur* was not a bad word. The girls who still lived at home would get experience of factory work and go on to more skilled and higher-paid jobs as China's modernization programme expanded, she explained. But in the meantime, their labour and that of millions more Chinese teenagers, who had for the most part finished middle school, was helping to build the motherland into a strong, developing nation.

Overnight we stayed at the Zhongshan Hot Springs Resort, a dramatic contrast with the radio factory. The two-storey guest houses were similar to motels in the United States but the surroundings were landscaped with traditional Chinese gardens, with lotus ponds and willows that seemed to weep into them with their million leaves like falling tears of green-gold in the late sun. The resort was financed by Hong Kong capital and administered by Hong Kong personnel so exclusively that only Hong Kong dollars were acceptable in the gift shop.

After breakfast the next morning we visited the nearby golf course, either the first or second to be laid out in the People's Republic. Financed by Japanese investors, it was managed by an Overseas Chinese who returned from a Manila golf course to accept a new responsibility to make money for his motherland. Nearby was an amusement park, still partly at blueprint stage, to provide fun and games for holiday-makers from Hong Kong and Macao. Already the Five-Legged Spider, the Twister, and the Astro-Fighter were geared up to make the world, in Disneyland style, spin or bounce or turn upside down. We were not tempted to ride the Loop-the-Loop Coaster, especially after we were informed that Premier Zhao Ziyang was not permitted by his security guard to loop upside down in a great circle route. 'Thank you, no,' we said to our amusement park guide, who offered us a free ride. 'We will follow your leader and keep both feet on the ground.'

As we proceeded on a circular route that brought us within a few miles of Macao and the South China Sea, we returned to Guangzhou by way of Foshan. The bountiful rice harvest lay in yellow sheaves all along our zigzag route. On a few side roads, closed to traffic, grain was being threshed with bamboo rods and stomping feet. The autumn haze, with the sun blotching through, turned the flat land into pale versions of Van Gogh's paintings of the French Midi.

In Foshan, twenty miles downriver from Guangzhou, we visited the Shiwan Pottery Works, famous around the world for glazed human figures, terracotta animals and birds, and useful vases and vessels. Here, as well as the craft shops we visited in Suzhou and elsewhere, there was much new pressure in comparison with the 1970s to spend US dollars and help to build up the foreign exchange essential for China's modernization programme. Our contribution had to be minimal. None the less, between Gertrude, Aiwen and myself, our collection of gifts and curios bulked large as we added two new holdalls to accommodate them. At Shiwan, we were introduced to the old coking and the new electronic furnaces; and to the department where highly skilled workers were engaged in contract productions, fantastic montages of human figures and landscapes, several of which were taking a year or more to complete.

In Foshan's free-market craft shops, we saw some of the latest papercuts. Millions were produced every year by craftspeople handling tiny knives and scissors to shape red, green and gold flowers and animals. Some of the less intricate were stamped out, a dozen at a time, on small punch presses.

Back in 1971, on his first trip to China, our son Chris had purchased a set of giant papercuts from Foshan to display at various art and craft exhibitions in the United States. The twenty-four panels, at least two feet by three, presented the history of the Chinese revolution in graphic detail: guerrilla war in sorghum fields, for example; the Red Army on the Long March over the Snowy Mountains and the Grasslands; the crossing of the Changjiang in the final phase of the Civil War; and, most impressive of all, an enormous red sun rising between giant sunflowers to symbolize the Chinese people's victory over feudalism at home and imperialism from abroad. In 1984, papercut subjects were more traditional: beauties and bodhisattvas, taboo during the Cultural Revolution; birds and flowers, instead of peasants on tractors and fishermen hauling in their nets.

Foshan was a microcosm of post-Cultural Revolution China. The famous Taoist monastery-turned-museum was in the final stages of restoration. Many of the old narrow streets were being widened into tree-lined boulevards. From the revolving cocktail lounge atop the Foshan Hotel, we had a slowly changing view of the city's trees and buildings, villages and ricefields beyond, and a network of the Zhujiang Delta's roads and creeks phasing out in the mist of a Chinese Indian summer. The new hotel, whose cocktail lounge turned hourly through the four points of the compass, was a joint project: labour and most materials were supplied by China; capital, architectural design and management by a patriotic Hong Kong millionaire. Our host, an economist from the Foreign Affairs Office of Foshan, explained the deal as a two-way profitable enterprise. In the first six years the Hong Kong investor received 70 per cent of the profits, the Chinese 30 per cent. In the following six years, percentages would be reversed. Finally, after twelve years, the hotel would be owned outright by the Chinese, with a competent staff trained in hotel management.

'In the West, your critics are saying that these transactions represent a return to capitalism. What is your opinion?' I asked.

'The West you talk about had two hundred years of industrial revolution, from steam to electronics. We have twenty years until the end of the century to accomplish the same development, turning a backward economy into a prosperous one. But we are succeeding. Even during the Cultural Revolution, which set us back in many disastrous ways for years, our productive power went up in the basic industries. Between 1965 and 1975, production of coal and steel more than doubled. Electricity went up from 67,600 million kilowatt-hours to 195,000. Since then, production figures have doubled. We are still a poor country. Our transport and communication systems are inadequate. But the enthusiasm and creativeness of our people have now recovered after a very dark period.'

'But foreign capital investments . . .'

'They are part of the solution. We use them to advance our whole socialist system. That is what we mean by the open door.'

'Some people in the US are confused by your new use of the phrase "open-door policy",' I noted. 'It used to mean, in the West's interpretation, a door kept open by the gunboats of England, France and the United States – from the outside.'

'Yes, but now we are in control of our own economy, and we open the door from the inside. All parties benefit from our joint enterprises.'

Pui Ying Middle School Rediscovered

Our visit to the Guangzhou area had reached the halfway point on Mrs Xu's ten-day schedule, when our agenda was abruptly knocked out of kilter by the biggest surprise of our whole trip. On the sixth morning the plan was to show Gertrude what was left of Pui Ying Middle School, converted after the revolution into a marine parts factory, and the house in which I was born, converted into the factory office.

Our driver, not too familiar with the south side of the Zhujiang, stopped at a one-pump petrol station to ask directions. Then confidently he drove along the Tongfu Zhonglu, as broad a thoroughfare as Fati could boast and as lively a shopping artery as we saw anywhere in China. Since Fati was not a priority tourist area, its physical layout had changed very little since I had known it as a boy. In front of seafood stores live fish and eels splashed in tubs, caged chickens cackled or crowed in front of poultry shops, pigs in pens by butchers' shops squealed as if they knew what fate had in store for them – all part of Fati's animated food markets. Free-market vegetable and fruit stands offered locally grown lichees and bananas on the stem, and autumn chestnuts to roast. Traditional pharmacists offered herbal remedies for every disease known in the subtropics. There were furniture stores specializing in bamboo, dumpling and fast-food wagons – even ice-cream pedlars on street corners.

Our driver had to weave through a crowd that used the thoroughfare for an overflow pavement as they shopped for their noon and evening meals. Parents held their children securely by the hand as they passed candy-hawkers, firecracker stands, and birds twittering and hopping about in their cages hung out in front of pet shops. Elders were fishing from bridges as we crossed canals, which were crowded, as in the old days, with sampans in which people still lived – the smallest houseboats in the world. But there was no evidence of the extremes of rags or riches that characterized early-twentieth-century China, and no visible beggars. Most of the children were round-cheeked and bright-eyed, different from the skinny urchins, pot-bellied with worms, whom I had known in the streets of Fati in my own childhood days.

'Aren't we going too far?' I asked. 'When we were here in 1975, I remember crossing only two creeks.'

A rapid fire of Cantonese between Xu Xiufang and our driver was interpreted by Yang Aiwen to mean, 'No, he is following directions.' But we did not turn into a narrow street half closed off by stacks of planks and logs in front of a construction company and see the four-storey building of what was once Pui Ying's Severance Hall rising above the grey-tiled roofs of Fati. Instead, about five miles further downriver, our driver turned off the main thoroughfare into an access road and drove through an iron gate into school grounds I had never seen before. 'Pui Ying,' he announced, with a flourish of his hand to indicate mission accomplished.

Mrs Xu introduced us to the gatekeeper with a build-up that must have convinced him that we were very important visitors from the United States, at least at ambassadorial level. He went dashing off to inform the Principal while I looked around in amazement at a totally new school. 'Founded in 1879,' Aiwen read from an inscription on what was a brand-new science building. 'Pui Ying,' said Mrs Xu, delighted, and Li Rongsan gave me his usual broad smile. I was more than amazed to see a whole new campus in the background with a dozen school buildings and dormitories and, in the recreation field, girls as well as boys playing basketball. So this was Pui Ying in the 1980s! Formerly a boys' middle school, it was now, after the revolution, coeducational.

'Unbelievable,' I said to Gertrude in an aside. 'I thought Pui Ying had moved to Hong Kong before the Japanese occupation. But here it is, like a Chinese phoenix rising out of the ashes of the old school, with all these new buildings!'

I was still marvelling at the changes when Principal Luo Huangshen came out to greet us. His smile of welcome scarcely bridged the credibility gap that his eyes expressed as he searched mine with a doubting-Thomas reservation. He graciously bowed us into the official reception room, where we were soon joined by the whole senior administrative staff: Vice-Principal Rao Chingbao, Dean Ling Dawen, Party Secretary Hu Yingchi and Ma Shaoke, interpreter and head of the English Department. Official photographer and physics instructor Chen Dachaun made a graphic record of our meeting with flashbulbs and camera poised at different angles. It required the finesse of Yang Aiwen and Ma Shaoke to transmit all the verbal excitement expressed in our two-way exchange. Even then, we were not sure that Principal Luo and his astonished staff members were convinced that I was actually the grandson of Pui Ying's founder, Henry Varnum Noyes. Gertrude dispelled the last doubt by producing from her handbag a photograph that exactly matched my grandfather's photograph in the school bulletin.

'We have found you at a good time....' Principal Luo's discovery was supported by his staff with those cordial 'ahs' of approval which punctuate Chinese dialogue.

'I think we have found each other,' I laughed, 'through a happy accident. We set out to show my wife the old school – or rather, what is left of it – and the house in which I was born. But our driver brought us here!'

'It is a happy accident', the Principal agreed, 'that brings you and your wife to us at this time. It was only last month on our National Day that new policies of our government made it possible for us again to name our school Pui Ying. It was called the Eighth Middle School after the revolution. The change-back has been of great satisfaction to our graduates, particularly those who knew your father and grandfather. Our Alumni Association numbers ten thousand members, not only in China but also abroad in your country and many others. They have always thought of their alma mater as Pui Ying, so the renaming of our school has increased their loyalty and support.' Luo smiled at Gertrude as he added, 'Our Association now includes women as well as men, I am sure you will be glad to know. Now, if you wish, we will take a tour round the campus and you will see why we are considered a "key" school, as famous in South China during the present period as it was in your father's and grandfather's day.'

The Principal, Vice-Principal and school photographer ushered us through the physics and communications building, pleased with our surprise at the updated laboratory equipment and visual education department; also at the computer room, with twenty terminals for student instruction, and in the next classroom twenty electric typewriters.

'Many of our graduates go on to engineering or technical colleges,' explained Vice-Principal Rao. 'We are happy to make our contribution to the Four Modernizations, since our country greatly needs trained experts in these fields. Our standards are considered high, so we are classified as a model middle school.'

'It is a surprise to learn that you survived the Japanese occupation,' I said.

'Yes, we still maintained our identity here during the Japanese occupation of Guangzhou. While our main staff and student body set up temporary headquarters in north-west Guangdong Province, some classes continued to be held here in private homes. After the revolution, Pui Ying returned to Guangzhou and was renamed the Eighth Middle School. And now we are happy to take back our old name.'

'It seems that China is enjoying a renaissance in education and a reformation in religion at the same time.'

'Yes, it's a new period,' Luo agreed. 'We are free to believe or not to believe. It is a period of persuasion rather than compulsion in every branch of human activity here in China, particularly in the field of education.'

'My grandfather wrote home in the 1870s, at about the time of the founding of Pui Ying, that the Chinese needed a complete revolution in their way of thinking. They needed to be taught to think for themselves. He was, of course, criticizing the Confucian system, with its emphasis on mechanical memorization.'

'Yes, yes. We still have a long way to go in education as well as in everything else if we are to achieve our goal of modernization by the end of the century, but we are moving ahead as fast as we can on what we call the New Long March.'

'I am sure my father and grandfather would be impressed with your progress. They were interested, as you know, not only in promoting Bible study, but also in science and mathematics. I learned from my grandfather's letters that when Pui Ying was founded in 1879, the Four Books of Confucius were the only texts used in Chinese schools. When he first introduced mathematics and science into the curriculum, some parents even withdrew their sons. But by the 1890s the pendulum began to swing the other way. By this time, business contacts with the outside world and trade with other countries were becoming more important and parents wanted their sons to have a more liberal education, to include Western science and also mathematics. Henry Varnum had been a farm boy in his youth, impatient, when he came to China, with the prevailing ideal that a student should be frail, wear glasses and scorn physical work and exercise. So sports were always an important part of the routine from the founding days of this school. He believed that a healthy mind could develop at its best only in a healthy body. So did my father, who used to take the Pui Ying basketball team downriver to compete with Canton Christian College. I remember on one occasion he took the team to Hong Kong with me along as mascot at the age of seven.'

'Some of our graduates will be happy to hear more of the history of our school, which you remember so well. If you are to be here this coming Sunday, I am sure they will be honoured to invite you to their monthly luncheon. But before you leave let us show you the old gatehouse, which you may remember in its former location. We have transported it here in sections and reassembled it. You will also recognize the rock as a relic from the garden that your grandfather purchased back in 1878 as a location for Pui Ying. The characters engraved on the rock mean, "Listen to the whispering pine".'

An Alumni Banquet in Our Honour

Early next morning Mr Wai Ming Young, Secretary of the Pui Ying Alumni Association, came to our hotel room with a red and gold envelope in his hand. But before delivering it, he deeply scrutinized my face. In perfect English he asked, 'Are you a Christian?'

'In ethics, yes,' I answered him frankly. 'But I am not much of a churchgoer.' When I saw disappointment clouding his face, I went on to say, 'I am much interested in the history of the Christian Church in China, since my relatives were early missionaries here in Guangzhou, as you well know. In Nanjing, my wife and I spent an evening with Bishop and Mrs Ting to learn more about what has happened in recent years. Chinese Christians who remained loyal to their religion must have gone through trial by fire during the Cultural Revolution, which Bishop Ting said was neither cultural nor a revolution.' Mr Young's unhappy expression did not soften, so I went on, as if delivering a lay sermon, 'The Bishop is a modern-day prophet, predicting that the Three-Self Movement will be as important for the future of Christianity as the Reformation was for its past. What do you think?'

Mr Young's answer caught me off guard. 'Ting is a communist!'

'I think not,' I countered. 'I read some of his sermons on the flight down from Nanjing. He believes in the doctrine of original sin.'

Young was not convinced, but he didn't debate the matter further. It would have been difficult for him to convince me that original sin was one of the tenets of communism. Giving me a sudden affable smile, as if there could only be friendship and understanding between us, he handed me the red and gold envelope. 'From the Pui Ying Alumni Association, of which I am the secretary. We are most happy to invite you, Mrs Noyes and your friends to a luncheon Sunday noon. We would like you to tell about your family, what has happened to them.'

Sunday noon on our last day in Guangzhou, Mr Young ushered us into the banqueting hall where some ninety alumni and alumnae of Pui Ying were already seated at a dozen round tables, designated by year of graduation. A moment's hush was followed by mutual applause, which continued as we were guided to the head table. Principal Luo received us with the double handshake of old friends and introduced us to two other honoured guests from the United States, Mr and Mrs Kenneth Mei of the Kuo Feng Travel Agency. Mei was himself a graduate of Pui Ying. I was honoured in addition by being seated next to the oldest alumnus present, Chan Shichai, born in 1898 in Guangzhou.

'I knew you when you were a child,' said Chan, with a grandfatherly smile. He made a gesture to show how tall I was at the age of eight. 'I loved your father. He taught me mathematics and I have been a mathematics teacher all my life until I retired. He set me on a good path. As long as I live I will think of him every day.'

'How old are you now?' I asked.

'Eighty-seven,' he answered with pride, as if it was a triumph for a Chinese to have lived so long through so many troubled years.

'Going on a hundred?'

'I am trying,' he sighed, 'but it is not easy!'

Mr Mei and I were both invited to speak after the last dim sum delicacy was served and we could eat no more. Chan Shichai informed me in a loud whisper, translated quietly by Yang Aiwen, that Guangzhou was famous for its 2,364 dim sum dishes, as Mr Mei was bringing greetings from the United States and wishing all graduates of Pui Ying and ourselves a long and happy life. He also issued an open invitation to his fellow alumni to visit the United States and guaranteed a warm welcome from the Overseas Chinese in New York and San Francisco.

Since Mr Young had asked me to speak about my family, I said when my turn came that two of my brothers, Bill and Dick, both born in Fati in our house on the old Pui Ying campus like myself, were still living, but that my youngest brother, Geoff, had been killed in the same war that had killed many of the relatives and friends of the alumni. There was a moment of silence and deep communion with memories of loss. Then, on a happier note, I congratulated the members of the Alumni Association for continuing to support Pui Ying, and Principal Luo and staff for their role in educating a younger generation to participate in modernizing their economy and educational system.

Gertrude and I then went from table to table, shaking hands with all the 'old boys', their wives and the younger 'old girls'. They were doctors, scientists, teachers, chemists, engineers, physicists, mathematicians, many of whom had moved inland to Chongqing to help win the war against the Japanese and were now doing important work in China's new modernization programmes back in Guangzhou. Some of them conversed with us in English. A few had known my father and grandfather, and shook hands with a special warmth. All twelve surviving members of the class of '39 stood up while their secretary presented us with a triangular pennant which had been specially designed to honour Pui Ying's hundredth birthday back in 1979. Its eagle, with wings spread, still glances sideways at me from my study wall, as if to remind me to try, like Chan Shichai, to live to be a hundred.

I was happy, as we left the dining hall with a standing ovation, that my father's life had not been wasted: Chan's affection for him was testimony enough. I was happy also that for five generations my family had contributed, in its own small and contradictory way, to the modernization of education in China.

All too soon that evening we were waiting our call at the Baiyun (White Cloud) Airport for the flight to Beijing. When it came with a rasp and a roar in both Cantonese and Putonghua, we had time for a last embrace and handshake with Xu Xiufang and Li Rongsan. 'Yang Aiwen told us, when we arrived in Shanghai four weeks ago,' I said in parting, 'that we were to have the best vacation in our whole lives. And now, thanks to you all and your ten-day plan, we've had it. It's your turn to visit us in San Francisco.'

As we flew north into clouds, salmon-coloured in the sun's reflected light over Guangzhou, my thoughts went back to 1975 when I had first travelled the same air route to Beijing at the evening hour. It was a time of half-day, half-night as we soared between heaven and earth: the meditative hour when memories flash back in video sequences spanning a lifetime. Curiously, the sharpest memory was not of my family, who had lived for so many years in Guangzhou, but of my visit with seventy-six-year-old Chen in the Riverside Apartments. When I asked him what he thought was the main difference between the old China and the new, he had replied quite simply, 'Now we care for one another.'

If that were not so, and the Chinese people were to lose the sense of collectively caring for one another, what would be the use of computer terminals and revolving cocktail lounges – or of education?

✸ 9 ✸

Celebrations in Beijing

November was a month of surprises. Two days before we took flight for Beijing, Aiwen knocked excitedly in the early morning to announce: 'You are invited to make a speech in the Great Hall of the People....' Out of breath, she added, 'For three minutes!'

'In the Great Hall? I can't believe it. What on?'

'To talk about distribution of Chinese books in the United States, your hardship experiences, the thirty-fifth anniversary of CIBTC...'

'In three minutes?' I interrupted.

'Perhaps five?' she added, with a question mark.

My first draft Gertrude thought too personal. Aiwen said it did not show 'enough suffering'. On the night flight between Guangzhou and Beijing I had time to revise our joint project to exclude subjectivities and include 'more suffering'. In the process I had time to reflect on an honour that came to me as a climax to a long association with China, the amazing changes that had taken place since I was born in Guangzhou in 1910, and the new relations between the American and Chinese peoples in the 1970s and 1980s.

As we touched down at Beijing airport and ran the gauntlet of guidelights, we began to reach for scarves and overcoats while the pilot was announcing a temperature of zero degrees outside. Yang Aiwen and other passengers were returning to the deep freeze of the northern capital with sunny, yellow bananas in mesh bags. As we trooped into the waiting room with bags bulging with gifts for friends and relatives, a second major surprise was awaiting us: we saw the head of son Chris towering above the crowd.

I turned to Aiwen accusingly. 'You knew he was coming!'

She laughed. 'I promised to keep a secret.'

'I'm here', Chris explained, 'at the invitation of *Renmin Ribao* to draw up a new contract for our distribution in the US and also to discuss the special North American edition, to begin next spring. In addition to Chinese scholars in the US who want to keep in touch with the motherland,' Chris explained to Aiwen, 'distribution is to be enlarged to include Overseas Chinese and Chinese Americans, most of whom can't read the reformed characters. So the North American edition will be printed in the traditional characters. I've also had time to line up about a dozen sessions for you, Dad, with publishers of foreign-language books and magazines and three banquets before the big events of the weekend. They are all interested in co-publishing – but also, they are all short of cash.'

At the end of the week, formal celebrations for the thirty-fifth anniversary of CIBTC opened with a concert in the Hall of the Chinese People's Political Consultative Conference. It was a pleasant change, after rushing to meet appointments all week, to sit back and enjoy the performance of some of the top talent from Beijing television. They not only performed for us, but the programme was also broadcast on sound and sight waves out to the farthest borders of the People's Republic – a potential audience of one billion!

The most popular song of the evening, 'I Love You, China', was still making music in our ears the next morning as we gathered in the headquarters of CIBTC for a friendly welcome by President Wang Qinyun. In his report on the history of the firm, formerly known as Guoji Shudian, Wang described the early difficult years in reopening information channels which had been closed by civil war. Year by year since then export of publications had increased, until thirty-five years later CIBTC's staff of 600 did business with 163 foreign countries in some fifty different languages. 'Our achievements are your achievements,' he concluded, with traditional Chinese courtesy. 'We welcome you as international members of our own family of book publishers and distributors.'

In the informal reception that followed we met members of the international family, as well as original founders of CIBTC, advisers and senior staff members, many of whom we knew personally from previous visits. Delegates from abroad came from Africa, Australia, Canada, England, France, Germany, Hong Kong, Italy, Japan, Latin America, Pakistan and the United States. M. Bergeron from Paris told us that his Phoenix Bookstore had been burned twice by anti-China fanatics but, he smiled grimly, rose from its ashes on both occasions to develop a larger clientele than before. The delegate from Pakistan said that whatever problems we might have in the West could not hold a candle to his problems back home, with raids and book burnings. We met Mr Lo of Commercial Press in Hong Kong, Jade Tang from Guanghua Books and Eva Skelley from Collet's, both from London; also Mr Yasui of the Oriental Bookstore, who had been my host in Tokyo for four days in 1975. We were happy to see that our associate Mei Yuan Xu and her co-worker from Li Min Bookstore in Los Angeles had arrived safely.

In different foreign-language groups with an interpreter, we were taken on a tour through sample book and magazine display rooms. CIBTC had modernized since my trip in 1975. With an irrepressible pride in China's Four Modernizations, our young guide piloted us through computer rooms, explained new microfilm services, and even showed us how the new telex terminals were operating with messages coming in from England and Australia. 'We are a developing country,' he explained. 'It may take us more than twenty years to catch up with the West, but we are modernizing as rapidly as possible.'

'*You Banfa!*' I responded.

He gave me an appreciative smile. 'Yes, we are finding a way!'

Back at the Xiyuan Hotel for an early lunch, Chris and I had time to summarize our separate negotiations of the week before the afternoon reception in the Great Hall of the People.

'How did you make out with *Renmin Ribao?*' I asked.

'Great. They express full confidence in us and plans for launching the North American edition are settled. The opener will be next spring at the San Francisco Chinese Consulate, with a formal reception at which the Editor-in-Chief Qin Chuan will be guest of honour. It will obviously be a prestigious affair. Also, CIBTC is arranging to send Ex-Manager Cao Jianfei to San Francisco to host a celebration for CB&P's twenty-fifth anniversary next spring, also at the Consulate. What about your negotiations?'

'Since we are due at the Great Hall in an hour and a half, I'll have to leave the details for San Francisco. But it's been a rewarding experience wherever we went to meet heads of the publishing bureaux in Shanghai, Nanjing and Guangzhou. They all expressed concern with new possibilities in the period ahead – and bountiful goodwill. In Beijing, our discussions were more practical. As an aside, though, I should mention that we talked with American, Italian and Japanese engineers at the various hotels where we stayed. Their role strikes me as a good deal simpler than ours. They were all involved in joint enterprises with their Chinese counterparts. China needs their advanced techniques and gives budget priority to joint enterprises in science and industry; and, in spite of foreign-currency problems, funds are made available. But "cultural engineers" like ourselves,' I laughed, 'who bring advanced techniques in book publishing and distribution, will have to knock harder on the door before it opens wider for us. The situation, though, is much more favourable to change since the stereotypes of the Cultural Revolution have been replaced by more flexible perspectives. I have a strong hunch that this thirty-fifth-anniversary affair was planned by CIBTC to help upgrade foreign-language publications and their importance for foreign relations in the priorities of the State Council. It is significant that the Head of the Propaganda Department and the Minister of Culture, both members of the State Council, are scheduled to attend this afternoon's reception, since I have been asked by CIBTC to mention them by name at the beginning of my speech. The State Council, as I understand, is the highest government body of China between sessions of the National People's Congress.

'Books and particularly periodicals for the export market

may not provide much of a profit to help solve China's need for foreign currency in the short run. But in the long run – and I was sure I had agreement from most of the publishers I talked to – publications perform a most important function. The Chinese magazines we have distributed in the US have stimulated the tourist trade: tens of thousands of Americans have visited China in the past few years. Also, dozens of US business people have opened up joint enterprises here and made investments which speed up China's industrial and electronic revolution. Many of them may have got the idea from reading *China's Foreign Trade* or *Beijing Review*. Besides, these periodicals provided the China experts with information that made them recognize in the early days that China was a major key to East–West relations and the orientation of the US to commercial developments in the Pacific Basin – to the advantage of both the American and Chinese economies, and to international peaceful relations. I make these points in my five-minute speech this afternoon.'

'Are you ready?'

'As ready as I will ever be. Of course I am reading it in English, and Yang Aiwen will give the Chinese. It will be obvious from my remarks that immediate profits from publications are not going to be of major importance in financing the modernization directly, but that foreign-language publications are responsible for the influx of millions of dollars annually in foreign exchange.'

'How do we show this on our balance sheet?' Chris asked, with a laugh and a quick glance at his watch. 'We'll have to rest our case there for the moment.'

Promptly at 1:45 p.m., as scheduled, Yang Aiwen, Gertrude, Chris and I mounted the steps at the main entrance of the Great Hall of the People. For me it was a moment of external calm but internal excitement as I reached into my inside breast pocket to be sure that my written speech was with me. Then the grandeur of the Great Hall and the immensity of Tian An Men Square overwhelmed thoughts of self.

The square was the creation of a revolutionary people, with the Monument to the Revolutionary Heroes at its centre honouring the millions who had died to liberate the nation from the tyranny of oppressors at home and abroad. It was spacious enough – the largest square of its kind in the world – for a million representatives of the Chinese people, including fifty-six minority nationalities, to celebrate International Workers' Day on 1 May and the founding of the People's Republic on 1 October. It was here at the Tian An Men Gate that supplicants used to kowtow to an emperor or empress who lived in a Forbidden City, one of the most complex and beautiful in the world, where dragon power had reigned for centuries in the Hall of Supreme Harmony. Now, Chairman Mao looked out over the square from a huge framed portrait below the balcony of the same gate. It was here, on 1 October 1949, that the Chairman – surrounded by leaders of the Chinese revolution: Zhou Enlai, Zhu De, Liu Shaoqi, Deng Xiaoping and many others – spoke to the future of the Chinese people: 'Our nation will from now on become one of the family of peace- and freedom-loving nations.'

China had become such a nation in the years that followed Mao's death, and the eight stormy years of re-evaluation during the Cultural Revolution, between 1976 and 1984. On that afternoon of the first day of December, as we mounted the steps of the Great Hall, he was still being honoured by a silent queue of mourners, four abreast, as they filed into the Mausoleum at the south end of the square. Mao Zedong Thought was also still celebrated by China's current legislators in their Constitution and in the Great Hall when they met in deliberation to plan the future of the most populous nation on earth. In Deng Xiaoping's definition, Mao Zedong Thought was 'the crystallization of the Chinese people's revolutionary struggle over half a century'. According to Deng, Mao's positive contributions were primary, his errors secondary. 'That's why we will for ever keep Chairman Mao's portrait on Tian An Men Gate as a symbol of our country and will always remember him as a founder of our Party and our state.'

These words came back to me as we passed under the five-star seal of the People's Republic. At the entrance of the Great Hall, People's Liberation Army men – in their green uniforms, red shoulder straps, red stars shining from their caps, and with cheeks blown red by the north-west wind –

reminded us that China still had to be vigilant in protecting its government from internal and external enemies.

As we passed through the high-ceilinged corridors with scrolls and framed paintings from early dynasties and modern times, it was apparent that the leaders of the revolution had valued China's historic culture and were making it available and meaningful to the Chinese people as a whole. After signing the visitors' book, beautifully bound in a Song-dynasty-style fabric, we gradually edged our way through the crowd towards the reception room. Here we met Shao Gongwen and Cao Jianfei, who greeted us as long-time friends. On previous trips they had been our hosts but had since retired from management, though continuing to serve CIBTC as advisers. Their successors, President Wang Qing-yun and Vice-President Ma Canxiong, were on hand to welcome us and introduce us to four distinguished represen-tatives of the government and the Party: Deng Liqun, Head of the Propaganda Department of the State Council; Hu Yushi, Founding Member of the Council of Friendship with Foreign Countries, a ninety-five-year-old senior citizen who had sponsored the Industrial Co-operative Movement, Indusco, with Edgar Snow and Rewi Alley in the 1930s; Zhu Muzhi, Minister of Culture and Member of the State Council; and Zhou Peiyuan, President of the Chinese People's Association for Peace and Disarmament and Vice-Chairman of both the Chinese Academy of Science and the Chinese People's Political Consultative Congress. In the reception room, with an audience enlarged from the morning assembly at CIBTC headquarters, were gathered representatives from all the foreign-language publishers whose books and periodicals we had distributed for twenty-five years.

The friendly atmosphere seemed to warm the cool, high-ceilinged hall as President Wang welcomed us all with a radiant smile. Son of a farming family, he looked as if he had stamina enough to plough a field or preside over a hundred meetings. With his infectious enthusiasm he elevated book distribution as a key link to developing friendly relations with peoples around the world. The Minister of Culture, Zhu Muzhi, raised the same theme to a higher political level and congratulated CIBTC for its many years of service in informing peoples abroad of the achievements of the People's Republic of China.

Speeches were brief: soon we moved on into the adjoining banqueting hall. It was immense, with round tables already loaded with dim sum specialities, silver dishes overflowing with candied fruits, bonbons in red and gold wrappings and bottles of maotai and red wine. I was steered by a friendly hand at my elbow – whose, I was too nervous to notice – to one of the head tables.

The climax of our five-week visit had finally arrived for me – also a peak moment in my life. All the problems of organizing distribution of Chinese publications in the United States – the cross-country sales trips year after year, the days and nights spent worrying about security, finance and politics and the necessity of walking a tightrope suspended between a capitalist and a socialist economy – were now, in a historic moment, being richly rewarded. I was too elated and nervous to touch food or drink, delicious as they looked. Listening to our Japanese friend deliver his speech, I knew that mine would come next and wished he would talk for ever.

But the time came all too soon when Yang Aiwen and I confronted the two microphones and our audience. There was a brief applause from all over the banqueting hall, particularly from the tables where Gertrude and Chris and our friends from Los Angeles were seated. I wished that my daughter Nicolette and the whole staff of CB&P had been with them. Then, after a moment of silence, I began to speak in a voice that was picked up by the loudspeakers and came booming back to my ears like the voice of a stranger. 'Mr Wang Qingyun, President of China International Book Trading Corporation, and Mr Ma Canxiong, Vice-President,' I began, 'we thank you for inviting us to celebrate your thirty-fifth anniversary here in the Great Hall of the People. To you and the distinguished leaders of the Party and the government ...' – my voice faltered as I fumbled through a pronunciation of their names which Yang Aiwen was quick to improve – '... and to your many friends and advisers,' I went on with more confidence, 'and the members of the CIBTC staff with whom we have had cordial relations for twenty-five years, we are happy to bring best wishes and congratulations from the staff of China Books & Periodicals and our friends in the United States.' As I paused for Yang Aiwen to interpret, I could hear our speech being translated into Japanese, French, Italian and other languages at different tables.

There was a murmur of approval as I went on to say, 'We from abroad are all mutually involved in the important task of distributing books and periodicals from China in our countries. These publications, and also art works, bring our multinational peoples together in world friendship. China's developments in the past, and now in the period of the Four Modernizations, are an inspiration to all of us.' Applause encouraged me to continue with new self-confidence and to enjoy the warm rapport between microphones and audience. 'Distributing publications from China has not always been easy for us in the outside world. Nor was it easy to distribute progressive books and magazines here in China before the revolution. We have all heard stories of those days from old friends, many of whom are present at this banquet. So our difficulties and hardships unite us here today. We have all been obliged to deal with police agents' attacks on our stores, with threats of burning and assassination by reactionaries who hate China and her socialist achievements.'

As Aiwen translated, my eyes wandered across the audience to spot our friends from France, Pakistan and Africa. When I went on to say, in the words of the popular song, 'But we love you, China!' the audience burst into applause.

'We are glad', I continued, 'that we have spent the past quarter century supplying the people of the United States with books and magazines from the Foreign Languages Press and the New World Press, exported to us by CIBTC. These publications have been of decisive importance in helping create a favourable atmosphere in the United States for China's regaining her rightful seat in the United Nations and in the normalization of relations between our two governments.' Again applause. Finally, I enlarged on the scope of reference to include all present with cheerful testimony to the value of lives spent in enlightening the peoples of the world with the five principles of peaceful coexistence that the late Premier Zhou Enlai had presented at the Bandung Conference in 1956. I concluded, 'We are truly happy, on this anniversary occasion, to share achievements with you who live in China and you from abroad who have participated in similar developments in your countries. We gather here today, therefore, as representatives of many peoples and nationalities – a United Nations of Book Dealers – to celebrate the thirty-fifth anniversary of China International Book Trading Corporation.'

The final celebration followed on Sunday evening with a state banquet, again in the Great Hall of the People. The featured guest to speak in the reception chamber before the banquet was Zhou Peiyuan. In the informal talk over a cup of jasmine tea before Zhou's address, I was introduced to him for the second time, this time to have a friendly talk seated on one of those Ming- or Qing-dynasty sofas built with a craftsman's skill to be a superb historical relic, rather than upholstered for comfort.

Zhou Peiyuan was as distinguished a senior citizen in appearance as his titles gave him a right to claim. His face, still firm in his mid eighties, had an expression of self-confidence and inner contentment. His smile encouraged me to ask about the function of the Chinese People's Political Consultative Congress, of which he was a vice-president. Was it like the US Senate or the British House of Lords? His smile broadened with amusement as he answered my question in perfect American-English, which he had mastered at the California Institute of Technology in his student days at the beginning of the 1920s. The Congress, he explained, was the first governing body of China after the revolution. It set up the National People's Congress in 1954, five years after the People's Republic of China was founded: 'People abroad do not have much understanding of our political system. They think we have only one party, but in fact the National People's Congress was set up by eight political parties, the largest being the Communist Party and the second in size the China Democratic League. The Chinese People's Political Consultative Congress was the prior organization which drew up our first Constitution and paid due attention in the process to the interests of minority nationalities, women and children, and people of religion.'

'Is the Consultative Congress now only an advisory body?'

'Mainly. But in China we have great respect for advisers, and they for ethics and social welfare. Therefore the National People's Congress is very responsive to our recommendations. People's democracy is a concept people abroad may have difficulty in understanding because of the so-called Cultural Revolution, which violated many of its principles. But we are back on a more even keel now. Educators, intellectuals, scientists and believers in religion are once more respected and play a constructive role for society as a whole, including workers and farmers who constitute the majority. We feel, therefore, that China can assume her fitting role in international affairs....' His explanation was interrupted as he was called to the podium to give us his views on world peace.

No novice in the peace movement, Zhou Peiyuan had represented China abroad at numerous peace conferences at which the threat of nuclear war was a main issue. It was his main theme that evening: 'Our objective is to work with people of the world to safeguard peace, strive for disarmament, realize the total prohibition and destruction of nuclear weapons, oppose the arms race and prevent a third world war.'

I was happy to find my place card next to Zhou Peiyuan's at the head table after we moved into the banqueting hall. The mood of the celebrants was a joyful one as they found their places at the eight large round tables in a hall with ancient paintings enlivening the walls and a high ceiling that seemed a mile above our heads. A succession of superb dishes were served: chicken salad with a rich herb dressing, prawns swimming in a sharp creamy sauce and many more delicacies in course after course. I lost count when I reached bursting point and had to lay my chopsticks defensively across my bowl and plant the palm of my hand over my maotai glass. There was time, before a music programme and a multitude of toasts, to discuss with Zhou Peiyuan China's role at the United Nations and her relationships to other Third World countries. 'We are hopeful', he said, 'that world peace can be assured. It is in the interests of all, and in China we have no need to bolster our economy with more and more lethal weapons. Quite the contrary! We are turning back many munitions factories, military installations and airfields to civilian service and production and reducing our armed forces by one million in the year ahead. We have a great deal to learn from Western science, but not how to make more and more dreadful weapons to kill.'

'And we have a great deal to learn from China, also. Not only acupuncture and moxibustion, but how to apply the principles of peaceful coexistence to guide our own foreign policy.'

Zhou Peiyuan nodded appreciation and was about to respond when the musical programme cut off further conversation. Our robust young baritone of the Friday evening concert was rattling the microphone as he tested a few notes in full voice, then waved to his soprano partner to join him. They rocked the hall with their songs, calling on the festive crowd to sing along with them. Once more they sang 'I Love You, China', while the audience responded in chorus with feet tapping and hands clapping with the beat. Our Italian delegate made a dash for the microphone in the midst of the applause. The next item on the programme, at his suggestion, was 'O Sole Mio'. With the gusto of an amateur tenor from Milan, his voice harmonized with Chinese baritone and soprano in a trio that was joined by the audience in a dozen different keys. The formal programme was transformed into a spontaneous song festival followed by an amateur hour of singing book dealers from all over the world.

The banquet ended with toasts floated on wine and maotai, 'To China International Book Trading Corporation!' and a final joyful toast in a dozen languages, 'To world peace! *Ganbei!*'

As we waited for our van on the chill northern steps of the Great Hall, the full moon was silvering Tian An Men Gate and casting shadows towards us across the square. Stars flashed in and out between islands of cloud jet-propelled by the wind across an ocean of sky towards the east, towards the North American continent six thousand miles away.

All too soon, our CAAC flight two nights later was jetting across the Pacific six and a half miles up, outspeeding clouds from the China coast and, before midnight, crossing the international dateline. It was Wednesday already in Beijing, but still Tuesday in San Francisco.

One by one the passengers, including Gertrude, had dozed off, but I was too elated from our week of negotiations and banquets in Beijing to sleep. I cupped my hands on the window to look out into the universe. There were no visible objects except moon and stars – no clouds now – to tell me we were moving.

Below, the greatest ocean in the world shows a gleaming surface of ebony in moonlight. Sky and sea have reached a yin–yang unity for peaceful coexistence. Why not human societies? As many as two billion people of a hundred diverse nationalities may be sleeping around the Pacific rim, at least half of them in the People's Republic of China. Why do they, or we, need star wars? Or any kind of war?

After a short night the sun, which had set behind us, rose unclouded up ahead. The Golden Gate and the Bridge, a silken thread, emerged from the Pacific as we sank like a gull over the Farallon Islands, circled the shoulders of San Mateo County, and rolled smoothly into San Francisco airport. It would take us three days to overcome jet lag and a week more to deal with cultural and culinary shock.

And then, back to work – after 'the best vacation of our lives'!

Glossary

Modern Chinese Transliterations (Pinyin) of Names and Places with Traditional Equivalents

Beijing = Peking
Chang Jiang = Yangtze River
Chonqing = Chungking
Ci Xi = Tzu Hsi (Dowager
  Empress)
Deng Xiaoping = Deng Hsiao-
  ping
Du Fu = Tu Fu
Guangdong = Kwangtung
Guangxi Zhuang = Kwangsi
  Chuang
Guangzhou = Canton
  (Kwangchow)
Guomindang = Kuomintang
  (KMT)
Huang He = Yellow River
Jiang Qing = Chiang Ching
  (Mao's wife)
Jiangxi = Kangsi

Li Bai = Li Po
Liu Shaoqi = Liu Shao-chi
Mao Zedong = Mao Tse-tung
Nanjing = Nanking
Qinghua = Chinghua
Shenzen = Shumchun
Shijiazhuang = Shihchiachuang
Sichuan = Szechwan
Suzhou = Soochow
Tianjin = Tientsin
Xian = Sian
Xinhua = Hsinhua
Xu = Hsu
Yanan = Yenan
Zhengzhou = Chengchow
Zhongsan = Chungsan
Zhou Enlai = Chou En-lai
Zhujiang = Pearl River

Abbreviations and Chinese Terms Used

cadre = government or Party functionary
CB&P = China Books & Periodicals
CIBTC = China International Book Trading
    Corporation
KMT = Kuo Min Tang
Meiguo = the beautiful country (America)
PLA = People's Liberation Army
Putonghua = the people's language, formerly Mandarin

Index